KIDS' BIBLE FACTS AND Q&A

Fun and Fascinating Bible Reference for Kids Ages 8 to 12

ED STRAUSS

starts on page 3!

starts on page 161!

ISBN 978-1-62416-630-3

Lists of scripture translations used are found on the pages immediately following the Facts and Q & A title pages.

Cover credits: 1st Image: Barbour Publishing; 2nd Image: Google; 3rd Image: WikiMedia; 4th and 5th Images; iStock

Published by Barbour Publishing, Inc., P.O. Box 719, Uhrichsville, Ohio 44683 www.barbourbooks.com

Our mission is to publish and distribute inspirational products offering exceptional value and biblical encouragement to the masses.

Printed in the United States of America.
Versa Press, East Peoria, IL 61611; October 2013; D10004167

KiDS'
Bible
Facts

INTRODUCTION

Welcome to *Kids' Bible Facts*, a book of Bible information of all kinds. These pages are full of facts about familiar people, places, and things, but they're also stuffed with little-known and sometimes surprising details. (Did you know, for example, that all the gold in God's temple was looted *eight* times? Or that one king of Judah had 28 sons and 60 daughters?)

What's in this book specifically?

- *Who's That?*—short biographies of the greatest men and women, heroes and villains in the Bible, everyone from Eve to Felix, from Barak to Balak.
- *Peoples & Places*—details on people groups like the Ammonites, Canaanites, Edomites, Hittites—all the "ites"—and the far-flung, mysterious lands that these people lived in long ago.
- *And That Means. . .*—definitions of unusual Bible words like *atonement, impute*, and *covenant*. Once you've read these, you'll find it a whole lot easier to understand the Bible.
- *Features*—short accounts of well-known Bible characters doing amazing things you never heard about, as well as some crazy unknowns doing insane stuff that you just *know* they're not going to get away with!
- *I Love Lists!*—with titles like: "Eight People Who Came Back from the Dead," "Four Dusty, Desert Donkey Details," "10 Times That People Lived in Caves," and much, much more!
- *Fun Facts*—interesting and downright zany information, like how King Solomon had a round table 2,000 years before King Arthur, or how one father named his sons Huppim and Muppim. (If either of those happens to be your name, we're laughing *with* you, not *at* you!)

You'll notice throughout *Kids' Bible Facts* that each type of entry is color-coded—by looking at a headline, you can tell at a glance whether the entry is a biography, a definition, a "fun fact" or whatever. And when you see a colored word within the text, that means there's related information somewhere on the two-page "spread" you're looking at. Be sure to read the related items for the best understanding.

This handy little fact-finder will help you learn quickly what's what and who's who in the Bible. We trust you'll find it such fascinating reading that you'll come back to it again and again—and learn what's in your own Bible better and better.

Aaron

Moses' older brother. God used Aaron and Moses to bring plagues on Egypt to try to convince Pharaoh to free the Israelites. Aaron later became high priest of Israel. (See: Exodus 7:1–7; 28:1–2.)

Abednego

King Nebuchadnezzar threw Shadrach, Meshach, and Abednego into a furnace for refusing to worship his idol, but God protected them. The king then made them officials of Babylon. (See: Daniel 3.)

King Nebuchadnezzar threw three men into t fiery furnace, but sees *four* in the flames—on looking "like the Son of God" (Daniel 3:24 KJV

STRANGE BUT TRUE!
The Babylonians had bizarre ways of making decisions and getting directions. They killed a sheep, cut out its liver, and studied its markings and color for "messages." (See: Ezekiel 21:21.)

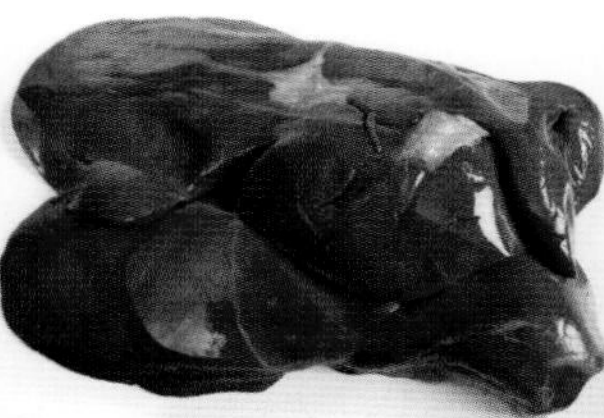

Four Powerful Priests Who Took Bold Action

1. Aaron ran in and saved the Israelites from a plague.
2. Phinehas speared an idolater and stopped a plague.
3. Jehoiada took over the government from the evil queen Athaliah.
4. Zechariah, son of Jehoiada, rebuked King Joash.

(See: Numbers 16:46–50; 25:1–11; 2 Kings 11:1–19; 2 Chronicles 24:17–23.)

And that Definition Means...

Worship

The Hebrew word for *worship* means "to bow down before someone" to show how much you honor them. We also worship God by praying, praising Him, by speaking about how great He is, or about the wonderful things that He has done. Worship also can be singing songs of praise to God. (See: Psalm 95:6; 145:1–12; 147:1.)

Egypt (Egyptians)

Egypt is a dry land in Africa, but the Nile River valley was very fertile. The Israelites lived there 430 years; Jesus was there when He was a child. (See: Exodus 12:40–41; Deuteronomy 11:10; Matthew 2:13–15.)

ABEL

The first son of Adam and Eve. Abel, a shepherd, pleased God by sacrificing a lamb to Him. This caused his brother Cain to kill him in a fit of jealousy. (See: Genesis 4:1–15.)

THE NAME GAME!
The Israelites had only a *first* name and no middle name, so while there were guys named "Buz" (Genesis 22:21) and guys named "Bunni" (Nehemiah 11:15), you never hear of a "Buz Bunni."

ABIATHAR

The only priest to survive a massacre, Abiathar fled into the wilderness to join David as a fugitive. He later became a high priest of Israel. (See: 1 Samuel 22; 1 Chronicles 15:11.)

ABIGAIL

The wise wife of foolish Nabal. Abigail's quick thinking and generosity saved her whole household. After Nabal died of a heart attack, she married David. (See: 1 Samuel 25.)

THE NAME GAME!
What's in a name? One foolish Bible villain was named *Nabal*, meaning "fool." A New Testament Christian was named *Philologus*, meaning "lover of words." (See: 1 Samuel 25:25; Romans 16:15.)

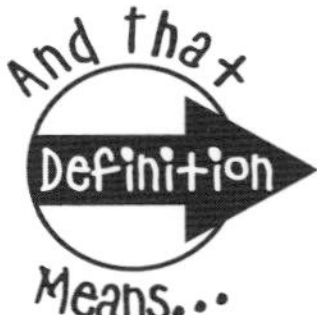

CONCUBINE

In ancient days, some men had more than one wife. Others chose to simply take a *concubine*—a slave who didn't have rights like a wife, but who slept with him and bore him children. If a man wished to get rid of his concubine, he gave her gifts, set her free, and sent her away. Abraham did this with his two concubines: Hagar and Keturah. (See: Genesis 16:1–4; 21:9–14; 25:5–6; 1 Chronicles 1:32.)

SACRIFICE

To give up something that is dear to you, or that costs you something. In the Law of Moses, the sacrifice God asked for was an animal—usually a lamb or a goat from the flock. In fact, *zebach*, which is the Hebrew word for *sacrifice*, means "a slaughtered animal." Paul said that Jesus was our Passover lamb sacrificed for us. (See: Genesis 22:1–18; Leviticus 1:2–5; 1 Corinthians 5:7.)

Lambs were often sacrificed in Old Testament times—and Jesus, the best sacrifice of all, was called "the Lamb of God" (John 1:29).

The world's oldest person of modern times, Jeanne Calment of France, celebrates her 117th birthday. She was 122 when she died in 1997.

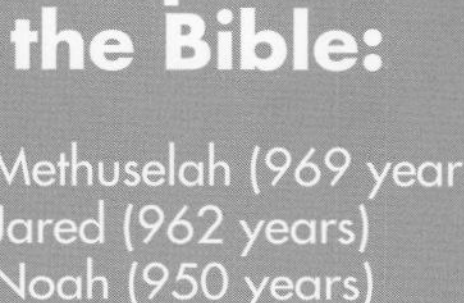

Eight Oldest People in the Bible:

1. Methuselah (969 years)
2. Jared (962 years)
3. Noah (950 years)
4. Adam (930 years)
5. Seth (912 years)
6. Kenan (910 years)
7. Enosh (905 years)
8. Mahalalel (895 years)

(See: Genesis 5:5, 8, 11, 14, 17, 20, 27; 9:29.)

Abraham Battles Five Invading Kings

Abraham had such huge flocks and herds that he needed 318 servants to watch over them. Since Canaan was a wild land full of bandits and raiders, these shepherds were also trained fighters. Good thing they were! One day five foreign kings invaded eastern and southern Canaan and carried off loot and prisoners—including Abraham's nephew Lot. Abraham called his Amorite allies, and together they chased the kings, caught up with them, and scattered their armies in a stunning battle. They recovered Lot and the other prisoners, as well as all the goods and loot that those armies had taken. (See: Genesis 13:5–6; 14.)

FUN FACTS!
Conquering kings used to carry thrones around with them, and their officials lugged fancy seats along so they could sit in the gates of the cities that they conquered. (See: Jeremiah 1:15; 39:3.)

FUN FACTS!
Abraham and Isaac grazed their flocks in the Negev. Dangerous grazing! The Negev was "a land of. . . lions and lionesses, of adders and darting snakes" (Isaiah 30:6 NIV). (See also: Genesis 20:1; 24:62.)

Abimelech

Two kings of the Philistines were named Abimelech: One let Abraham and Sarah live in his city, Gerar, and the other let Isaac and Rebekah live there. Another Abimelech, an Israelite, was crowned king of Shechem. (See: Genesis 20; 26; Judges 9.)

FUN FACTS!
If you thought that Saul was the first Israelite to be king, you are mistaken. Abimelech was the first king in Israel. But all he ruled was the city of Shechem. (See: Judges 9:6.)

Abishag

The most beautiful woman in Israel. Abishag was brought to old King David to keep him warm in bed. Later, Prince Adonijah was killed for asking to marry her. (See: 1 Kings 1:1–4; 2:13–25.)

Like Abishag, Shunit Faragi is the most beautiful Israeli woman of her time. She represented her country in the 2008 Miss Universe contest.

Abishai

King David's nephew and Joab's brother. Abishai was very loyal to David but cruel to his enemies. Abishai's solution was usually to kill people. (See: 1 Samuel 26:5–9; 2 Samuel 16:5–12; 1 Chronicles 2:16.)

And that

Means...

Angels

Angels are beings with supernatural powers who serve God and man. They bear His messages to mankind and protect believers. Angels were never human and people don't become angels when they die, but angels often look like humans when they appear. (See: Judges 13:3–6; Psalm 34:7; Luke 1:18–19; Hebrews 1:7, 14.)

STRANGE BUT TRUE!
The astonishing thing about angels is that, although they're far mightier and more amazing than people, they're here to *serve* us! (See: Hebrews 1:7, 14; 2:6–7.)

The old Philistine city of Gaza is still around and often in the news. Smoke rises above buildings in this 2009 photo following an Israeli/Palestinian battle.

Philistia (Philistines)

The Philistines ruled five cities—Gath, Gaza, Ekron, Ashdod, and Ashkelon—on the coast west of Israel. They were enemies of the Israelites for most of their history. (See: Joshua 13:3; Judges 13:1; 1 Samuel 31:1.)

Cities Buried by Burning Sulfur

The citizens of Sodom and Gomorrah were wealthy and were so oppressive that the poor cried out to heaven against them. On top of that, they had very dirty minds. When God sent two angels to Sodom, the people there tried to hurt them. That was it! At dawn the next day the angels dragged Lot and his family out of the city; then there was an ear-splitting roar and God rained scorching sulfur down on Sodom and the neighboring sinful cities. Thick black smoke rolled into the sky, and those wicked cities were gone. (See: Genesis 18:20–21; 19:1–29; Ezekiel 16:49–50.)

THE NAME GAME!

Shinab was the king of Admah, one of the cities destroyed along with Sodom and Gomorrah. This king had an odd name: *Shinab* means "father's tooth." (See: Genesis 14:2; Deuteronomy 29:23.)

Ten Times That People Lived in Caves

1. Lot and his daughters lived in a cave after the city of Sodom was destroyed.
2. The five Amorite kings who fled the Israelite army hid in the cave at Makkedah.
3. Israelites hid from the Midianites.
4. Samson stayed in a cave in the rock of Etam.
5. Israelite soldiers hid from the Philistines.
6. David and 400 men lived in the cave of Adullum.
7. David and his men hid in a cave at En Gedi.
8. Obadiah hid 100 prophets of God in two caves.
9. Elijah spent the night in a cave on Mount Sinai.
10. The poor in Job's day fled to caves.

(See: Genesis 19:24, 30; Joshua 10:16; Judges 6:2; 15:8; 1 Samuel 13:6; 22:1–2; 24:1–3; 1 Kings 18:4; 19:8–9; Job 30:3–6.)

Abner

The commander of King Saul's army. After Saul's death, Abner was about to unite the Israelites under David when Joab, David's nephew, killed him. (See: 2 Samuel 2–3.)

Abraham

Father of the nation of Israel and spiritual father of those who believe in God. Abraham was 100 years old when his son Isaac was born. (See: Genesis 17:1–8; 21:5; Romans 4:1–16.)

FUN FACTS!
Once a ram was grazing on top of Mount Moriah when its curly horns were caught in a thicket. Abraham saw the ram, grabbed it, and sacrificed it to God. (See: Genesis 22:13.)

Absalom

A son of King David. He wanted to be king, so he gathered an army and fought his father—and died. Absalom was famous for his good looks and long hair. (See: 2 Samuel 14:25–26; 15–18.)

FUN FACTS!
When Prince Absalom wanted to be popular with the Israelites, he wouldn't let them bow down to him. Instead, he grabbed them and kissed them. (See: 2 Samuel 15:5–6.)

Absalom's beautiful long hair gets caught in a tree branch in this painting from the 1500s. Soldiers from his father's army killed him while he hung there, trapped.

Altar of Burnt Offering

A small platform that animals were sacrificed and burned on. Abraham, Elijah, and others built altars by piling rough stones together. God told the Israelites to build an altar of wood and cover it with bronze. When the temple was built in Jerusalem, the altar of burnt offering stood outside the temple's front doors. (See: Exodus 27:1–2; 1 Kings 18:30–32.)

Jesus talks with a woman from Samaria—a very unusual thing for a Jewish teacher to do. But He wants her to know the way to salvation.

Places & People

HEBREWS

Descendants of a man named Eber. Abraham was called a Hebrew, and so were his descendants. When the Hebrews lived in Egypt, they began to be called the children of Israel. (See: Genesis 11:16, 26; 14:13; Exodus 1:9.)

STRANGE BUT TRUE!

Anyone looking into Abner's tomb would've seen one skeleton but two skulls. Why's that? When Ish-bosheth (son of Saul) was beheaded, King David put his head in Abner's tomb. (See: 2 Samuel 4:12.)

Eight Famous Encounters at Wells and Pools

1. Abraham's servant, Eliezer, met Rebekah at the town well.
2. Philistine herdsmen drove Isaac away from two wells.
3. Jacob met his future wife, Rachel, at a well.
4. Moses drove nasty shepherds from a well in Midian.
5. Generals of two armies, Joab and Abner, met at the pool of Gibeon.
6. A woman once hid two of David's spies down in her well.
7. Jesus spoke with the Samaritan woman at Jacob's well.
8. Jesus healed a lame man at the Pool of Bethesda.

(See: Genesis 24:10–18; 26:19–22; 29:1–12; Exodus 2:15–21; 2 Samuel 2:12–16; 17:17–19; John 4:4–10; 5:1–8.)

Seven Powerful Promises That God Made to Abraham

1. Abraham would be a blessing to everyone on earth.
2. God would give him the entire land of Canaan.
3. Abraham's offspring would be as numerous as the dust and the stars.
4. Abraham's descendants would be slaves 400 years, then be set free with great riches.
5. Abraham would live a long, peaceful life.
6. God would bless Ishmael and greatly increase his descendants—the Arabs.
7. His aged wife Sarah would miraculously have a son.

(Genesis 12:3; 13:14–17; 15:5, 13–15, 18–21; 17:20; 18:9–10,14.)

ACHAN

Everything in the city of Jericho had been dedicated to God, but Achan took some treasure and clothes for himself, and this caused Israel to be defeated in Ai. Achan was killed for his sin. (See: Joshua 7.)

ADAM

The very first man. Adam was created by God, and he and Eve were the ancestors of all human beings. They lived in the Garden of Eden until they sinned. (See: Genesis 2–3.)

STRANGE BUT TRUE!
Energy-beam swords are not just science fiction! When the Garden of Eden was still on earth, God had a cherubim with a flaming sword guarding it. (See: Genesis 3:24.)

Adam and Eve cry after God kicks them out of the Garden of Eden in this painting from the 1400s.

ADONIJAH

When David was dying, Prince Adonijah declared himself king. Solomon became king instead, however. Adonijah was later killed for asking to have Abishag as his wife. (See: 1 Kings 1; 2:13–25.)

STRANGE BUT TRUE!
King Arthur wasn't the first king to have a round table. Two thousand years earlier, King Solomon had a *mesab*, which means "a circular, round table." (See: Song of Solomon 1:12.)

CURSE, THE

In the beginning, when God first created the earth and everything in it, "it was very good" (Genesis 1:31 KJV). After Adam and Eve sinned, however, God punished them. Not only did they begin to grow old and die, but God said, "Cursed is the ground because of you" (Genesis 3:17 RSV). That's when things like thorns and thistles and mosquitoes became problems. (See also: Genesis 2:17.)

FALL, THE

When God created Adam and Eve and placed them in the Garden of Eden, they were perfect and without sin, without death or sickness or anything evil. When they disobeyed God, however, they fell from that wonderful state and began to suffer from sin, death, and sickness. This is called the Fall. (See Curse, above.) Jesus will one day restore man's perfect state. (See also: Genesis 3:11–19; Revelation 21:4.)

EDEN

No one knows exactly where the land of Eden was, though many people think it was in Iraq. God created a paradise there, the Garden of Eden, and Adam and Eve lived there. (See: Genesis 2:8–14.)

Five Thorn and Thorn-bush Names

Thorn bushes grew all over Israel. They were so common that parents named their kids after them:

1. *Soco* also means "thorny."
2. *Shamir* means "sharp point" or "thorn."
3. *Asnah* means "thorn bush."
4. *Hakkoz* means "thorn."
5. *Hassenaah* means "thorny."

(See: 1 Chronicles 4:18; 24:24; Ezra 2:50, 61; Nehemiah 3:3.)

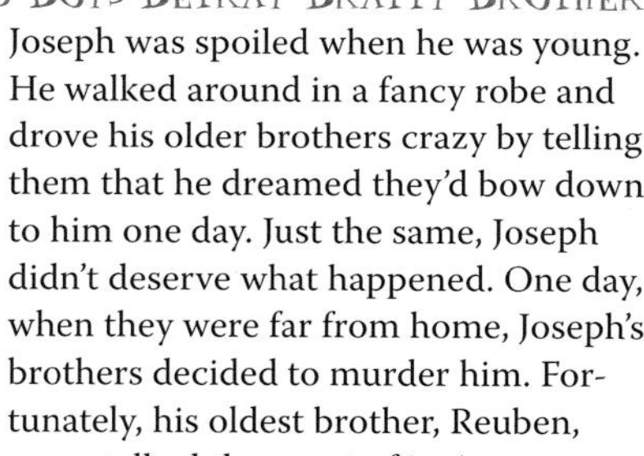

BAD BOYS BETRAY BRATTY BROTHER

Joseph was spoiled when he was young. He walked around in a fancy robe and drove his older brothers crazy by telling them that he dreamed they'd bow down to him one day. Just the same, Joseph didn't deserve what happened. One day, when they were far from home, Joseph's brothers decided to murder him. Fortunately, his oldest brother, Reuben, talked them out of it. Another brother, Judah, then had the "bright idea" of selling Joseph as a slave to a caravan headed down to Egypt—so they did. Then the brothers lied to their father Jacob that a wild animal had killed Joseph. (See: Genesis 37.)

FUN FACTS!
When Joseph first arrived in Egypt he was a slave. About 13 years later he was the master, and he made all the *Egyptians* slaves. (See: Genesis 37:36; 47:20–23.)

Joseph, wearing only a cloth around his waist, is sold as a slave by his brothers. They hated Joseph for being their father's favorite.

AHAB

An idol-worshipping king of the northern kingdom, Israel. Ahab married Jezebel, the wicked princess of Sidon, and she pushed him into doing all kinds of evil things. (See: 1 Kings 16:29–33; 21.)

FUN FACTS!
Could you sit down and eat lunch if 450 false prophets had just been killed in front of you? King Ahab did. He must've had one tough stomach! (See: 1 Kings 18:19, 40–42.)

AHASUERUS

The Persian king who married Esther, a young Jewish woman. "Ahasuerus" (Esther 1:1 KJV) was very likely the Jews' name for the Persian king "Xerxes" (Esther 1:1 NIV). (See also: Esther 2:17.)

THE NAME GAME!
One of King Xerxes' servants had an unusual name—"Carcas" (Esther 1:10). That sounds a lot like *carcass.* And the odd thing is, his name means "vulture."

A Jewish boy dresses like King Ahasuerus for the holiday of Purim. Purim celebrates the Jews' escape from a plot to destroy them about 600 years before Jesus.

AHAZ

A king of Judah in the days of the Assyrian Empire. Ahaz paid the Assyrians gold to be on his side. Later, he made a copy of one of their pagan altars and worshipped on it. (See: 2 Kings 16.)

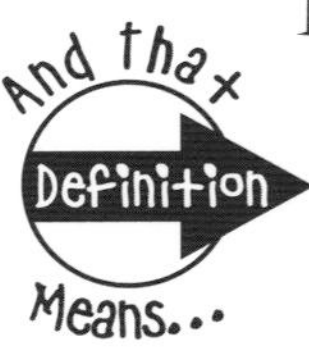

IDOL, IDOLATRY

An *idol* is an object that supposedly represents an invisible god or goddess. Idols were usually made out of wood, stone, or metal and in the shape of humans or animals. *Idolatry* is the worship of these pagan gods and their idols, and God forbade idolatry. God mocked idols, saying that they were totally useless. (See: Exodus 20:3–4; Isaiah 44:9–20.)

From Prison House to Powerhouse

First Joseph's brothers hated him so much that they sold him as a slave. Talk about rejection! Joseph was a faithful, hardworking slave in Potiphar's house in Egypt but then Potiphar's wife falsely accused him of trying to hurt her. Potiphar was furious and threw Joseph in jail. There Joseph helped a prisoner, Pharaoh's wine taster, by interpreting his dreams. . .but when the man got out he forgot all about Joseph. When Joseph was about as low as he could get, suddenly he was called to the royal court to interpret Pharaoh's dream. Next thing you know, Joseph was the second most powerful man in Egypt. (See: Genesis 37, 39–41.)

FUN FACTS!
Joseph was 17 when he was sold as a slave into Egypt and 30 when he finally got out of prison. He'd been a slave and prisoner for 13 years. (See: Genesis 37:2, 36; 41:39–40, 46.)

Six Pagan Temples Right inside the Land of Israel

1. The temple of Baal in Shechem
2. The temple of Ashtoreth in Beth Shan
3. The temple of Baal in Samaria
4. The temple of Baal in Jerusalem
5. The temple of Dagon in Beth Shan
6. The Samaritans built a temple on Mount Gerizim. They first dedicated it to God, then rededicated it to Jupiter to please the Greeks.

(See: Judges 9:3–4; 1 Samuel 31:10; 2 Kings 10:23, 27; 11:18; 1 Chronicles 10:10; John 4:19.)

Eight Dramatic and Unusual Dreams

1. God told King Abimelech that he was basically dead meat.
2. In a dream, God told Laban to keep his mouth shut.
3. Joseph dreamed about sheaves of grain bowing down.
4. Pharaoh's wine taster and his baker had very odd dreams.
5. Pharaoh dreamed about cannibal cows.
6. A soldier dreamed about a giant barley cake smashing a tent.
7. Nebuchadnezzar dreamed about a tall, multi-metal statue.
8. An angel warned Joseph to escape with his family to Egypt.

(See: Genesis 20:3–7; 31:24; 37:5–7; 40:8–19; 41:17–21; Judges 7:13–15; Daniel 2:1, 31–35; Matthew 2:13.)

Many people around the world created idols. These wooden "tiki" carvings are from Hawaii.

Ahaziah

A king of Judah. He was a son of wicked Queen Athaliah and worshipped Baal. Ahaziah was killed by Jehu while visiting his cousin, King Joram of Israel. (See: 2 Kings 8:25–29; 9:14–29.)

STRANGE BUT TRUE!
Another wicked man named Ahaziah, a king of Israel, was in the upper room of his palace where he fell through the wooden lattice and hit the ground, fatally injuring himself. (See: 2 Kings 1:2.)

Amaziah

A king of Judah who worshipped God until he defeated the Edomites. Then he worshipped the Edomites' gods. He became proud and was defeated by King Jehoash of Israel. (See: 2 Chronicles 25.)

Amos

A prophet of God in the days when Israel was prosperous. Amos preached against the selfish rich, warning them that God would judge them. (See: Amos 1:1; 6:1–7; 7:10–17.)

Prophet, Prophecy

A *prophet* was a man who gave a message from God. A female prophet was called a *prophetess.* Sometimes their prophecies simply warned that God would punish people if they didn't obey. Other times, prophets talked about things that would happen in the future. For example, Isaiah prophesied about Jesus' death and burial hundreds of years before Jesus was born. (See: Isaiah 53; Jeremiah 35:17.)

A chariot race is among the highlights of the 1959 movie *Ben-Hur*. Actor Charlton Heston (racing the white team) plays an angry man who meets Jesus and learns about forgiveness.

Places & People

Edom (Edomites)

Esau (Edom) was a son of Isaac. He conquered the land southeast of the Dead Sea and called it Edom. The Edomites often fought wars with Israel. (See: Genesis 25:30; Numbers 20:14–21.)

THE NAME GAME!
Talk about names with beautiful meanings! A man named *Me-Zahab* ("waters of gold") had a granddaughter named *Mehetabel* ("God is doing good"), the queen of Edom. (See: Genesis 36:39.)

FUN FACTS!
Queen Athaliah was the only woman to rule Judah, but she was so evil and outrageously wicked that it's fortunate she only reigned six years. (See: 2 Kings 11:1–3.)

Five Deadly Chariot Rides

1. The Egyptian chariot army was drowned in the Red Sea.
2. Jabin's chariot army was wiped out in the River Kishon.
3. King Ahab was mortally wounded in a chariot.
4. Jehu killed King Joram with an arrow in his chariot.
5. King Ahaziah was mortally wounded in his chariot.

(See: Exodus 14:1–28; Judges 4:1–2, 14–15; 5:21; 1 Kings 22:34–35; 2 Kings 9:21–24, 27–28.)

Eight Queens—the Magnificent and the Misguided

1. Bathsheba, who sinned with King David, was the mother of King Solomon.
2. Zeruah, widow of a common man, was the mother of King Jeroboam.
3. Naamah, a foreigner from Ammon, was Solomon's queen and the mother of King Rehoboam.
4. Maacah, a goddess-worshipper, was Rehoboam's queen and the mother of King Abijah.
5. Azubah, a good Jerusalem girl, was Asa's queen and the mother of King Jehoshaphat.
6. Athaliah, one of history's nastiest women, was Jehoram's queen and the mother of King Ahaziah.
7. Zibiah, Ahaziah's queen, was the mother of godly King Joash.
8. Zebidah, good King Josiah's queen, was the mother of King Jehoiakim.

(See: 1 Kings 1:28–30; 11:26; 12:20; 14:21; 15:1–2, 13; 22:41–42; 2 Kings 8:25–26; 12:1; 23:36.)

ANDREW

One of the 12 apostles of Jesus. Andrew was Simon Peter's brother and, like Peter, used to be a fisherman and a disciple of John the Baptist. (See: Matthew 4:18–20; John 1:35–42.)

APOLLOS

Apollos was a highly educated Jew from Egypt. He was taught by Priscilla and Aquila in Ephesus, then became a leader in the church at Corinth. (See: Acts 18:24–28; 1 Corinthians 3:5–6.)

ARISTARCHUS

A little-known but faithful friend of the apostle Paul. Aristarchus was caught in a riot in Ephesus, then traveled with Paul to Greece, Jerusalem, and Rome. (See: Acts 19:1, 29; 20:1–4; 27:1–2.)

FUN FACTS!
Once some sailors tried to escape a doomed ship in a lifeboat, but the apostle Paul stopped them. Good thing! Otherwise all the passengers would've drowned. (See: Acts 27:30–32.)

And that Definition Means...

APOSTLE

Apostle means "messenger" or "ambassador." Jesus had about 120 disciples or followers, and from them He chose 12 to be His apostles. Jesus sent His apostles out to preach the gospel, perform miracles, and cast out demons. Later, other men such as Paul were called apostles, too. (See: Matthew 10:1–8; Luke 6:12–16; Acts 1:15; Ephesians 1:1.)

Lifeboats hang over the side of a ship, in case of trouble.

OBEDIENCE

The Bible talks a great deal about the importance of keeping (obeying) God's commands. The Jews were told that they would be blessed if they obeyed the Law of Moses and cursed if they disobeyed it. Jesus said, "If you love me, you will obey what I command" (John 14:15 NIV). (See also: Deuteronomy 28.)

STRANGE BUT TRUE!
God once told an army to dig ditches in the desert. It sounded strange—*very* strange—but they obeyed Him and won a huge battle as a result. (See: 2 Kings 3:15–24.)

Deliverer Jumps the Gun

When Moses was a baby, he was adopted by Pharaoh's daughter. He was educated in all the wisdom of the Egyptians and became a powerful prince. When he learned that he was actually a son of Hebrew slaves, he went out to see how his people were doing. They were expecting a deliverer to come along about this time and set them free, so Moses figured (correctly) that he must be it. But in his haste he killed an Egyptian slave driver, and when Pharaoh found out, he tried to execute Moses. Moses had to flee into the desert and wait 40 years to be the deliverer—and *this* time he did things God's way. (See: Exodus 2; Acts 7:20–36.)

STRANGE BUT TRUE!
The archangel Michael once got in an argument with the devil. Guess what they were arguing about? The body of Moses! (See: Jude 1:9.)

Ephesus (Ephesians)

In Paul's day, Ephesus was a large city on the west coast of what is now Turkey. Paul preached the gospel there and a riot broke out. Paul later wrote a letter to the Ephesians. (See: Acts 19; Ephesians 1:1.)

Most Christians worship in church buildings today. But in the time of the apostle Paul, believers worshipped in each others' homes.

Four People Who Had Churches in Their Homes

1. Priscilla and Aquila in Rome
2. Priscilla and Aquila in Ephesus, Asia
3. Nympha in Colosse
4. Philemon in Colosse

(See: Romans 16:3–5; 1 Corinthians 16:19; Colossians 4:15; Philemon 2

I Love Lists!

Asa

A king of Judah in the early days of the southern kingdom. Asa was a good king who got rid of idol-worship. He was constantly fighting with King Baasha of Israel. (See: 1 Kings 15:9–24.)

Asaph

A Levite in the days of David and Solomon, he sang before the Ark of God and led praise services in the temple. He wrote 12 psalms. (See: 1 Chronicles 16:4–5; Psalms 50, 73–83.)

FUN FACTS!
King Solomon spent seven years building the temple of God. It took him 13 years—nearly *twice* as long!—to build his own magnificent palace. (See: 1 Kings 6:37–38; 7:1.)

Asherah

A disgusting goddess whom people believed was the wife of Baal. The Canaanites—and later the Israelites—worshipped her and set up "Asherah poles" (1 Kings 14:15 NIV). (See also: Judges 3:7.)

STRANGE BUT TRUE!
When Baal-worshippers *really* wanted their god to notice them and answer prayer, they slashed themselves with swords and spears till they were red with blood. (See: 1 Kings 18:26–28.)

Ark of the Covenant

Also called the Ark of God. The Ark was a gold-covered wooden chest with two golden cherubim on its lid. It was only three and a half feet long but it symbolized the presence of God. The Israelites stored special things inside the Ark, such as a jar of manna, Aaron's rod, and the stone tablets of the Ten Commandments. (See: Exodus 25:10–22; 1 Samuel 4:4, 11; Hebrews 9:3–5.)

STRANGE BUT TRUE!
Once a huge crowd of disrespectful men opened the lid of the Ark of the Covenant and looked inside—and God struck them dead, just like in the Indiana Jones movie! (See: 1 Samuel 6:19.)

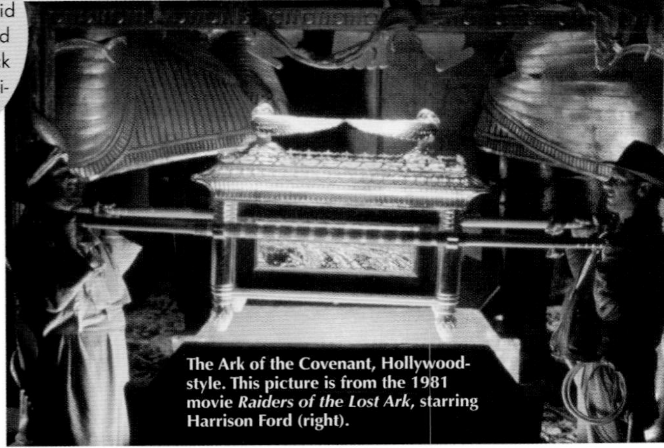

The Ark of the Covenant, Hollywood-style. This picture is from the 1981 movie *Raiders of the Lost Ark*, starring Harrison Ford (right).

Egyptians mummify the body of Joseph, as they had done with his father, Jacob, years before (Genesis 50:2).

Seven Asherah-Smashing, Baal-Bashing Heroes

1. Gideon tore down the Asherah pole and the altar of Baal.
2. The Israelites in Jephthah's day ditched their Baal and Asherah idols.
3. Elijah had the Israelites kill the prophets of Baal.
4. Jehu killed the prophets of Baal and demolished their temple.
5. In King Joash's day, the Israelites tore down the temple of Baal.
6. King Josiah burned Asherah poles and dumped the priests of Baal.
7. Asa destroyed idol altars, smashed sacred stones, and cut down Asherah poles.

(See: Judges 6:25–28; 10:6–7, 16; 1 Kings 18:19, 40; 2 Kings 10:23–27; 11:17–18; 23:4–6; 2 Chronicles 14:2–5.)

I Love Lists!

Greater Than the Magicians of Egypt

When Moses and Aaron appeared before Pharaoh, Aaron threw down Moses' staff, and it morphed into a snake. Pharaoh wasn't impressed. His court magicians did the same thing. Aaron struck the Nile, and all the water turned to blood. The magicians did the same. Aaron stretched his hand over the Nile, and swarms of frogs came out. The magicians summoned frogs, too. *Then* God caused gnats to fill the land. The magicians tried all their magic spells but couldn't do what God had done. They were also completely powerless to copy the next six plagues God sent on Egypt. (See: Exodus 7:8–12, 20–22; 8:5–7, 16–19.)

STRANGE BUT TRUE!
When Moses and the Israelites left Egypt, they were carrying a mummy with them—Joseph's embalmed body and bones. (See: Genesis 50:26; Exodus 13:19.)

ATHALIAH

The only ruling queen of Judah. When her son—King Ahaziah—died, evil, idolatrous Athaliah killed all of her grandsons (so she thought) so that she could become queen. (See: 2 Kings 11.)

FUN FACTS!
The Bible says about idols: "They have mouths, but they speak not, they have eyes, but they see not, they have ears, but they hear not" (Psalm 135:16–17 RSV). They're good for nothing!

BAAL

The chief pagan god of the Canaanites. Baal was supposedly the god of rain and crops and cattle. His followers had strange, sick ways of worshipping him. (See: 1 Kings 18:25–28.)

BAAL-ZEBUB

Baal-Zebub was originally a Philistine god. By Jesus' day, the Jews considered Beelzebub to be "the prince of demons" (Matthew 12:24 NIV), Satan himself. (See also: 2 Kings 1:2.)

FUN FACTS!
The Israelites worshipped an idol of a golden calf. Big mistake! But it was okay for them to make *statues* of 12 bulls because they didn't worship them. (See: Exodus 32; 1 Kings 7:25.)

This idol was made by Aztecs in South America more than 600 years ago.

And that Definition Means...

PASSOVER FEAST

In Egypt the angel of death "passed over" the houses of the Israelites who had put the blood of a lamb on their doorposts. God told the Israelites to celebrate the Passover Feast every year to remember what He had done for them. At this feast, the Jews ate lamb, unleavened (flat) bread, and bitter herbs. Jesus turned the Passover Feast into the Lord's Supper. (See: Exodus 12; Matthew 26:17–29.)

FUN FACTS!
When the Israelites left Egypt, hundreds of thousands of them carried containers of uncooked unleavened bread dough, wrapped in clothing, on their shoulders. (See: Exodus 12:33–34.)

FEAST OF UNLEAVENED BREAD

Leaven is an old word for *yeast,* which bakers mix into bread dough to make it rise. *Un*leavened bread is flat bread without yeast. The Feast of Unleavened Bread is a feast that lasted one week and followed immediately after Passover. In Jesus' day, the entire time was referred to as either Passover or the Feast of Unleavened Bread. Yeast symbolized evil and hypocrisy, and Paul wrote that Christians should be sincere and truthful. (See: Exodus 23:15; Matthew 26:17; 1 Corinthians 5:6–8.)

Fooling and Foiling Pharaoh

When Moses brought the Israelites out of Egypt, God led them south. . .then told them to head back north. It was a deliberate act to fool Pharaoh and make him think they were wandering around in confusion. Then God told the Israelites to camp by the Red Sea. He wanted it to look like they couldn't cross and were trapped. Pharaoh fell for it and sent his army after them. That night God opened up the Red Sea—a wall of water on the left hand and a wall on the right—and the Israelites safely crossed. When the Egyptians followed them into the seabed, however, the walls of water came crashing down and drowned them. (See: Exodus 13:17–14:31.)

Six Pagan Gods the Israelites Foolishly Worshipped

1. Golden calves
2. Baal
3. Ashtoreth
4. Asherah
5. Molech, the god of the Ammonites
6. Chemosh, the god of Moab

(See: Exodus 32; Judges 2:11, 13; 3:7; 1 Kings 11:5, 7; 12:25–30.)

Ammon (Ammonites)

Ben-Ammi was a son of Lot, and his descendants, the Ammonites, lived in the land of Ammon east of the Jordan River. King David fought them. (See: Genesis 19:36–38; 2 Samuel 10:1–11:1; 12:26–31.)

These carvings of the Egyptian pharaoh Rameses are more than 3,000 years old.

Balaam

A prophet famous for owning a talking donkey. Balaam boasted that he saw visions from God, but he compromised with idol-worshippers for money. (See: Numbers 22; Jude 1:11.)

FUN FACTS!
An Israelite named Caleb claimed his people could "swallow" their enemies. Balaam described the Israelites as a wild ox that "devour[s] hostile nations" (Numbers 24:8 NIV). (See also: Numbers 14:6–9.)

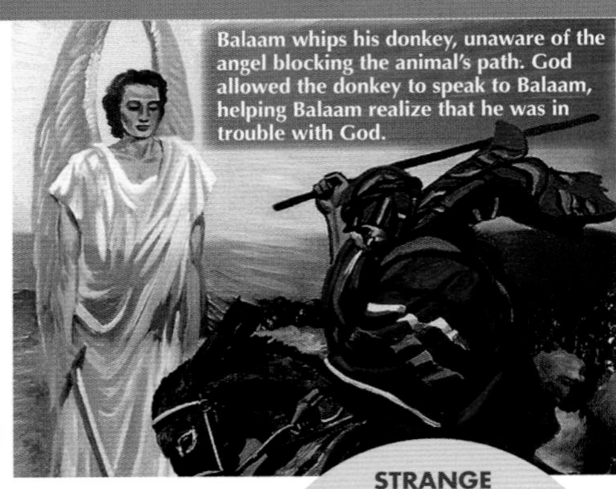
Balaam whips his donkey, unaware of the angel blocking the animal's path. God allowed the donkey to speak to Balaam, helping Balaam realize that he was in trouble with God.

STRANGE BUT TRUE!
Some folks think that animals are more sensitive than people because Balaam's donkey saw an angel way before Balaam did. But then, Balaam's donkey could also *speak*! (See: Numbers 22:23–33.)

Balak

The king of Moab in Moses' day. Balak was afraid of the Israelites camped on his border, so he offered Balaam great riches if he would come curse them. (See: Numbers 22:1–21; 24:10–11.)

Barabbas

A notorious Jewish criminal. When Pilate said he'd release one prisoner at Passover, Jesus' religious enemies asked him to release Barabbas instead of Jesus. (See: Matthew 27:15–26; Mark 15:7.)

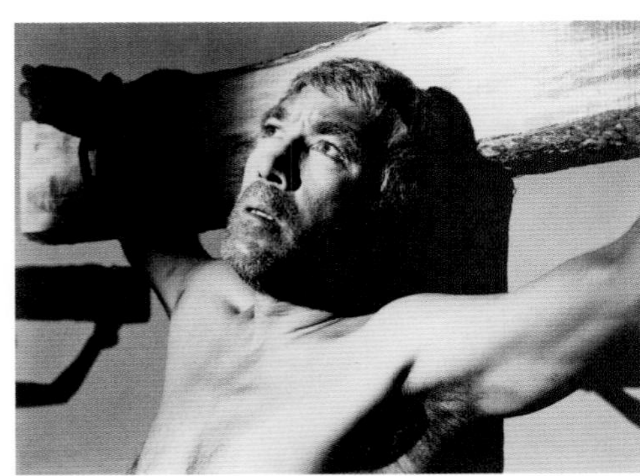
Actor Anthony Quinn plays Barabbas in a 1961 movie. In the story, Barabbas becomes a believer in Jesus—and is crucified during the Romans' persecution of Christians.

Lord's Supper

Jesus' final Passover meal with His disciples is called the Lord's Supper or the Last Supper. Jesus gave new meaning to this Passover meal when He told His disciples that drinking the wine was symbolic of drinking His blood (receiving salvation) and that eating the bread was symbolic of eating His body. We often call the Lord's Supper "communion." (See: Mark 14:12, 22–24.)

War against the Amalekites

In Moses' day, fierce warlike nomads called Amalekites lived in the Sinai desert. When the Israelite slaves came out of Egypt with no fighting experience, the Amalekites attacked them. Moses stood on a nearby hill to watch the battle and held the staff of God over his head. As long as he held it up, the Israelites were winning. When he got tired and let it drop, the Amalekites started winning. Aaron and Hur realized what was happening, so they rolled a stone under Moses for him to sit on, then stood on either side of him, holding up his hands until sundown, and the Israelites won the battle. (See: Exodus 17:8–16.)

Kadesh-barnea

Sometimes just called Kadesh, this oasis was in the desert south of Israel. It usually belonged to the Amalekites, but the Israelites lived there for many years. (See: Genesis 14:7; Numbers 20:1.)

Nine Cases of Famous Folks Who Washed Their Faces, Hands, and Feet

1. The Lord and two angels washed their feet.
2. Eliezer and his men washed their feet.
3. Joseph's brothers washed their feet.
4. Joseph washed his face.
5. A Levite, his wife, and his servant washed their feet.
6. Bathsheba bathed in her enclosed courtyard.
7. Elisha used to help Elijah wash his hands.
8. Pilate washed his hands.
9. The Pharisees washed their hands often.

(See: Genesis 18:1–4, 16; 24:32; 43:24, 30–31; Judges 19:19–21; 2 Samuel 11:2; 2 Kings 3:11; Matthew 27:24; Mark 7:3–4.)

Four Times Animals Taught People a Thing or Two

1. Balaam's donkey rebuked him for his madness.
2. Job told his friends that the animals, the birds, and the fish could teach them.
3. The oxen knew their masters better than Israel knew God.
4. Birds knew better than God's people what they were supposed to do.

(See: Numbers 22:25–33; Job 12:7–8; Isaiah 1:3; Jeremiah 8:7.)

Barak

When Jabin, a Canaanite king, conquered northern Israel, Deborah commanded Barak to fight Jabin, but Barak said he'd only go if she came with him—so she did. (See: Judges 4–5.)

STRANGE BUT TRUE!
The main god of the Greeks was Zeus. Once, when Barnabas and Paul had healed a lame man in the city of Lystra, the people there thought that Barnabas was Zeus. (See: Acts 14:8–18.)

Barnabas

A leader in the early church. Barnabas was full of the Holy Spirit and very generous. He traveled around with the apostle Paul, preaching the gospel. (See: Acts 4:36–37; 11:19–25; 13.)

Bartimaeus

A blind man who begged by the roadside near Jericho. When Jesus passed by, Bartimaeus wouldn't stop calling out to Him, so Jesus healed him, giving him sight. (See: Mark 10:46–52.)

THE NAME GAME!
It's not kids' faults what their parents name them. One Christian in the New Testament was called *Nereus*. His folks had named him after a Greek sea god! (See: Romans 16:15.)

Confess

Confess means to speak out loud and tell others about something. The Bible says that we are to "confess. . . 'Jesus is Lord' " (Romans 10:9 NIV). This means to publicly speak about our faith in Jesus. We are also told: "confess your sins to each other" (James 5:16 NIV). That way, others can know to pray for us so that we can be healed.

Anakim and Other Giants of Canaan

Goliath wasn't the only giant in the Bible. There were tons of other giants. In fact, there were *six entire nations* of giants. There were: **(1)** the Anakim of southern Canaan (Numbers 13:28, 33; Joshua 11:21); **(2)** the Rephaim of northern Canaan in the hill country of Ephraim (Joshua 17:15); **(3)** the Anakim of Gath and other cities on the coast (Joshua 11:22; 1 Samuel 17:4); **(4)** the Emim of Moab, east of the Dead Sea (Deuteronomy 2:9–11); **(5)** the Zamzummim of Ammon, east of the Jordan River (Deuteronomy 2:19–21); and **(6)** the Rephaim of Bashan, east of the Sea of Galilee (Genesis 14:5; Deuteronomy 3:4–5, 11).

CANAAN (CANAANITES)

Noah cursed Canaan, a son of Ham. Canaan settled in the land of Canaan, which is now called Israel. His descendants, the Canaanites, were very wicked. (See: Genesis 9:20–25; Leviticus 18:24–25.)

FUN FACTS!
Once Israel did "more evil than the nations had done whom the LORD destroyed before the people of Israel" (2 Kings 21:9 RSV). God had kicked out the Canaanites. Now He kicked out the Israelites.

Four War Songs That Women Sang

1. Miriam led the women in a victory song over Pharaoh.
2. Deborah sang a song about defeating Jabin and Sisera.
3. Women sang about Saul and David defeating the Philistines.
4. Women sang sad songs about King Josiah's death following his defeat in battle.

(See: Exodus 15:20–21; Judges 5; 1 Samuel 18:6–7; 2 Chronicles 35:25.)

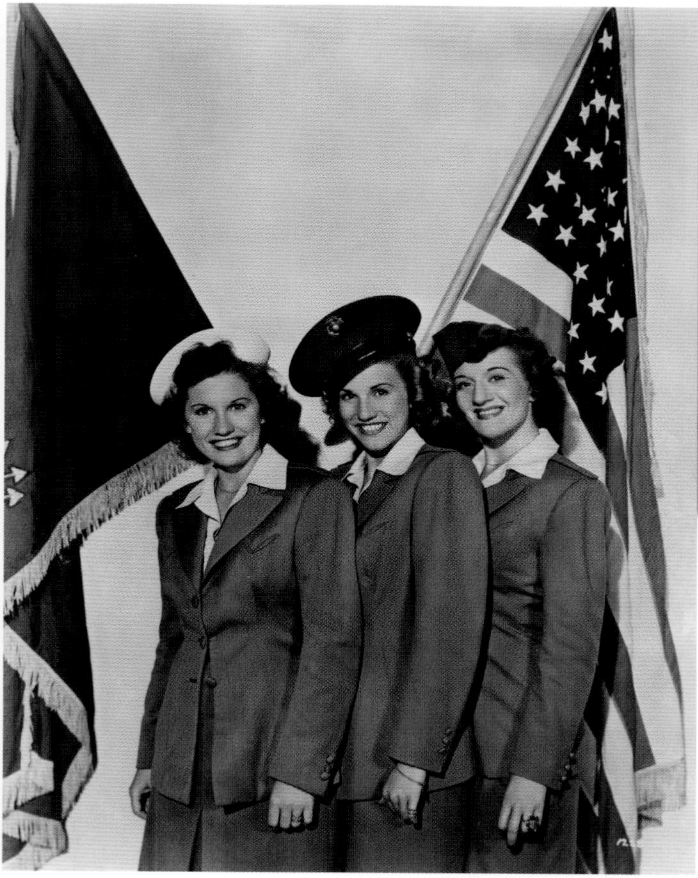

The Andrews sisters sang war songs to encourage Americans during World War II.

BARUCH

The son of a noble family and a close friend of the prophet Jeremiah. Baruch was Jeremiah's secretary and wrote down Jeremiah's prophecies. (See: Jeremiah 36:4; 45.)

BATHSHEBA

Bathsheba was married to one of David's warriors, Uriah the Hittite, but David had Uriah killed so that he could marry her. Bathsheba became the mother of Solomon. (See: 2 Samuel 11; 12:24.)

FUN FACTS!
The Bible says that Asahel, David's nephew, was "as fleet-footed as a wild gazelle" (2 Samuel 2:18 NIV). Not literally, of course. He was *fast*, but he couldn't run 50 miles an hour.

BELSHAZZAR

A descendant of Nebuchadnezzar, king of Babylon. King Belshazzar was feasting with a thousand nobles when a hand wrote a mysterious message on the palace wall. (See: Daniel 5.)

SCRIBE

Originally, a *scribe* meant a professional letter-writer or secretary. Baruch was the prophet Jeremiah's scribe. Some scribes specialized in writing out copies of the Law of Moses, and they did it so much that they became really familiar with the Law. Eventually some scribes became teachers. Another name for *scribes* was "teachers of the law," and by Jesus' day, unfortunately, many of them were hypocrites (Matthew 23 NIV). (See also: Jeremiah 36:4.)

An elderly rabbi does the work of a scribe, fixing faded letters on a scroll of scripture.

THE BAD, MAD GRAB FOR LAND

When God told the Israelites to march into Canaan and take over the land, they decided to send spies in first. Fine. But when the spies came back with fearful stories, the people rebelled and decided *not* to march into Canaan. As punishment, they were told to wander in the desert 40 years until they all died. Then the Israelites decided that, well, they *would* invade after all. Moses said, "Do not go up, because the LORD is not with you" (Numbers 14:42 NIV), but they went anyway. They marched north, encountered the enemy, and. . .were completely defeated. (See: Numbers 13–14; Deuteronomy 1:19–35.)

FUN FACTS!
When the Israelites invaded Canaan, God told them to drive out all the Canaanites. They failed to do that, and years later the Canaanites ruled and mistreated them. (See: Judges 4:1–3.)

Places & People

BABYLON (BABYLONIANS)

Babylon was a gigantic city in what is now Iraq. It was the capitol of the Babylonian Empire. Its king, Nebuchadnezzar, conquered Judah and took the Jews to Babylon. (See: 2 Kings 25:1–11.)

FUN FACTS!
If you ever find a couple of cute little bear cubs and want to take them home, *forget* it! Don't even ask your mom. The mama bear will go absolutely wild. (See: 2 Samuel 17:8.)

FUN FACTS!
Talk about fast! Elijah once outran a horse-drawn chariot on a 20-mile run from Mount Carmel to the city of Jezreel—and it was pouring rain! (See: 1 Kings 18:44–46.)

Three Plagues Where Many People Died at Once

1. A small plague killed the 10 unbelieving spies.
2. A plague in the Israelite camp killed 14,700 people.
3. A plague killed 70,000 people throughout Israel.

(See: Numbers 14:37; 16:49; 1 Chronicles 21:14.)

Four Fearful, Snarling Bear Thoughts

Once, lots of Syrian brown bears lived in the forested hills of Israel and were a huge problem:

1. David killed a bear that was carrying off one of his sheep.
2. Two bears mauled a gang of 42 loud, mocking youths.
3. A mother bear robbed of her bear cubs will be furious.
4. God will tear apart the wicked like an angry she-bear.

(See: 1 Samuel 17:34–36; 2 Kings 2:23–24; Proverbs 17:12; Hosea 13:8.)

BENJAMIN

The youngest of Jacob's 12 sons. Rachel was the mother of Joseph and Benjamin and died giving birth to Benjamin. He was Joseph's favorite brother. (See: Genesis 35:16–18; 43:26–34.)

FUN FACTS!
When Joseph invited his 11 brothers to dinner, he gave his youngest brother, Benjamin, *five* times as much food as the others! Ben must've been stuffed! (See: Genesis 43:34.)

THE NAME GAME!
Joseph's brother Benjamin named two of his sons "Muppim" and "Huppim" (Genesis 46:21). That's *not* where the Muppets came from!

Kermit the Frog and Miss Piggy. . .no relation to the Bible's Muppim.

BEZALEL

A highly skilled craftsman in Moses' day. He worked in metals, wood, and stone and made the Ark of God and other items for the Tent of Meeting. (See: Exodus 31:1–11; 35:30–35.)

A modern craftsman, like the Bible's Bezalel, works on a piece of jewelry.

BOAZ

A rich farmer in Bethlehem and relative of Naomi. After Naomi's sons died, Boaz married Ruth, Naomi's daughter-in-law. Boaz was the great-grandfather of King David. (See: Ruth 2:1–12; 4:13–22.)

TENT OF MEETING

Also called the *tabernacle* in the King James Bible. When the Israelites were wandering in the desert, they needed a place to keep the Ark of the Covenant and other holy objects. They also needed a place to worship God. God instructed Moses to build a large tent where He could meet with them. This tent had a large fence made of cloth around it. (See: Exodus 26; 29:42.)

Ground and Fire Gobble Up Grumblers

Once Korah, Dathan, and Abiram and 250 other Israelite leaders rose against Moses and Aaron. "Why have you set yourselves up as leaders?" they asked. "We're *all* holy!" Moses told everyone to appear before God the next day. When Korah and his followers showed up at the doorway of the Tent of Meeting, God warned all the Israelites to stand clear. As soon as everyone had moved a safe distance away, the ground opened up and swallowed Korah, Dathan, Abiram, and their households. Then fire scorched out from the Lord and burned up the 250 other rebels. After that it was *pretty clear* that God had chosen Moses and Aaron, not these other "holy" guys. (See: Numbers 16:1–35.)

FUN FACTS!
When millions of Israelites lived in cloth tents in the desert, you'd think fire was bound to break out in the tent camp sometime, right? Well, it did at least once. (See: Numbers 11:1–3.)

FUN FACTS!
When the Israelites lived 40 years in the desert, a pillar of cloud hovered over the Tent of Meeting. Each night it glowed like a pillar of fire. (See: Numbers 9:15–16.)

Five Times People Gave Clothing as Presents

1. Jacob gave his son Joseph a "coat of many colours" (Genesis 37:3 KJV).
2. Joseph gave his brother Benjamin five sets of clothes.
3. Samson gave his wedding guests 30 sets of clothing.
4. Naaman gave Gehazi, Elisha's servant, two sets of clothing.
5. A father gave his returning son the best robe he had.

(See: Genesis 45:22; Judges 14:19; 2 Kings 5:19–23; Luke 15:22.)

Three Famous Gatherings in the City Gates

Ancient cities were surrounded by walls, and elders often held important meetings in the busy gates:

1. Abraham talked to the Hittites in the gates of Hebron about buying a burial place.
2. Job often sat with the elders of Uz in the city gates, judging cases.
3. Boaz discussed buying Naomi's land and marrying Ruth in the gateway of Bethlehem.

(See: Genesis 23:1–11; Job 29:7–17; Ruth 4:1–11.)

Caesar

Caesar was the last name of a leading Roman family and became a title of all Roman emperors. Caesar Augustus and Tiberius Caesar are mentioned in the New Testament. (See: Luke 2:1; 3:1.)

Tiberius Caesar

Caiaphas

Caiaphas was the high priest of Israel in Jesus' day. He was a selfish leader who sentenced Jesus to death to keep peace with the Romans. (See: John 11:47–50; Matthew 26:57–66.)

Cain

The oldest son of Adam and Eve. Cain killed his brother Abel in a jealous rage, so God set a mark on Cain and made him a permanent wanderer. (See: Genesis 4:1–17.)

The murderer Cain wanders the earth—his punishment from God—in this painting from 1880.

High Priest

The *high priest* was a man from the tribe of Levi who came before God to pray and to make sacrifices for the sins of his people. Moses' brother Aaron was the first high priest. When a high priest died, his son usually became high priest. Not all high priests were godly men; for example, Caiaphas condemned Jesus to death (See: Exodus 28:1; Numbers 20:25–28; Matthew 26:57–66).

The Amazing Bronze Serpent

When the older, rebellious generation had all died, the young Israelites headed in to conquer Canaan. But as they were crossing the desert, they began complaining, "There is no water! And we detest this miserable food!" (Numbers 21:5 NIV). Then venomous snakes bit them and many Israelites died. When the people repented, God had Moses hammer a snake out of bronze and hold it up on a pole, and whoever looked at it was healed. Hundreds of years later, however, the Israelites began worshipping the bronze serpent as a god. Dumb mistake. King Hezekiah took a hammer and smashed it in pieces. (See: Numbers 21:4–9; 2 Kings 18:4.)

FUN FACTS!
When the Canaanites of Arad heard that the Israelites were passing by, they surprise-attacked them. Big mistake. The Israelites counter-attacked and wiped out their cities. (See: Numbers 21:1–3.)

The cottonmouth snake, found in the eastern United States, can kill with its venom.

Five Painful Snake Bites

1. Venomous snakes bit and killed Israelites in the wilderness.
2. "Whoever breaks through a wall may be bitten by a snake" (Ecclesiastes 10:8 NIV).
3. God threatened to send vipers to bite the evil Israelites.
4. Sometimes as men rested by a wall they were bitten by snakes .
5. Paul was bitten by a viper on Malta but suffered no ill effects.

(See: Numbers 21:4–9; Jeremiah 8:17; Amos 5:19; Acts 28:1-6)

STRANGE BUT TRUE!
The only people in the Bible who held conversations with animals were Eve, who chatted with a serpent; and Balaam, who argued with his donkey. (See: Genesis 3:1–5; Numbers 22:21–30.)

Places & People

Caesarea

King Herod built a city with a good harbor on the northern coast of Israel. He named it after the emperor, Caesar, and the Romans made it the provincial capitol. Cornelius lived there. (See: Acts 10:1–2.)

AWESOME FEAT!
King Hezekiah wanted a secure water supply, so he had a tunnel cut through 1,700 feet of rock to bring water from a spring outside the city to a pool inside Jerusalem. (See: 2 Chronicles 32:30.)

CALEB

One of the 12 spies sent into Canaan. Only Caleb and Joshua brought back a good report. Many years later, at age 85, Caleb conquered the city of Hebron. (See: Numbers 13; Joshua 14:6–14.)

CORNELIUS

A Roman centurion who received a vision from God. Cornelius then asked Peter to come to his house and preach the gospel. Cornelius, his family, and his friends all became Christians. (See: Acts 10.)

FUN FACTS!
Tanners cleaned animal skins and made them into leather. They had a stinky job and their homes smelled. The apostle Peter stayed several days in a tanner's house. (See: Acts 9:43.)

A man dresses up like a Roman soldier of the apostle Peter's day.

CYRUS

The ruler of the Persian Empire who allowed the Jews to leave Babylon and return to Judah. Isaiah had prophesied about Cyrus hundreds of years earlier. (See: Ezra 1:1–4; Isaiah 45:1.)

SYNAGOGUE

A Jewish house of worship. When the Babylonians destroyed the temple of God and took the Jews to far-off lands, the Jews began to meet together on Sabbaths and to pray and read and teach the Law. Eventually they built special buildings to do these things in. In Jesus' day, there were synagogues all over Israel—all over the Roman Empire, in fact. (See: Diaspora—below; see also: Luke 4:16; Acts 15:21.)

DIASPORA

The Jews living scattered among the Gentile nations. After the Jews were taken to Babylon, some returned home to Judea. Many others continued living in foreign nations, from Egypt to Persia to Greece. In Paul's day, there were Jews living in every major city of the Roman Empire. (See: Esther 8:9–17; John 7:35; Acts 15:21; James 1:1.)

The Dude Who Was Dumber Than His Donkey

Balaam could hear from God yet he was buddy-buddy with idol-worshippers. He took the spiritual gifts of God lightly. So when the king of Moab called Balaam to put a curse on the Israelites and Balaam went, God sent an angel to kill Balaam. His donkey saw the angel and ran off into a field. Then she scraped against a wall to run past. Finally, she just lay down in the road. Balaam began beating her, and suddenly his donkey began speaking. Instead of cluing in that something unusual was happening, Balaam began arguing with his donkey. That's when the angel appeared to Balaam and laid things out plain—*real* plain. (See: Numbers 22:1–35.)

STRANGE BUT TRUE!

Once, Abraham stood under a tree and watched God and two angels eating lunch. Seriously! They had milk, curds, beef, and bread for the main course. (See: Genesis 18:6–8.)

FUN FACTS!

God said that the land of Canaan was a good land, but that the Canaanites who lived there were so wicked that the land would vomit them out. (See: Leviticus 18:28.)

Four Dusty, Desert Donkey Details

Thousands of years ago, tons of wild asses (donkeys) roamed the deserts near Canaan. Here's what the Bible says about them:

1. Hungry donkeys bray (call out) in the desert.
2. A wild donkey's colt can't be born as a man.
3. Poor people scrounge for food in the desert like wild donkeys.
4. Wild donkeys laugh at tame donkeys that have to work.

(See: Job 6:5; 11:12; 24:5; 39:5–8.)

Rome (Romans)

Rome was the capital city of the Roman Empire. Paul was taken to Rome as a prisoner and preached the gospel there. He also wrote a letter to the Romans. (See: Acts 28:16–20; Romans 1:1–7.)

The apostle Paul probably recognized the Temple of Saturn in Rome—it was built 500 years before his time, and parts of it are still standing.

DAGON

A Philistine god. Samson destroyed Dagon's temple in Gaza. When the Ark of God was placed in Dagon's temple in Ashdod, his idol fell down before it. (See: Judges 16:21–30; 1 Samuel 5:1–4.)

STRANGE BUT TRUE!
The Philistines captured the Ark of the Covenant and put it in the temple of Dagon. The idol of Dagon fell over and lay flat before the Ark. They set Dagon up again, but he fell down again. (See: 1 Samuel 5:1–4.)

Many believe the Philistine god Dagon was like a male mermaid—half man and half fish.

DAMARIS

A Greek woman from Athens. When Paul preached to philosophers at the Areopagus (Mars' Hill), several men, as well as Damaris, became Christians. (See: Acts 17:19, 34.)

AWESOME FEAT!
When Samson lost his strength, the Philistines gouged out his eyes. When his strength returned, Samson killed 3,000 Philistines "for [his] two eyes" (Judges 16:28 NKJV). (See also: Judges 16:21–30.)

DANIEL

A Jewish youth taken as a prisoner to Babylon. After telling King Nebuchadnezzar his dream and interpreting it, Daniel became the king's chief adviser and the ruler over Babylon. (See: Daniel 1:1–6; 2.)

CHRISTIAN

Those who believe in and follow Jesus Christ. In the book of Acts, *Christians* are usually referred to as "the believers" or "the disciples"—and "the disciples were called Christians first in Antioch" (Acts 11:26 KJV). To be a Christian begins with accepting Jesus as your Savior and Lord. Then you must obey and follow Jesus. (See: 1 John 2:6.)

FASTING

To go without food, or to avoid eating certain kinds of food. People fast to get their minds off of physical things and to focus on prayer to God. Daniel fasted for 21 days, eating "no delicacies" (Daniel 10:3 RSV). Jesus once fasted for 40 days. (See: Matthew 4:1–4.)

Spies Beneath the Piles of Flax

One time, Joshua sent two spies into Jericho to check out the city's defenses, but they were spotted. The spies ducked into the house of a sinful woman named Rahab, but the king sent soldiers there to arrest them. Rahab had a linen-making business (linen threads come from the flax plant), and she had flax drying on the flat roof of her house. Quickly, Rahab took the men up onto her roof and covered them with heaps of flax. The soldiers searched but didn't find them, and thanks to Rahab's sending the soldiers another direction, the two spies then escaped and took their report back to Joshua. (See: Joshua 2.)

FUN FACTS!
Many Israelites lived east of the Jordan River, and when the men went off to war, they left their families behind—and didn't see them for five or six years! (See: Numbers 32:1–6, 16–18; Joshua 22:1–4.)

FUN FACTS!
A clan of Israelites living in the town of Beth Ashbea specialized in growing crops of flax and weaving their threads into linen clothes. (See: 1 Chronicles 4:21.)

Olives were an important crop for people of biblical times.

Seven Famous and Somewhat Fantastic Trees

1. The tree of life
2. The tree of the knowledge
3. The great tree of Moreh—also called the soothsayers' tree
4. The great oaks of Mamre
5. The olive tree that refused to be king
6. The cedar treetop transplanted by an eagle
7. The enormous tree in King Nebuchadnezzar's dream

(Genesis 2:9; 3:1–7, 22; 12:6; 13:18; 14:13; Judges 9:8–9, 37; Ezekiel 17:1–4; Daniel 4:10–12; Revelation 2:7; 22:2.)

DARIUS

King Darius the Mede was an ally of the Persians, and his army conquered the city of Babylon. Darius was tricked into throwing Daniel into the lions' den. (See: Daniel 5:30–31; 6.)

STRANGE BUT TRUE!
God sent an angel with the answer to Daniel's prayer, but a demon prince blocked him for 21 days. Finally the archangel Michael helped the angel break through. (See: Daniel 10:12–13.)

DAVID

David was a shepherd when he was a youth in Bethlehem. He later became King Saul's musician and bodyguard, then became the second king of Israel. (See: 1 Samuel 16; 2 Samuel 5:1–5.)

FUN FACTS!
The Israelites beat grain to break off the covering (chaff), then tossed the grain in the air to let the wind blow the chaff away. David prayed that his enemies would be like chaff. (See: Psalm 35:4–5.)

David ruins his rule as Israel's king by stealing his neighbor's wife, Bathsheba. When he should have been out fighting a battle, he stayed home—and saw the beautiful woman bathing next door (see 2 Samuel 11).

FUN FACTS!
In King Saul's day, there were no blacksmiths in Israel. Then, 400 years later, there were no blacksmiths in Israel again. They all went off to Babylon. (See: 1 Samuel 13:19; 2 Kings 24:14.)

DEBORAH

A prophetess and a judge of Israel. When Jabin, a Canaanite king, invaded Israel, Deborah commanded Barak to defeat Jabin. Afterward she wrote a famous battle song. (See: Judges 4–5.)

JUDGMENT

A decision or ruling by judges and rulers. When he was king of Israel, "David executed judgment and justice" (2 Samuel 8:15 KJV). *Judgment* also means God's decision or ruling on a matter: "The judgments of the LORD are true and righteous" (Psalm 19:9 NKJV). *Judgment* also means a disaster God sent upon people to punish them, such as when God judged Sodom. (See: Genesis 19:24–25.)

GREAT WHITE THRONE OF JUDGMENT

The final Judgment at the end of the world when God will judge the unsaved. (Believers are judged earlier at the "judgment seat of Christ," see page 140.) (See also: Revelation 20:11–15)

The Day a Flooding River Dried Up

The Jordan River is normally not wide or deep, but when the snow melts and rains fall in spring, it overflows its banks onto a flood plain nearly a mile wide. And *this* was the time God picked for the Israelites to cross. They had no way of knowing, but it seems that hours earlier a landslide had blocked the river 20 miles upstream at a town called Adam. Talk about miraculous timing! The instant God's priests walked into the water, the last of the water ran past and the river dried up! The dam held *just* long enough for all the Israelites to cross over, then the water broke out and the river flooded again. (See: Joshua 3–4.)

FUN FACTS!
When God dried up rivers and seas, two things happened: (1) the Israelites crossed on dry land, and (2) the stranded fish died and rotted. (See: Exodus 14:21–22; Joshua 3:15–17; Isaiah 50:2.)

Ten Prophetesses (Lady Prophets)

1. Miriam
2. Deborah
3. Huldah
4. Noadiah—she was a bad one!
5. Isaiah's wife
6. Anna

7–10. Philip's four daughters

(See: Exodus 15:20; Judges 4:4; 2 Kings 22:14; Nehemiah 6:14; Isaiah 8:3; Luke 2:36–38; Acts 21:9.)

Jordan River

This river flows south from the Sea of Galilee into the Dead Sea, and formed the eastern border of Canaan. The Israelites crossed it during flood season, and John baptized people there. (See: Joshua 3:14–17; Matthew 3:4–6).

Judgment—in the form of legal decisions—is often shown as a woman holding a scale.

Delilah

A Philistine woman whom Samson loved. The Philistine lords offered Delilah money to betray Samson, so she pestered him until he told her the secret of his strength. (See: Judges 16:4–21.)

STRANGE BUT TRUE!
Samson could kill a lion with his bare hands and rip off city gates without getting tired. But Delilah's constant nagging made him "tired to death" (Judges 16:16 NIV). (See also: Judges 14:5–6.)

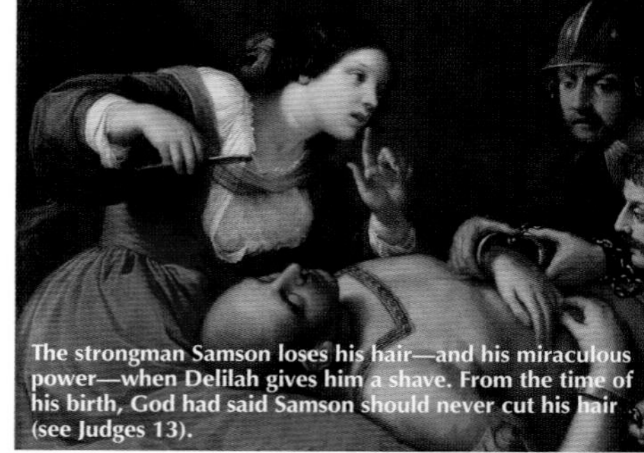
The strongman Samson loses his hair—and his miraculous power—when Delilah gives him a shave. From the time of his birth, God had said Samson should never cut his hair (see Judges 13).

Demas

When Paul was in prison, Demas was one of his closest helpers. Later on, however, Demas "loved this present world" (2 Timothy 4:10 NKJV) and deserted Paul. (See: Philemon 1:23–24.)

Demetrius

A silversmith in Ephesus who made silver shrines of the goddess Artemis (Diana). Demetrius started a riot when Paul taught that manmade gods were not real. (See: Acts 19:23–41.)

Day of Atonement

One day a year, the high priest would go into the Holy of Holies with the blood of a goat to atone for the sins that the Israelites had committed in ignorance. This day was called Yom Kippur or the Feast of Atonement—even though they fasted on this day. (See: Atonement and Holy of Holies, both found on page 46.) God then covered the sins of the Israelites and forgave them. (See: Leviticus 16; Hebrews 9:7–8.)

Scapegoat

On the Day of Atonement, the high priest took two goats: the first goat was sacrificed (killed). The high priest then symbolically placed the sins of the nation on the second goat. Then the scapegoat (*escape*-goat) was driven out into the wilderness. These days a scapegoat means anyone who is picked out and blamed for other people's mistakes. (See: Leviticus 16:1–22.)

STRANGE BUT TRUE!
People once believed in satyrs (half-goat, half-human beings), so when they read that the *sair* danced in ruined cities, they thought the Hebrew word *sair* meant *satyr* (Isaiah 13:21 KJV).

A camouflaged soldier waits in ambush.

Five Ambushes from Bushes and Buildings

1. The Israelites ambushed the Canaanite city of Ai.
2. The Israelites ambushed the Benjamites in Gibeon.
3. The king of Aram tried to ambush the king of Israel several times.
4. King Jeroboam's armies ambushed King Abijah's army.
5. More than 40 men waited to ambush the apostle Paul.

(See: Joshua 8:12; Judges 20:28–29; 2 Kings 6:8–10; 2 Chronicles 13:13–15; Acts 23:20–21.)

I Love Lists!

Tiny City a Hard Nut to Crack

After God had helped them win a great victory at Jericho, the Israelites came to the city of Ai (*Ay*-eye). Since the city was so small, Joshua sent only 3,000 soldiers against it. To everyone's surprise, the men of Ai came rushing out, killed 36 Israelites, and drove the rest of Israel's army off. Joshua was stunned. Why hadn't God helped them win such an easy battle? Then he found out why. All the treasures of Jericho were supposed to have been given to God, but an Israelite named Achan had kept some for himself. He had stolen from God! When the Israelites dealt with *that* sin, then God helped them defeat Ai. (See: Joshua 7:1–8:29.)

AWESOME FEAT!

Ox goads were long poles with a metal point for poking lazy oxen. A superhero named Shamgar once killed 600 Philistines with an ox goad. (See: Judges 3:31.)

DINAH

A daughter of Jacob and Leah. The Canaanite prince of Shechem hurt her, then spoke kindly to her and wanted to marry her. Dinah's brothers killed all the men in Shechem in revenge. (See: Genesis 34.)

FUN FACTS!
There are 66 names in a list of Jacob's descendants. The only females included in this all-boy list are his two granddaughters, Dinah (Genesis 46:15) and Serah (Genesis 46:17). (See also: Genesis 46:8–26.)

EBED-MELECH

An Ethiopian (Cushite) official in King Zedekiah's court. When he learned that Jeremiah had been cast into a mud-filled pit, he got permission to rescue him. (See: Jeremiah 38:1–13.)

ELEAZAR

The third son of Aaron. Eleazar became chief priest after Aaron's death. He helped Joshua divide the land of Canaan among the tribes of Israel. (See: Exodus 6:23; Numbers 20:28; 34:17.)

AVENGE, AVENGER

In ancient times when someone killed a person, a man in the dead person's family would kill the murderer to get even. He was the avenger. God says that He will avenge us when people hurt or persecute us, so we are to love our enemies and not to take vengeance on them ourselves. (See: Numbers 35:14–25; Romans 12:19–21.)

WACKY, WEIRD WEATHER AT WAR

Once five Amorite kings attacked Israel's allies, the Gibeonites, so Joshua marched his army to Gibeon by night and surprised the Amorites early the next morning. The Amorites were so panicked that they took off running down the road. The Israelites chased them and began cutting them down.

Then weird, wild, weather broke loose. The sky grew dark with storm clouds, and God began hurling down huge, baseball-sized hailstones on the terrified Amorites. More Amorites died from being hit by hailstones than were killed by the swords of the Israelites. (See: Joshua 10:1–11.)

FUN FACTS!
When the King James Bible asks, "Hast thou entered into the treasures of the snow?" it's *not* asking, "Have you been to Santa Claus's toy factory at the North Pole?" (See: Job 38:22.)

God bombed Amorite soldiers with hailstones like these during a battle against Joshua.

Millstones are grooved to help grind grain into flour.

Eight Weird War Weapons

1. The Red Sea parted, then washed back, drowning the Egyptians.
2. Giant hailstones wiped out the Amorite armies.
3. Swarms of angry hornets drove the Canaanites out of Canaan.
4. A woman dropped a millstone on King Abimelech's head.
5. Samson used the jawbone of a donkey as a weapon.
6. God caused loud thunder to panic the Philistines.
7. Forest trees killed King David's enemies.
8. God caused the loud, fake noise of an army attacking, which sent the Arameans fleeing.

(See: Exodus 14:21–28; Joshua 10:11; 24:12; Judges 9:52–53; 15:14–16; 1 Samuel 7:10; 2 Samuel 18:6–8; 2 Kings 7:5–7.)

CUSH (CUSHITES)

Cush was a kingdom south of Egypt, in the land that is today called Sudan. Candace was queen of Cush (sometimes mistakenly called Ethiopia) in New Testament times. (See: Acts 8:26–27.)

FUN FACTS!
The kings and armies of Judah had a secret escape route out of Jerusalem. In King Zedekiah's day, it was a secret gate in the palace garden, between the two city walls. (See: 2 Kings 25:2–4.)

FUN FACTS!
Jacob's body was brought from Egypt and buried in Mamre. His son Joseph's bones were brought from Egypt and buried in Shechem, a different city. (See: Genesis 50:13–14; Joshua 24:32.)

ELI

A later descendant of Aaron and a high priest. Eli's sons were wicked, and he didn't control them, so God took away his family's right to be high priests. (See: 1 Samuel 2:11–36.)

ELIEZER

Abraham's steward (overseer of his belongings). Eliezer was most likely the servant who went to Haran to find a wife for Abraham's son Isaac. (See: Genesis 15:2; 24:1–67.)

ELIJAH

A prophet of Israel (the northern kingdom) in the days of King Ahab. Elijah called for a drought on the land and called fire down from heaven. (See: 1 Kings 17:1; 18:36–38; 2 Kings 1:7–12.)

STRANGE BUT TRUE!
The prophet Elijah apparently started the trend of dressing in animal-hair robes. Hundreds of years later, prophets still dressed that way. (See: 2 Kings 1:7–8; Mark 1:6.)

Elijah (center) watches fire from heaven burn up the sacrifice he put on the altar to God. Meanwhile, priests of the false god Baal dance around their altar, trying to get a similar response.

HOLY OF HOLIES

Also called the Most Holy Place. It was a small room in the heart of the temple where the Ark of the Covenant was kept, and where God's presence was. A thick curtain kept the people out. Once a year on the Day of Atonement, the high priest entered this room to pray for God to forgive the sins that the people had done in ignorance. (See: Exodus 26:31–35; Leviticus 16; Hebrews 9:1–8.)

ATONE, ATONEMENT

A Bible translator invented the word *atone* (at-one) to show how Jesus makes peace between us and God. Sin separates us from God, but when Jesus died on the cross, He *atoned* for our sins. He made us "at one" with God. *Kaphar*, which is the Hebrew word for *atone*, means "to cover." Jesus' blood covers our sins. (See: Exodus 30:10; 32:30; Romans 3:23; 6:23.)

Surprise Attack on Hazor

After God helped the Israelites defeat the Amorite kings down south, the Canaanites of the north became alarmed. Normally, all their little cities and kingdoms fought among themselves, but now Jabin, king of Hazor, sent out word to all the kings of the north, and they gathered to fight Israel. Joshua didn't wait for this monster army to march south. He quickly marched his army north, caught the Canaanites before they were ready, and obliterated their armies—all in one blow! Then with the soldiers of Hazor and the other cities gone, Joshua was able to easily capture their unguarded cities. (See: Joshua 11:1–15.)

Amorites

Thousands of years ago, desert tribes called Amorites settled in Canaan. Abraham was friends with them. Later the Amorites became wicked and Joshua battled them. (See: Genesis 14:13; Joshua 10:5–10.)

FUN FACTS!
When the false god Baal didn't answer his prophet's prayers, Elijah mocked them saying, "Shout louder! . . . Maybe he is sleeping and must be awakened" (1 Kings 18:27 NIV).

THE NAME GAME!
When God told Abraham that his 90-year-old wife Sarah would have a baby, Abraham fell to the ground laughing—so God told him to name his son *Isaac*, meaning "he laughs." (See: Genesis 17:15–19.)

Three Fattest Men in the Bible

1. Eglon king of Moab was a "very fat man" (Judges 3:17 NKJV). (See also: Judges 3:21–22.)
2. Eli was so "heavy" (1 Samuel 4:18 RSV) that he died when he fell off his chair.
3. Regarding rich men, Psalm 73:7 (KJV) says, "Their eyes stand out with fatness."

Six Times Fierce, Miraculous Fire Fell

1. Fire came out from the Lord and killed 250 rebellious men.
2. The fire of the Lord fell on Elijah's sacrifice on Mount Carmel.

3–4. Elijah called down fire *two times* to kill 100 men.

5. God sent down fire from heaven on David's sacrifices.
6. God sent down fire when Solomon dedicated the temple.

(See: Numbers 16:35; 1 Kings 18:38; 2 Kings 1:9–12; 1 Chronicles 21:26; 2 Chronicles 7:1.)

ELISHA

A prophet who worked closely with Elijah and inherited his cloak when he was caught up into heaven. Elisha did even more miracles than Elijah. (See: 1 Kings 19:19–21; 2 Kings 2:1–22.)

FUN FACTS!
Ever had someone stare at you so long that you wondered what you did wrong? The prophet Elisha stared at Hazael so long that Hazael was ashamed. (See: 2 Kings 8:10–11.)

STRANGE BUT TRUE!
The only time the Bible talks about anybody sneezing is when it mentions that a young boy sneezed seven times in a row—after Elisha brought him back to life! (See: 2 Kings 4:35.)

ENOCH

A godly man who lived before the Flood. Enoch "walked with God" (Genesis 5:22 KJV), and when he was 365 years old, God took him to heaven—alive! Enoch didn't even die. (See: Genesis 5:18–24.)

EPAPHRAS

The apostle Paul's "dear fellow servant" (Colossians 1:7 NIV) and the minister of the church at Colosse. He was always praying for God to help his fellow Christians. (See: Colossians 4:12–13.)

THE NAME GAME!
Epaphras was the faithful Christian minister of the church of Colosse. But what a name for people to call you all day long! *Epaphras* means "handsome" or "charming." (See: Colossians 1:7.)

CHURCH

The Greek word for "church" is ekklēsia, which means the community of believers "called out" from the world to follow Jesus. When Paul preached the gospel in a new city, one of the first things he did was to organize fellowships of new believers—churches. The church is Christ's body here on earth, representing Him to the world. (See: Body of Christ, page 130; see also Acts 14:21–23.)

HEAVEN

A place of perfect peace, health, and joy that lasts forever. The saved will live in heaven in the presence of God, Jesus, and the holy angels. Right now, heaven is a spiritual place only, but one day God will come down to a new earth to dwell with people. Heaven will then be a supernatural spiritual/physical place on earth. (See: Revelation 7:15–17; 21:1–7, 12.)

King Solomon uses his wisdom to figure out which woman is the mother of a living child. Read the whole story in 1 Kings 3:16–28.

Two Arguments over Babies

There are two times in the Old Testament where two women each had a baby; one baby died and one baby was alive, and the women argued about the living baby.

1. In King Solomon's day
2. In the prophet Elisha's day

(See: 1 Kings 3:16–27; 2 Kings 6:26–30.)

Feature

Rooting out the Forest Giants

In Joshua's day, the hills of Canaan were covered with thick forests. The Canaanites lived down in the fertile plains and had speedy chariot armies. Now, when the Israelites entered Canaan, members of the tribe of Manasseh complained that there were so *many* of them that they had no room to live. Okay then. Joshua gave them a choice: either fight the chariot armies in the plains or pick up their axes, go up into the hills, and clear some farmland. The people of Manasseh chose the forests. They had to fight the giants (Rephaim) living up in the hills, but it must've beat dodging iron chariots. (See: Joshua 17:14–18.)

REALLY GROSS!

These days, people wash their cars to make them look nice and shiny. In Israel, men washed their chariots when they were bloody from battle. (See: 1 Kings 22:37–38.)

Epaphroditus

When Paul was in prison, the Christians of Philippi sent Epaphroditus with money to help him. While he was in Rome, Epaphroditus became so sick that he nearly died. (See: Philippians 2:25–29.)

Esau

The son of Isaac, and Jacob's twin brother. Esau was the oldest brother but didn't really care for his birthright, so he sold it to Jacob for a bowl of stew and some bread. (See: Genesis 25:21–34.)

STRANGE BUT TRUE!
Esau was so incredibly hairy that to run your fingers along his arm was about the same as petting a goat. *Seriously!* (See: Genesis 27:11–16, 21–23.)

Esther

A beautiful Jewish woman living in the capital of Persia. When King Ahaseurus (Xerxes) needed a new queen, he picked Esther. She later saved her people from being killed. (See: Esther 2:17; 7–8.)

A young Jewish girl dresses as Queen Esther for a Purim celebration.

Birthright

In Israel, the firstborn son received the birthright—the right to a double share of his father's property. The firstborn Esau traded his huge birthright to his younger brother, Jacob, for one bowl of stew. The Prodigal Son was not the oldest son, so he received a smaller inheritance—fortunately, since he wasted it! (See: Genesis 25:24–34; Deuteronomy 21:15–17; Luke 15:11–13.)

Seventy Kings Scrapping for Scraps

When the Israelites came into Canaan, they had to deal with some very nasty characters. Take Adoni-Bezek, for example: He was the Canaanite king of Bezek, and he constantly made war against neighboring cities. Whenever he captured a king, he cut off his thumbs and big toes and kept him as a prisoner. Only dogs ate scraps that fell from the table, but to humiliate the conquered kings, Adoni-Bezek forced them to fight for food and scramble for scraps under his palace table. That was one *huge* mess of scraps! No wonder the Israelites cut off Adoni-Bezek's big toes and thumbs. (See: Matthew 15:27; Judges 1:1–8.)

FUN FACTS!
Two rulers Adoni-Zedek, a king of Jerusalem, and Adoni-Bezek, a king of Bezek fought the Israelites. Betcha can't say "Adoni-Zedek and Adoni-Bezek" real fast ten times. (See: Joshua 10:1–10; Judges 1:4–6.)

PHILIPPI (PHILIPPIANS)

Philippi was one of the most important cities of Macedonia (northern Greece). Paul preached the gospel there and later wrote a letter to the Philippians. (See: Acts 16:11–12; Philippians 1:1.)

FUN FACTS!
The ancient Persians had a Pony Express. They had an excellent road system, and when they had urgent messages, they sent messengers on the swiftest horses. (See: Esther 8:10, 14.)

The first person martyred (killed for following Jesus) is Stephen, stoned by people who hated his preaching (Acts 6:8–7:60).

Four Mentions of Ridden Horses

1. The royal horses of Persian messengers
2. The warhorses of Uz
3. The mount of the apostle Paul
4. White horses of Jesus and the armies of heaven

(See: Esther 8:14; Job 39:19–25; Acts 23:23–24; Revelation 19:11–14.)

Five Very Tough Punishments

1. Burning—for a man who marries a woman and her mother
2. Stoning—for being a medium, for blasphemy, for gathering wood on the Sabbath, for idolatry
3. Throwing captured enemy soldiers off a cliff
4. Hanging—of Haman, who had built the gallows for Esther's cousin Mordecai
5. Sawing people in two

(See: Leviticus 20:14, 27; 24:16; Numbers 15:32–36; Deuteronomy 13:6–10; 2 Chronicles 25:12; Esther 7:9–10; Hebrews 11:37.)

Eve

The first woman and the wife of Adam. Eve was created from one of Adam's ribs. Satan, as a serpent, convinced her to disobey God and eat the forbidden fruit. (See: Genesis 2:20–3:24.)

Ezekiel

A prophet who lived in Babylon and had some of the most bizarre visions in the Bible. Ezekiel also did some very odd things in order to obey God. (See: Ezekiel 1:3–28; 4:1–17; 12:1–7; 37:1–14.)

STRANGE BUT TRUE!
Ezekiel once had a vision of a valley filled with dry bones. There was a tremendous rattling and clanking when the skeletons suddenly reassembled! (See: Ezekiel 37:1–10.)

FUN FACTS!
Ezekiel was some prophet! God told him to dig through the temple wall to get into the temple. Later, God told Ezekiel to dig through the wall of his house to get out. (See: Ezekiel 8:7–8; 12:5–7.)

In one of the creepiest scenes in the Bible, the prophet Ezekiel watches a bunch of old skeletons come back to life.

Ezra

A wise scribe who traveled from Babylon to Judah to teach the Law of Moses to the Jewish people. Ezra spoke strongly against Jews marrying nonbelievers. (See: Ezra 7; 9–10.)

Original Sin

The original (very first) sin was when Adam and Eve disobeyed God and ate the fruit of the tree of the knowledge. This brought the curse and death into the world. Adam and Eve then had sinful natures, and all humans after them did as well. (See Curse, page 14, and Sinful Nature, page 132; see also: Genesis 3; 1 Corinthians 15:21–22.)

Outwitting Sisera's Chariot Army

When the Israelites took over Canaan, they didn't finish driving out the Canaanites. Big mistake. Several years later, the Canaanite king, Jabin, overran northern Israel. His general, Sisera, had 900 chariots and cruelly crushed the Israelites for 20 years. The Israelites had no chariots. What to do? God set a trap: He had the Israelites lure Sisera's army into the flat Kishon River valley. Sisera was delighted. This was an ideal chariot battlefield. But then a sudden rainstorm broke, the river overflowed its banks, and his chariots were useless in the mud. The Israelites wiped out the entire Canaanite army. (See: Judges 4:1–16; 5:4, 21.)

FUN FACTS!
God said that He could've helped Israel drive out the Canaanites in one year, but He didn't do it, or the land would have quickly filled up with wild animals. (See: Exodus 23:27–29.)

Judah

After Solomon died, the nation of Israel split into two kingdoms—the northern tribes were called Israel, and the southern tribe, Judah, was called Judah. Many years later the Romans called the land *Judea*. (See: 1 Kings 12:16–20; Matthew 2:1.)

A Christian rock group, Stryper, was known as a "hair band." Can you guess why?

Six Men and Their Hair

1. Esau was completely covered with hair when he was born.
2. When Samson's hair was cut, he lost his strength.
3. Absalom had such long hair that it weighed five pounds.
4. Ezekiel cut off all his hair and burned some of it.
5. Nebuchadnezzar, a king of Babylon, had hair that was long, dirty, and matted together.
6. Ezra pulled some of his hair out in grief.

(See: Genesis 25:24-25; Judges 16:17–20; 2 Samuel 14:25–26; Ezekiel 5:1–4; Daniel 4:33; Ezra 9:3.)

FELIX

The Roman governor of Judea. When Paul's Jewish enemies accused Paul of crimes, Felix didn't hand Paul over to them—but he didn't set Paul free either. (See: Acts 24.)

FUN FACTS!
The Roman governor Felix was afraid of the gospel message, but often talked with Paul because he hoped that Paul would offer him a bribe. Paul didn't, by the way. (See: Acts 24:25–26.)

This bronze coin is from the time of Felix.

FESTUS

Festus replaced Felix as governor. When Paul insisted on being judged by Caesar, Festus held a court hearing first to find out from Paul exactly what had happened (Acts 24:27; 25–26).

GABRIEL

A high-ranking angel who often took messages to Israel. He made announcements to Daniel, to Zechariah, and to Mary, the mother of Jesus. (See: Daniel 9:20–27; Luke 1:18–19, 26–37.)

The angel Gabriel is often shown with a horn—since many people believe he'll blow the trumpet on God's day of judgment of the earth.

ALTAR OF INCENSE

A short stand covered with gold. Sweet-smelling incense was burned on it twice a day. This altar was inside the temple, and burning incense on it symbolized believers' prayers rising to God. Zechariah was burning incense to God when the angel Gabriel appeared to him. (See: Exodus 30:1–8; Luke 1:8–11, 19; Revelation 8:3.)

Midianite Invasion! Time for a Miracle!

When the Israelites disobeyed God, God allowed the armies of Midian to invade their land. Countless raiders swept into Israel before harvest and let their livestock eat all the Israelites' crops. The Israelites fled into caves and mountains. They were starving. This went on for seven years, year after year. They were desperate! Finally, God sent an angel to a farmer named Gideon. The angel told him to raise an army and attack the Midianites. God whittled Gideon's army down from 32,000 men to a mere 300 to make sure that the Israelites understood that it would take a miracle of *God* for them to win—and they did! (See: Judges 6–7.)

THE NAME GAME!
In Gideon's day, the Midianites were ruled by four princes—Zeeb, Zebah, Zalmunna, and Oreb. Seems like names starting with *Z* were popular with Midianite princes. (See: Judges 8:3, 12.)

Midian (Midianites)

Midian was a son of Abraham, and the Midianites lived in the deserts south of Israel. Moses lived in Midian for 40 years. (See: Genesis 25:1–2; Exodus 2:15–22.)

FUN FACTS!
Claudius Lysias claimed that he'd rescued Paul from a mob when he learned that Paul was a Roman citizen. What a lie. He only found out Paul was a Roman when he was about to torture him. (Compare Acts 21:31–40; 22:24–29 with 23:26–27).

Five Times God and Angels Appeared on Earth as Men

1. The Lord and two angels appeared as men to Abraham.
2. Jacob wrestled with a "man" who was actually God.
3. The angel of the Lord appeared to Gideon.
4. The angel of the Lord appeared to Manoah once and his wife twice.
5. Two "men" (angels) talked to the women at Jesus' tomb.

(See: Genesis 18:1–2; 19:1; 32:22–30; Judges 6:11–22; 13:2–21; Luke 24:1–6.)

Four Things the Israelites Burned as Fuel

1. Wood, mostly dry sticks
2. Thornbushes, because there were so many of them
3. Dried cow poop
4. Shields, bows, arrows, war clubs, and spears

(See: Numbers 15:32; 1 Kings 17:10–12; Ecclesiastes 7:6; Ezekiel 4:15; 39:9.)

Gamaliel

A highly respected Jewish rabbi. Gamaliel taught Paul when Paul was young and prevented the Sanhedrin (ruling Jewish council) from killing the apostles. (See: Acts 5:33–40; 22:3.)

Gedaliah

A friend of the prophet Jeremiah. After the Babylonians conquered Judah, they appointed Gedaliah governor. He was killed because he trusted people too much. (See: Jeremiah 40:1–41:3.)

Gehazi

The servant of the prophet Elisha. At first, Gehazi was a faithful servant, but later he was cursed with leprosy for being greedy. (See: 2 Kings 4:8–37; 5:20–27; 8:4–6.)

FUN FACTS!
Gehazi once asked a mom, "Is your child all right?" (2 Kings 4:26 NIV). She answered, "Everything is all right" (2 Kings 4:26 NIV). Everything *wasn't* all right, however. Her son had just died.

Like Jews and Gentiles, white people and African-Americans were once separated by custom—even being forced to use different drinking fountains.

FUN FACTS!
When the olives were ripe, Israelite farmers beat the branches of the trees with sticks to make the olives fall. There were always some olives on the top branches that wouldn't fall. (See: Isaiah 17:6.)

Court of the Gentiles

The Jews built God's temple to worship God in, and Gentiles (non-Jews) were not allowed in it. God knew that people from every nation would be drawn to Him, however, so the Jews allowed the Gentiles to enter the courtyard just outside the temple (Revelation 11:2 KJV). This was called the Court of the Gentiles. (See: Isaiah 56:7; Acts 21:28.)

JOTHAM'S FABLE

The people of Shechem wanted Gideon to rule over them, but he refused. Then they wanted Gideon's worthless son Abimelech for their king, so he killed all of his 70 brothers. Only Jotham escaped. Abimelech then went to Shechem to be crowned. Jotham had a dangerous message, so he stood atop a nearby hill and shouted it out as a story—a fable about how the trees wanted a king, but the olive tree refused. The fig tree refused. Even the grape vine refused. Only the worthless, ground-crawling, prickly thornbush accepted. (The thornbush was Abimelech.) Then Jotham basically said, "May Abimelech destroy you, and may you destroy Abimelech!" And that's what happened. (See: Judges 8:22–23; 9:1–21, 56–57.)

FUN FACTS!
Gideon was fighting to save Israel, but the elders of Succoth mocked him and refused to give his army food. After the battle, Gideon whipped the elders with thorns and briars. (See: Judges 8:4–16.)

DAMASCUS

Damascus was a very important, ancient city in Syria. One time the apostle Paul escaped the city by being lowered in a basket through an opening in the wall. (See: Acts 9:19–25.)

The towers of a Muslim mosque, built more than 500 years ago, rise above modern-day Damascus.

Six Deaths That Were Barely Avoided

1. Nabal and his farm workers barely avoided being killed.
2. Jeremiah's friends talked his enemies out of killing him.
3. Ten men avoided being killed and thrown in a water pit.
4. Joseph, Mary, and Jesus fled Bethlehem just in time.
5. Jesus escaped before He could be thrown down a cliff.
6. Paul escaped death in Damascus through an opening in the wall.

(See: 1 Samuel 25:1–34; Jeremiah 26:7–24; 41:4–8; Matthew 2:13–16; Luke 4:28–30; Acts 9:23–25.)

GIDEON

The son of a wealthy Israelite farmer who lived in Gilead. Gideon doubted that God would use him to win a war and asked God for many signs. God then used Gideon to win an amazing battle. (See: Judges 6–7.)

STRANGE BUT TRUE!
In Gideon's day, 9,700 soldiers stuck their faces down in the water and lapped like a dog when they were thirsty. They were kicked out of the army as a result. (See: Judges 7:2–8.)

Ever find a Bible in the drawer of a hotel dresser? It was put there by a group called The Gideons, named after the Bible hero.

GOD THE FATHER

The first person in the Trinity. The other persons are God the Son (Jesus) and God the Holy Spirit. Jesus called God His Father. (See: Trinity, page 68; see also: John 14:7–11; 20:17)

FUN FACTS!
God poked fun at Israelites who burned part of a block of wood to roast meat and bake bread, then carved an idol out of the leftover wood and bowed down to it. (See: Isaiah 44:9–20.)

GOLIATH

A giant who lived in the Philistine city of Gath. Goliath was over nine feet tall. He challenged the Israelites to send a warrior to fight him, so David fought and killed him. (See: 1 Samuel 17.)

ABBA

An Aramaic word meaning "daddy." (Aramaic is the language that Jesus and His disciples spoke.) Before He was crucified, Jesus prayed in the Garden of Gethsemane, crying out to God, "Abba, Father." The apostle Paul used the word *Abba*, too, saying that we are children of God and that we should address Him as our Father. (See: Mark 14:36; Romans 8:14–15; Galatians 4:6.)

David's slingshot knocked Goliath down. . .but the teenager used the giant's own sword to cut off Goliath's head!

ELDERS

In the Bible, elders means a council of older, wise people—usually men—chosen to rule. In Old Testament times, elders were older men who ruled a town or city in Israel. Gideon once whipped 77 elders of Succoth for not giving bread to his exhausted troops. Elders also helped rule all Israel. In New Testament times, elders were wise, mature men who were chosen to rule the individual churches. (See: Numbers 11:16–17; Judges 8:4–16; Titus 1:5–6.)

Feature

OUTLAW BECOMES GENERAL

Gilead, chief of the land of Gilead, had a wife and several sons, but he also had a son, Jephthah, by another, bad woman. When Gilead died his sons chased Jephthah away, saying, "You're not going to get any of the inheritance!" The elders of the land agreed, so Jephthah went to the land of Tob. There he became a mighty warrior and the leader of a band of adventurers. Later when the land of Gilead was overrun by enemies, the elders had to humble themselves—oh, how embarrassing!—and ask Jephthah to lead their armies. After defeating the enemy, Jephthah ruled Gilead for six years. (See: Judges 11:1–11, 32–33; 12:7.)

GATH

One of the five cities of the Philistines. Gath was the home of the giant Goliath. David visited Gath twice before he became king. (See: 1 Samuel 17:4; 21:10; 27:1–3.)

STRANGE BUT TRUE!
David visited Gath, and when the Philistines recognized him, he pretended that he was crazy. David drooled in his beard and scratched the door like a dog. (See: 1 Samuel 21:10–15.)

Eight Times the Israelites Vanquished Giants

1. The Israelites defeated the giants Ahiman, Sheshai, and Talmai.
2. The Israelites killed monstrous Og.
3. David killed the giant Goliath.
4. Abishai, David's nephew, killed the giant Ishbi-Benob.
5. Sibbecai the Israelite killed the giant Saph.

6–7. Elhanan from Bethlehem killed Goliath Junior and also killed Lahmi, Goliath's brother.

8. Jonathan, David's nephew, killed a multi-fingered, multi-toed giant.

(See: Numbers 13:22; 21:32–35; Deuteronomy 3:3–11; Judges 1:10; 1 Samuel 17; 2 Samuel 21:15–21; 1 Chronicles 20:5.)

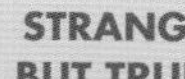

I Love Lists!

Habakkuk

A prophet when the Babylonians were about to conquer Judah. Habakkuk first asked God why He didn't punish evildoers—then asked why He used the Babylonians to punish them. (See: Habakkuk 1.)

FUN FACTS!
Habakkuk said that when the Red Sea came crashing down, drowning Pharaoh's chariots and horses, God was trampling the sea with *His* chariots and horses. (See: Habakkuk 3:8, 15.)

Hagar

Sarah's Egyptian slave. Sarah thought she couldn't have children, so she gave Hagar to Abraham as a concubine (lesser wife). Hagar bore Abraham a son named Ishmael. (See: Genesis 16.)

FUN FACTS!
Hagar wasn't *really* a big lady, but Paul compared her to a mountain. In Galatians 4:25, Paul said that Hagar was like Mount Sinai, where God gave Moses the Law.

Haggai

A prophet who lived after the Jews returned from Babylon. God's temple had been destroyed, so Haggai and another prophet named Zechariah encouraged the Jews to rebuild it. (See: Haggai 1:1–12; Ezra 5:1–2; 6:14.)

Dedicate

To set something apart for a special use. "To dedicate" is sometimes called "to consecrate," especially if a ceremony goes along with it. God told the Israelites to dedicate their firstborn sons to Him. We are to dedicate our lives to God. Romans 12:1 (KJV) talks about offering our bodies as a "living sacrifice" to God. (See Sanctify, page 144; see also: Exodus 13:1–2.)

Offering

The Law of Moses told the Jews to offer (give) God offerings. This could mean offering bread to God. Often, however, an offering meant a lamb or goat or some other animal that was sacrificed (killed) on the altar. Sometimes God commanded the Israelites to give an offering of gold and other valuables. (See: Exodus 25:1–7; Leviticus 1:2–5; 7:11–12.)

FUN FACTS!
Abraham once stood guard over the dead bodies of animals he'd sacrificed and drove off the vultures and other birds of prey that swooped down to eat them. (See: Genesis 15:9–11.)

Samson's Fantastic Fox-Fire Feat

A Philistine father once made Samson furious by giving away Samson's bride to another man. In retaliation, Samson went out, caught 300 foxes, and tied them tail to tail in pairs. He then attached a torch to every pair of tails and set the foxes loose. The freaked-out, fearful foxes fled like fiends trying to flee the fiery torches—with both foxes in each pair trying to run different directions! With 150 fox-teams running wild, they burned down miles of Philistine fields and vineyards and olive groves. Now think how much *work* that was to catch those 300 foxes in the first place. You try catching just *one*! (See: Judges 15:1–5.)

A typical North American red fox.

Five Water Discoveries in the Desert

1. Hagar, dying of thirst, discovered a well in the desert.
2. Anah found hot springs in the desert while grazing donkeys.
3. God brought water out of a rock at Massah for Moses and the thirsty Israelites.
4. At Kadesh, using Moses, God once again brought water from a rock.
5. God caused water to spring out of the ground for Samson.

(See: Genesis 21:15–19; 36:24; Exodus 17:1–7; Numbers 20:1–11; Judges 15:16–19.)

STRANGE BUT TRUE!

Freedom for a tooth! In Israel, if you were a slave but your master hit you and knocked out a tooth, you got to go free for that missing tooth! (See: Exodus 21:26–27.)

HAM

The youngest of Noah's three sons. Ham was the father of the Egyptians and other African peoples. Noah cursed Ham's son, Canaan. (See: Genesis 9:18–25; 10:6–20.)

HAMAN

A powerful man in Persia and an enemy of the Jews. Haman persuaded the Persian king to make a law to kill all the Jews, but the Jews were spared and Haman was killed instead. (See: Esther 3; 7.)

THE NAME GAME!
Aspatha means "horse-given." Now, what kind of father would call his son "horse-given"? Well, Haman, one of the greatest villains in the Bible, that's who. (See: Esther 9:6–10.)

HANNAH

The mother of Samuel. She promised God that if He gave her a son, she'd give the child back to Him. When Samuel was still a boy, Hannah took him to live at the Tent of Meeting. (See: 1 Samuel 1.)

TENT OF MEETING

The "Tent of Meeting" (Exodus 29:42 NIV) was also called the "tabernacle" in the King James Bible. When the Israelites were wandering in the desert, they needed a place to keep the Ark of the Covenant and other holy objects. They also needed a place to worship God. God instructed Moses to build a large tent where He could meet with them. This tent had a large fence made of cloth around it. (See: Exodus 26.)

FUN FACTS!
Talk about an unexpected job! The Israelites, led by Moses, headed off to Canaan to become farmers, but they first spent 40 years as shepherds in the desert. (See: Numbers 14:33.)

A model of the ancient tabernacle, set up in modern-day Israel.

The Tribe of Dan Migrates North

After much of Canaan had been conquered, Joshua divided the land between the tribes of Israel and told them to settle down. It was then up to each tribe to conquer the Canaanites remaining in its territory. The members of the tribe of Dan had a problem, however. The best land in their area was controlled by strong Amorite and Philistine armies, and the Danites were stuck up in the hills. As their population increased, they felt squeezed, so they sent out five spies. The spies found good, undefended land far to the north, so the Danites marched there, attacked the Canaanites, and won. Finally they had enough room to settle down. (See: Judges 1:34; 18:1–31.)

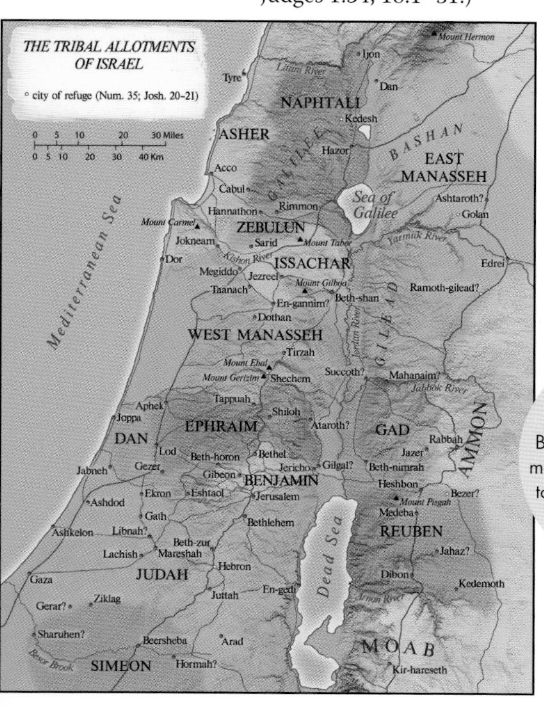

Crazy Stuff That Happened in Vineyards

1. Noah planted a vineyard, grew grapes, made wine, and got drunk.
2. Once 200 warriors hid in a vineyard, jumped out, and grabbed 200 dancing girls.
3. Elijah confronted King Ahab in Naboth's vineyard.
4. A farmer's lazy son finally decided to work in the vineyard.
5. Wicked workers killed the vineyard owner's servants and son.

(See: Genesis 9:20–21; Judges 20:47; 21:12–23; 1 Kings 21:17–24; Matthew 21:28–31, 33–41

FUN FACTS!

Dan was the northernmost town in Israel, and Beersheba was the southernmost, so when people wanted to say "all Israel," they said, "from Dan to Beersheba" (2 Samuel 17:11 NKJV).

FUN FACTS!

When Israelite farmers harvested their grain and ground it into flour, the very first thing they baked—a cake—had to be given to God. (See: Numbers 15:18–21.)

HEROD THE GREAT

An Edomite who became king of Judea in the days of the Romans. He rebuilt the Jewish temple but was a cruel, suspicious king. He tried to kill Baby Jesus. (See: Matthew 2:1–16.)

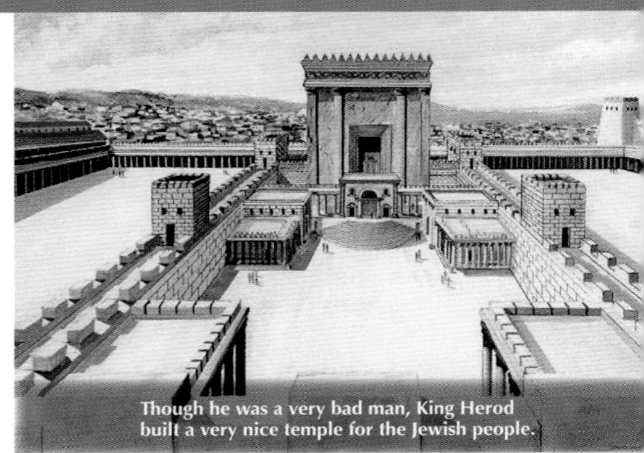
Though he was a very bad man, King Herod built a very nice temple for the Jewish people.

HEROD AGRIPPA

A grandson of Herod the Great. He was the King Herod who killed James, John's brother. He loved it when the crowds said he had "the voice of a god" (Acts 12:22 NIV), so God let him be eaten by worms and die. (See: Acts 12:1–4, 19–23.)

THE NAME GAME!
Herod Agrippa had a servant named "Blastus" (Acts 12:20). *Blastus* doesn't mean "please shoot us with a ray gun." It means "bud." More guys get called Bud than Blastus these days.

HEROD ANTIPAS

A son of Herod the Great. When John the Baptist criticized him for marrying his brother's wife, this Herod put John in prison. He then beheaded John and had his head brought back out on a platter. Later, he and his soldiers mocked Jesus. (See: Mark 6:17–29; Luke 23:6–12.)

DISCIPLE

A follower of a teacher, such as the disciples of John the Baptist. Usually in the New Testament, however, *disciple* refers to the followers of Jesus. Jesus' followers were not called "Christians" until later on. Jesus said that to truly be His disciples, we have to obey His teachings. He also said that His disciples would be known by their love for others. (See: Matthew 9:14; John 8:31; 13:35; Acts 6:7; 11:26.)

God's Ark Plagues the Philistines

The Ark of the Covenant was a gold-covered chest that symbolized the presence of God, so one day the Israelites carried it into battle, hoping it would help them win. Instead, the Philistines won the battle, captured the Ark, and took it to the city of Ashdod. Soon a plague hit Ashdod and people started getting tumors (painful swellings). Quickly the Philistines of Ashdod sent the Ark to Gath. Everyone there was struck with tumors, too, and panicked. They tried taking the Ark to Ekron, but the men of Ekron stopped them. They told their rulers to send the Ark back to the Israelites, loaded down with offerings of golden rats and models of tumors—so they did. (See: 1 Samuel 5:1–6:14.)

A rock badger looks out from his stony home.

Five Rodents Registered in the Writings

1. Bats—God told the Israelites not to eat bats.
2. Rats—the Philistines made small golden rats.
3. Rock badgers (coneys)—these rodents live in the rocks.
4. Moles—the wicked will throw their golden idols to the "moles" (Isaiah 2:20 KJV).
5. Mice—some Israelites cooked mice and ate them.

(See: Leviticus 11:13, 19; 1 Samuel 6:5; Proverbs 30:26; Isaiah 66:17.)

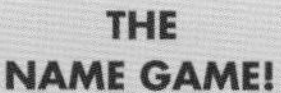

THE NAME GAME!
Esau had a funny nickname: *Red.* (*Edom* is Hebrew for "red.") He was called this after he traded his birthright for a stew made of red lentils. (See: Genesis 25:30.)

FUN FACTS!
James and John were brothers. James was the *first* of the apostles to die, and John was the *last* apostle to die. He lived longer than any of the other 12 apostles. (See: Acts 12:1–2.)

HEZEKIAH

A good king of Judah during the days of the Assyrian empire. When the Assyrians mocked God, Hezekiah prayed, and God sent an angel to wipe out the Assyrian army. (See: 2 Kings 18–19.)

An Assyrian Archer

HIRAM

The king of Tyre in the days of David and Solomon. Hiram sent workers and materials to David to build his palace, and later to Solomon to build God's temple. (See: 2 Samuel 5:11; 1 Kings 5; 7:13–15.)

STRANGE BUT TRUE!
When King Hezekiah was dying of a huge boil, God told the prophet Isaiah to put a poultice (a veggie pack) of mashed-up figs on his boil—and it cured him. (See: Isaiah 38:1–5, 21.)

HULDAH

A prophetess during the days of King Josiah. When the long-lost Book of the Law was found in the temple, Huldah gave tenderhearted Josiah a comforting prophecy. (See: 2 Kings 22:3–20.)

LAW, THE

The Law of Moses, the first five books of the Bible—Genesis, Exodus, Leviticus, Numbers, and Deuteronomy. God gave Moses the Law on Mount Sinai and commanded His people to obey it. The Jews called all the other books of scripture "the Prophets," and they called the entire Old Testament "the prophets and the law" (Matthew 11:13 KJV). (See also: Luke 24:44.)

SCRIPTURES

Scriptures means "the Writings"—the holy Writings that God gave to His people. For the Jews and the early Christians, the scriptures meant the Law and the Prophets in the Old Testament. After a while, however, Christians realized that the writings of Paul and the other apostles were *also* scripture, along with "the rest of the Scriptures" (2 Peter 3:15–16 NKJV). (See also: Luke 24:27.)

God Gives the Israelites a King

For hundreds of years Israel had no king except for God, and God used judges—wise, courageous men like the prophet Samuel—to lead them. But when Nahash, king of the Ammonites, began attacking, the Israelites were desperate for a king to lead them into battle. What they were asking for was wrong, but God had mercy and told Samuel, "Listen to them and give them a king" (1 Samuel 8:22 NIV). Just the same, after Saul was proclaimed king in a big celebration, God sent a heavy rain to ruin their crops. The people were sorry, but they had a king now, so Samuel told them *and* their king to follow God. (See: 1 Samuel 8:1–22; 11:14–15; 12:12–22.)

Five Bible Characters with the Same Name

1. A male Noah and a female Noah
2. A good Jonathan and a bad Jonathan
3. A bad Saul and a good Saul
4. A bad Judas and a good Judas
5. A bad Ananias and a good Ananias

(See: Genesis 6:9; Numbers 26:33; Judges 18:30; 1 Samuel 14:1; 16:1; Matthew 26: 14–15; Acts 5: 1–5; 9:10–20; 15:22.)

I Love Lists!

FUN FACTS!
When King David bought a hill, he paid 15 pounds of gold for it. When King Omri bought a hill some years later, he paid 150 pounds of silver for it. (See: 1 Kings 16:24; 1 Chronicles 21:25.)

FUN FACTS!
In Solomon's day, one shiny new chariot from Egypt cost 15 pounds of silver. Expensive! You could buy four Egyptian horses for that same price! (See: 1 Kings 10:29.)

A modern model of an ancient Roman chariot.

HOLY SPIRIT

The third person of the Trinity, also called the Spirit of God and the Comforter. Jesus promised to send the Spirit to live in the hearts of believers. (See: Trinity—below; see also: John 14:25–26; 16:5–14.)

FUN FACTS!
The Holy Spirit told an old prophet named Simeon that he wouldn't die before he saw the Savior of Israel—and sure enough, Simeon lived to see baby Jesus! (Luke 2:25–32).

HOSEA

A prophet of the northern kingdom of Israel. Hosea had a very unfaithful wife. Israel was rich and prosperous at this time, but Hosea rebuked it for turning from God. (See: Hosea 3–4.)

ISAAC

The son of Abraham and Sarah. Isaac was born by a miracle when his parents were both old. When Isaac was young, Abraham nearly sacrificed him on an altar. (See: Genesis 21:1–7; 22:1–14.)

FUN FACTS!
When they were old, both Isaac and Ahijah became blind. People tried to trick both of them. Isaac fell for it, but Ahijah wasn't fooled at all. (See: Genesis 27:1–29; 1 Kings 14:1–6.)

DISCIPLINE

Also called chastisement. In the Bible, discipline is not just punishment for breaking rules, but an important part of training to help us grow up to become mature, obedient Christians. Hebrews 12:4–13 gives an excellent explanation of God's discipline: "God disciplines us for our good, that we may share in his holiness" (Hebrews 12:10 NIV).

TRINITY

There is one God, but He exists in a *trinity* (three persons)—the Father, the Son, and the Holy Spirit. The Holy Spirit is one with God because He is God's very own spirit, and Jesus is also one with His Father. When Jesus was baptized, the Son was present, the Father spoke from heaven, and the Spirit descended. All three members of the Trinity were there. (See: Matthew 3:16–17; John 10:30; 1 Corinthians 2:10–11.)

A young boy acts out the story of William Tell—an expert Swiss archer forced to shoot an apple off his son's head.

Five Famous Archers

1. Ishmael, the son of Abraham, was an archer in the desert.
2. Jonathan, David's friend, was a famous archer.
3. An Aramean soldier killed King Ahab with a fluke arrow.
4. The prophet Elisha and the king of Israel shot a bow together.
5. The men of Lydia were "famous as archers" (Isaiah 66:19 NIV).

(See: Genesis 21:20; 2 Samuel 1:17–18, 22; 1 Kings 22:29–40; 2 Kings 13:15–17.)

Death Penalty for Eating Honey

Prince Jonathan had just won a battle, and the Philistines were now fleeing. Then King Saul did something dumb. He basically said, "Cursed be any man who eats food today before we beat the Philistines!" Soon the Israelites began getting weak as they chased the Philistines. Jonathan hadn't heard his father, so when he passed a beehive he grabbed some honey and ate it. Saul was so furious that he wanted to kill his own son—all for eating a little honey! Fortunately the Israelites stood up for Jonathan and talked Saul out of killing him. (See: 1 Samuel 14:1–46.)

FUN FACTS!
Ancient warriors used to go into battle all decked out in gold jewelry. The problem was, if the *other* army won and you were dead, the enemy got to take all your loot. (See: Judges 8:24–26.)

Five Prophets with No Names

1. The man of God from Judah
2. An old prophet
3. The prophet who spoke to King Ahab
4. The "strike me" prophet
5. The prophet who rebuked King Amaziah

(See: 1 Kings 13:1, 11, 20, 27; 20:13, 22, 28, 35, 37, 41; 2 Chronicles 25:14–15.)

Isaiah

A great prophet of Judah in the days of King Hezekiah and the Assyrian empire. Isaiah gave several amazing prophecies about the coming Messiah, Jesus. (See: Isaiah 7:14; 9:6–7; 53.)

REALLY GROSS!
The Lord describes things in a funny way at times. Speaking through Isaiah, God said He would make the Egyptians so dizzy they would be like a drunk man staggering around in his own vomit. (See: Isaiah 19:14.)

Ishmael

The son of Hagar, Sarah's Egyptian servant. Ishmael's father was Abraham. Ishmael was mean to young Isaac, so Abraham sent Ishmael and Hagar away. (See: Genesis 16; 21:8–21.)

Jacob

Twin brother of Esau. Jacob deceived his father, Isaac, to get Esau's blessing. Jacob's name was later changed to Israel, and his 12 sons were the ancestors of the 12 tribes of Israel. (See: Genesis 27:1–29; 32:28; 35:22–26.)

FUN FACTS!
When Jacob wanted to convince his blind father that he was Esau, Jacob wore one of Esau's robes. When Isaac caught the—ahem!—*smell* of Esau's clothes, he was convinced. (See: Genesis 27:15, 26–27.)

FUN FACTS!
When Jacob met his brother Esau many years after cheating him, Jacob gave Esau a huge present: 220 goats, 220 sheep, 50 cattle, 30 camels, and 30 donkeys. (See: Genesis 32:13–15.)

A camel rests in the deserts of India.

FUN FACTS!
What happened to all Jacob's camels? He had many camels when he entere Canaan, but some 20 years later, all his sons had to carr grain on was donkeys. (See: Genesis 32:7; 42:26.)

Messiah

And that Definition Means...

The Hebrew word *Messiah* means "anointed one," and the Greek word *Christ* also means "anointed one." When Jesus is called Jesus the Christ it means Jesus the Messiah. In Jesus' day, many Israelites were waiting for the Messiah, the anointed King, to arrive and bring truth and justice. They believed that the Messiah would be the Son of God. (See: John 1:41, 49; 4:25–26.)

Musician Escapes Out Window

When David was a young man, he married King Saul's daughter Michal. Now, one afternoon while David was playing his harp for the king, an evil spirit possessed Saul, and he tried to impale David with a spear. David escaped to his house, but Michal knew that her dad had gone berserk and that he wouldn't stop till David was dead. She urged David to escape out the window that night, then she put a dummy in his bed, covered it with clothes, and put goat's hair at its head. When Saul sent some men the next morning to arrest David, there was the dummy—but David was long gone. (See: 1 Samuel 19:9–16.)

Israel (Israelites)

God changed Jacob's name to *Israel*—which means "ruling with God." When Israel's descendants, the children of Israel (or Israelites), conquered Canaan, they renamed the land Israel. (See: Genesis 32:28.)

Six kids make up a big family today—but that's nothing compared to some of the Bible's families!

Five Men with Way, Way Too Many Wives, Listed from the Most to the Least

1. Solomon had 700 wives and 300 concubines (lesser wives).
2. Rehoboam had 18 wives and 60 concubines.
3. David had at least 6 wives and 10 concubines.
4. Abijah had 14 wives.
5. Gideon (Jerub-Baal) had "many wives" (Judges 8:30 RSV).

(see: 2 Samuel 3:2–5; 15:16; 1 Kings 11:3; 2 Chronicles 11:21; 13:21.)

Seven Bible Records for the Most Children, Listed from the Most to the Least

1. Rehoboam had 28 sons and 60 daughters.
2. Gideon (also called Jerub-Baal) had 70 sons.
3. Ahab had 70 sons.
4. Abijah had 22 sons and 16 daughters.
5. Jair had 30 sons.
6. Heman had 14 sons and three daughters.
7. Jacob had 12 sons and at least two daughters

(See: Genesis 35:22–26; Judges 8:30; 2 Kings 10:1; 1 Chronicles 25:5; 2 Chronicles 11:21; 13:21.)

JABIN

Two Canaanite kings were named Jabin. Joshua defeated the first Jabin, and many years later Deborah and Barak defeated the second one. (See: Joshua 11:1–10; Judges 4.)

JAEL

Heber the Kenite was friends with Jabin, but his wife Jael was on Israel's side—so when Jabin's general, Sisera, fled a battle and hid in Jael's tent, Jael killed him. (See: Judges 4:11–22; 5:24–27.)

Sisera "gets nailed" by Jael in this painting from the 1700s.

AWESOME FEAT!
The Canaanite general Sisera was killed by a woman. When he fled from a battle, hid in Jael's tent, then fell asleep, she hammered a tent peg through his head! (See: Judges 4:17–21.)

JAIRUS

The leader of a Jewish synagogue. His 12-year-old daughter died, but when Jesus came, after crossing Lake Gennesaret, He sent away the mourners and raised Jairus's daughter from the dead. (See: Mark 5:22–43.)

STRANGE BUT TRUE!
In Israel, when someone in a wealthy family died, like Jairus's daughter, often the families hired a "noisy crowd" (Matthew 9:23 NIV) of strangers called "wailing women" (Jeremiah 9:17 NIV) to come in and cry.

FORGIVENESS

Also called "pardon" and "remission of sins." To forgive someone who has wronged you means giving up your claim for repayment or revenge. Forgiveness also means letting go of grudges against others. When we repent of our sins, God forgives us. Jesus said that we should forgive others, just as God has forgiven us. (See: Matthew 18:21–35; Acts 2:38; Colossians 3:12–13.)

FUN FACTS!
In Joshua's day, Piram was an Amorite king who attacked Gibeon, Israel's ally. You get an idea of the kind of person Piram was by his name. It means "wild donkey." (See: Joshua 10:3.)

Abigail Saves the Fool and the Farm

Once a beautiful woman named Abigail was married to a pigheaded man named Nabal. (*Nabal* means "fool.") Nabal had 3,000 sheep, and when he sheared them to sell his wool, he threw a big feast. Now, for months David and his men had helped watch over Nabal's flocks, so now David asked if Nabal could spare anything from his feast. Instead of showing gratitude, Nabal hurled insults at David. Unfortunately, David decided to take revenge, but as his men were coming to wipe out Nabal and his hired hands, Abigail heard what had happened and quickly sent David a ton of food. Nabal died of a heart attack about 11 days later, and Abigail and David were married. (See: 1 Samuel 25.)

Galilee, Sea of

This small lake, also called Lake Gennesaret, is in north Israel. Four of Jesus' disciples were fishermen there, and Jesus often preached near it. (See: Mark 1:16–20; Luke 5:1–2.)

Fishing boats along the shore of the Sea of Galilee.

Eight People Who Came Back from the Dead

1. The widow of Zarephath's son
2. The Shunammite woman's son
3. A dead man touched by Elisha's bones (You gotta read this story found in 2 Kings 13:20–21!)
4. Jesus, the most important one of all—because His resurrection powers our own!
5. Jairus's daughter
6. Lazarus
7. Dorcas, also called Tabitha
8. Eutychus

(See: 1 Kings 17:10, 17–24; 2 Kings 4:8–37; 13:20–21; Matthew 28; Mark 5:21–43; 16; Luke 24; John 11:1–44; 20; Acts 9:36–43; 20:7–12.)

Six Things Israelites Did when They Heard Terrible News

1. Sprinkled dirt or ashes on their heads
2. Tore their clothing
3. Pulled out hair from their head and beard
4. Fasted from food and water
5. Dressed in rough, itchy sackcloth
6. Covered their heads

(See: Joshua 7:6; Ezra 9:3, 5; 10:6; Isaiah 22:12; Jeremiah 14:3.)

James

One of Jesus' 12 apostles. Jesus called him and his brother, John, the "Sons of Thunder." James, the first apostle to die, was killed by King Herod Agrippa. (See: Mark 1:19–20; 3:17; Acts 12:1–2.)

James

One of Jesus' younger brothers. At first, James didn't believe in Jesus. Later, James became the head of the church in Jerusalem. (See: Matthew 13:55; John 7:5; Acts 21:18.)

IMPORTANT IDEA!
One day Jesus is going to get married! Symbolically, that is. He will marry the Church, which is called the Bride of Christ. (See: Revelation 19:7–9; 2 Corinthians 11:2.)

James and John wade ashore to follow Jesus in this painting from the 1880s.

Japheth

One of the three sons of Noah. Japheth was the ancestor of the Europeans—from the Russians of the north to the Greeks in the islands of the south. (See: Genesis 10:1–5.)

Rebuke

To give a stern talk to someone, to give him or her a harsh lecture. The prophet Samuel gave King Saul a very stiff rebuke. Paul said that sometimes it's necessary to rebuke people, but that a young man should not harshly rebuke an older man; instead, he should explain things gently to him. (See: 1 Samuel 15:16–19; 1 Timothy 5:1; Titus 1:13.)

A Ghost Story

Even though King Saul himself had outlawed mediums, when he wanted to know how a battle against the Philistines would go—and God was no longer talking to him—Saul went to a medium at Endor one night. He asked the hag to bring up the spirit of the dead prophet Samuel. Of course, the "witch of Endor" couldn't summon godly Samuel, but God permitted the prophet to appear—scaring the medium out of her wits! Samuel then gave bad news to Saul: "Tomorrow you and your sons will be with me" (1 Samuel 28:19 NIV)—meaning they'd be *dead*! Sure enough, Saul and his three sons died on the battlefield the next day. (See: 1 Samuel 28, 31.)

FUN FACTS!
In Israel, shields were made of wood covered with leather. To make swords bounce off their shields, men rubbed olive oil on them. (See: 2 Samuel 1:21.)

Greece (Greeks)

Greece was—and still is—a country in southern Europe. Greece once had an empire that ruled much of the Middle East. In Jesus' day, Greece was just a province of the Roman Empire.

IMPORTANT IDEA!

If we want to serve God, we need to wear armor and helmets, carry a shield, and bear a sword. All of this is *spiritual* armor, of course! Read about it in Ephesians 6:11–17.

Suits of armor like this one protected soldiers centuries ago.

Seven Prophets Who Scolded Rulers

1. Samuel rebuked King Saul.
2. Nathan rebuked King David.
3. Ahijah rebuked King Jeroboam and his wife.
4. Jehu rebuked King Baasha.
5. Elijah rebuked King Ahab.
6. Micaiah rebuked King Ahab.
7. John the Baptist rebuked King Herod Antipas.

(See: 1 Samuel 13:11–14; 15:13–23; 2 Samuel 12:1–12; 1 Kings 14:1–14; 16:1–4; 17:1; 21:17–26; 22:15–28; Mark 6:17–20.)

Eight Famous Female Followers of Jesus

1. Zebedee's wife, the mother of James and John
2. Mary Magdalene
3. Mary, the mother of James and Joses
4. Salome
5. Joanna the wife of Cuza, King Herod Antipas's steward
6. Susanna

7–8. Mary and Martha, the sisters of Lazarus

(See: Matthew 20:20; 27:55–56; Mark 16:1; Luke 8:2–3; 10:38–39; 24:9–10; John 11:1–3.)

JEHOAHAZ

The son of Jehu, king of Israel. Because of his sins, God let the Arameans completely overrun Israel, but King Jehoahaz cried out to God, and the Arameans were defeated. (See: 2 Kings 13:1–9.)

JEHOIACHIN

One of the last kings of Judah. Jehoiachin (also called Jeconiah) ruled only three months, but the line of David—including Jesus—descends from him. (See: 2 Kings 24:8–16; 25:27–30; Matthew 1:12–16.)

FUN FACTS!
Shebna carved out a fancy tomb for himself among the kings of Judah—without permission. God said that he'd throw Shebna like a ball into a faraway country. (See: Isaiah 22:15–18.)

JEHOIADA

A high priest. Jehoiada hid baby Joash in God's temple for years. When Joash was seven, Jehoiada gathered a small army, declared Joash king, and had evil Queen Athaliah killed. (See: 2 Kings 11.)

TEN COMMANDMENTS

When God gave Moses the Law, it contained hundreds of commandments for the Jews to obey. But God wrote the ten most important laws on two stone tablets. These laws are known as the Ten Commandments. (See: Exodus 20:1–17; 31:18.)

FUN FACTS!
Nehushta was the mother of evil King Jehoiachin. She surrendered to the Babylonians with her son, then traveled as a fellow-prisoner with him to Babylon. (See 2 Kings 24:8, 12, 15.)

FUN FACTS!
King Manasseh was so foolish that he bowed down and worshipped the stars in the sky. He even built two altars to the stars inside God's temple. (See: 2 Chronicles 33:1–5.)

Actor Charlton Heston plays Moses, holding the Ten Commandments, in a movie from 1956.

Grasshoppers are big for bugs—but compared to a person, they're tiny. That's how the Israelites felt when they saw giants in the promised land!

Five Times People Were Compared to Insects

1. The Israelites felt "like grasshoppers" (Numbers 13:33 NKJV) next to the giants.
2. David compared himself to a "flea" (1 Samuel 26:20).
3. Bildad said "man, who is but a maggot" (Job 25:6 NIV) cannot be pure in heart.
4. The psalm writer said, "I am a worm, and no man" (Psalm 22:6 RSV).
5. The psalm writer prayed for the wicked to melt like a snail (or slug) (Psalm 58:8 KJV, NIV).

Gift-giving Guy Becomes King

David and his men had left their wives, children, and flocks in Ziklag (in Judah) to go to battle. When they returned, they found that Amalekites had raided Ziklag and taken everything. They chased the Amalekites, defeated them, and recovered everything—and then some! The Amalekites had raided many other towns in Judah and elsewhere, so David now had *huge* flocks and herds. David not only gave sheep and cattle back to the people they'd been stolen from, he sent some of the plunder as gifts to the elders of Judah. A short while later all the elders made David king of Judah. (See: 1 Samuel 30; 2 Samuel 2:1–4.)

Aram (Arameans)

Aram was a powerful kingdom in what is now Syria, north of Israel. The Arameans fought many battles trying to conquer Israel. Naaman was an Aramean. (See: 2 Kings 5; 6:8–24; 7:5–7.)

JEHOIAKIM

The disobedient king of Judah in the days of the prophet Jeremiah. Jehoiakim refused to listen to Jeremiah and burned his scroll of prophecies. (See: Jeremiah 22:18–19; 36.)

FUN FACTS!
Evil-Merodach was a Babylonian king. Despite his name, he was a *good* ruler who released Jehoiakim's son, King Jehoiachin of Judah, from prison and let him eat at his table. (See: Jeremiah 52:31–34.)

JEHORAM

A wicked king of Judah. He married evil Athaliah, Ahab's daughter. Disaster hit Judah in Jehoram's days and he died a painful death—his bowels fell out! (See: 2 Kings 8:16–24; 2 Chronicles 21:4–20.)

JEHOSHAPHAT

A good king of Judah who won great battles. He was an ally of the evil kings of Israel, however, so God destroyed his fleet of ships. (See: 2 Chronicles 20.)

FUN FACTS!
King Solomon's trading ships brought him tons of gold from Ophir, but when King Jehoshaphat built trading ships, God wrecked them. (See: 1 Kings 9:26–28; 2 Chronicles 20:35–37.)

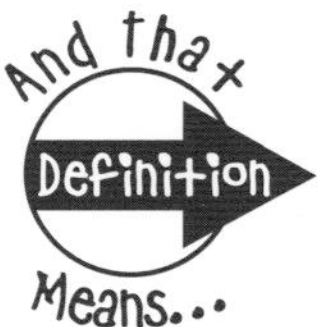

HALLELUJAH, ALLELUIA

A Hebrew word that means "praise the Lord." It is often translated as "praise the Lord" or "thank the Lord," though sometimes the original word *hallelujah* is used. (See: Psalm 106:1; Revelation 19:1.)

HOSANNA

Hosanna is a Hebrew word that means, "LORD, save us!" (Psalm 118:25 NIV). It was also a shout of praise to God. When Jesus rode triumphantly into Jerusalem on a donkey, the crowds shouted, "Hosanna to the Son of David! . . . Hosanna in the highest!" (Matthew 21:6–9 NKJV).

People lay coats and tree branches before Jesus, shouting "Hosanna!" as He rides into Jerusalem.

Taking the Ark to Jerusalem

For years the Ark of the Covenant had been at a city called Baalah. When King David wanted to bring it to Jerusalem, he had it put on a cart and oxen pulled it down the road. At one point the oxen stumbled and a man named Uzzah grabbed the Ark to steady it—and was struck dead! David was so afraid that he left the Ark there. Later on, he did things the *right* way. There were gold rings on the side of the Ark for poles to fit through, and David had God's priests carry the Ark with the poles on their shoulders. On the second try he was able to bring the Ark to Jerusalem. (See: 2 Samuel 6:1–15; 1 Chronicles 15:1–15.)

THE NAME GAME!

Talk about names that sound like chickens cackling, get these: *Bakbakkar*, *Bakbuk*, and *Bakbukiah*. They mean "searcher," "bottle," and "wasted by the Lord." (See: 1 Chronicles 9:15; Ezra 2:51; Nehemiah 12:9.)

FUN FACTS!

Two evil kings, Manasseh and Amon, weren't buried in the royal tombs with the other kings of Judah. They were buried in the palace garden instead. (See: 2 Kings 21:18, 25–26.)

Four People with Gross Diseases—REALLY GROSS!!

1. King Asa became so severely "diseased in his feet" (2 Chronicles 16:12 NKJV) that it killed him (2 Chronicles 16:11–13 NKJV).
2. Evil King Jehoram had such a horrible disease in his bowels that his bowels dropped out, killing him (2 Chronicles 21:18–19 NIV).
3. Job was attacked by Satan with "painful sores from the soles of his feet to the top of his head" (Job 2:7 NIV). "He sat in the midst of the ashes" (Job 2:8 NKJV) and scraped away the scabs and pus.
4. Proud King Herod Agrippa was "eaten by worms and died" (Acts 12:23 RSV).

Jehu

The energetic commander of Israel's army. God made Jehu the new king, told him to kill the evil rulers (Ahaziah and Jezebel), and to wipe out Baal-worship—so Jehu did. (See: 2 Kings 9–10.)

REALLY GROSS!
Rather than fight with the new king, Jehu, the elders of Samaria killed the 70 sons of the former king, descendants of Ahab, and delivered all 70 heads to Jehu in baskets. (See: 2 Kings 10:1–8.)

Jeremiah

A prophet in the final years of Judah. Jeremiah warned the people and the rulers of Judah to repent but they didn't. The lamenting Jeremiah is called the Weeping Prophet. (See: Jeremiah 1:1–10; 40:1–3.)

FUN FACTS!
The book of Jeremiah (39:10) tells us that one day some poor Israelites had nothing, and the next day they owned vineyards, houses, and fields. The former owners had been shipped off to Babylon.

Jeroboam

After King Solomon died, the northern tribes rebelled against his son, Rehoboam, and created their own nation called Israel. Jeroboam was northern Israel's first king. (See: 1 Kings 12.)

Gentile

Anyone who is not a Jew. The Hebrew word for "nation" or "people" is *gôyim*, so when God talked about other nations or peoples, he called them gôyim, or Gentiles. Since other nations were idol-worshippers, God told the Jews to keep separate from them. Later, Christ broke down the wall between Gentiles and Jews and allowed Gentiles to be saved also. (See: Ephesians 2:11–14.)

"Gentiles" come in all sizes, shapes, and colors. If you're not Jewish, you're a Gentile, too!

King David Builds an Empire

When David became king, Saul had just lost a big battle, and Israel was overrun by Philistines. Within 20 years, David controlled a huge empire that stretched from Egypt to the Euphrates River. How did he do it? Well, God did miracles to help him, the Israelites learned how to make iron weapons, *and* David was a superwarrior! It was one battle after another—each victory bigger and more spectacular than the last—until finally David was the undisputed ruler over an empire. Five hundred years later, the Persians still remembered how powerful Israel had been. (See: 1 Samuel 31:7; 2 Samuel 8:1–14; Ezra 4:18–20.)

Three Biggest Gatherings of False Prophets

1. Ahab gathered 450 prophets of Baal.
2. Jehu killed a huge crowd of prophets and ministers of Baal.
3. Ahab gathered 400 false prophets.

(See: 1 Kings 18:19–20; 2 Kings 10:18–25; 2 Chronicles 18:5.)

Bethlehem

The hometown of King David, son of Jesse. It was about five miles south of Jerusalem. Mary and Joseph traveled to Bethlehem to pay taxes, and Jesus was born there. (See: 1 Samuel 16:1; Luke 2:1–7.)

FUN FACTS!
Talk about the neighborhood going to the dogs. Jeremiah wrote that whenever Israelites abandoned their cities, guess who moved into the ruined houses? Jackals! (See: Jeremiah 9:11; 10:22.)

Bethlehem, where the "Prince of Peace" was born on the first Christmas, is a town now fought over by Jews and Palestinians.

FUN FACTS!
King Jeroboam was about to sacrifice to his idols when a prophet of God came along and prophesied against the altar. It immediately split in half. (See: 1 Kings 13:1–5.)

Jesse

The father of King David and ancestor of Jesus. Jesse was a well-to-do shepherd in Bethlehem who had eight sons and two daughters. David was his youngest son. (See: 1 Samuel 16:1–13; 17:12–19.)

Jesus

God's Son and the Son of Mary. Jesus went around Israel, preaching, teaching, and healing. He was crucified by His enemies but rose from the dead! (See: Matthew 1:18–25; 26–28; Acts 10:36–41.)

FUN FACTS!
A man named Sceva had seven sons who went around trying to cast out demons. They were pathetic and powerless, though, because they didn't really know Jesus. (See: Acts 19:13–16.)

The crucifixion of Jesus may be one of the most painted events in history. This picture is from the early 1500s.

STRANGE BUT TRUE!
The Midianite kings loved their camels, to be sure! Nothing was too good for the royal camels! They even hung gold chains around their camels' necks. (See: Judges 8:26.)

Jethro

The priest of Midian, also called Reuel. His daughter, Zipporah, married Moses. Later on, Jethro gave Moses wise advice on how to get organized. (See: Exodus 2:15–21; 18.)

Glorification

Glorification means "to share in Christ's glory" (Romans 8:17 NIV). Jesus had an incredible, glorious body after His resurrection. When believers are raised from the dead they will have new, eternal, glorious bodies, too. (See also Resurrection, page 90; see also: 1 Corinthians 15:40–44; Revelation 1:13–16.)

Sadducee

The Sadducees were leading men from wealthy families of priests. They believed in God but did not believe in angels or the resurrection from the dead. To the Sadducees, only this life was important. They were also really into the temple ceremonies. Jesus warned His disciples against the teachings of the Sadducees. (See: Matthew 16:5–12; Acts 23:8.)

Honor Guard of Heavenly Monsters

When God, through Moses, commanded the Israelites not to make idols of any creature in heaven or in earth, He didn't mean that they couldn't make statues and carve images of the cherubim. These awesome, weird creatures were like an honor guard around God's throne. For a bizarre description of these many-winged, multi-eyed monsters, read Ezekiel 1:4–14 and Revelation 4:6–8. God's presence dwelled in the Holy of Holies (in the most inner part of the temple), so workmen placed two 15-foot-tall golden statues of cherubim there, and put two small cherubim on top of the Ark of the Covenant. They then carved cherubim all over the inside walls of the temple. (See: Exodus 20:4; 1 Kings 6:23–35.)

FUN FACTS!

King Manasseh was so foolish that he had priests burn incense to the sun, and made idols of a horse and chariot for the sun, too. He must have gotten a little too much sun. (See: 2 Kings 21:5, 23:11; 2 Chronicles 33:7.)

Places & People

Nazareth

In Jesus' day, Nazareth was a small hilltop town in Galilee, north of Judea. Jesus grew up there as a child and, as a young man, was a carpenter there. (See: Matthew 2:22–23; Mark 6:3; Luke 1:26–27; 4:16.)

An old-time carpentry shop in Italy.

Seven Prophecies that Jesus Fulfilled

1. He was born in Bethlehem in Judea.
2. He was betrayed for 30 pieces of silver, which were then thrown down and used to buy a potter's field.
3. He was crucified ("pierced My hands and My feet") (Psalm 22:16 NKJV; Matthew 27:35 NKJV).
4. Enemies mocked Him, saying, "Let the LORD rescue him" (Psalm 22:7–8 NIV).
5. Men gambled for His clothes and divided them up.
6. He was buried in a rich man's grave.
7. He was dead for three days, then was raised to life.

(See: Psalm 22:18; Isaiah 53:9; Micah 5:2; Zechariah 11:12–13; Matthew 2:4–9; 20:18–19; 26:14–16; 27:3–10, 43, 57–60; 28:1–6; John 19:23–24.)

JEZEBEL

The evil, Baal-worshipping wife of King Ahab of Israel. She tried to slay all God's prophets but was later killed by order of Jehu. (See: 1 Kings 19:1–2; 21; 2 Kings 9:30–37.)

JOAB

King David's nephew. For many years, Joab was the commander of David's army. He was a brave soldier but was also very rough and merciless. (See: 2 Samuel 3:22–30; 18:1–15; 20:4–10.)

JOASH

As a baby, Joash barely escaped being killed by his murderous grandmother, Athaliah. Joash was hidden in God's temple until, at age seven, he became the king of Judah. (See: 2 Chronicles 22:10–24:27.)

FUN FACTS!
Josiah was only eight years old when he became king of Judah. That wasn't even the record! Joash was only a seven-year-old kid when he became king. (See: 2 Kings 22:1; 2 Chronicles 24:1.)

DAY OF THE LORD

Also called the day of God or the day of God's wrath. In the Old Testament this was the long-awaited day when the Lord would rescue Israel from her enemies and punish evildoers. The New Testament teaches that Jesus will judge the wicked after He returns. (See: Second Coming, page 104; see also: Isaiah 2:12–21; 2 Peter 3:10–13; Revelation 6:12–17.)

THE QUEEN OF SHEBA

The land of Sheba was down the Arabian coast from Israel, and in King Solomon's day it was ruled by a queen. We don't know her name, but we do know what she was very, very curious. When Solomon's ships passed her country, sailing to Ophir, she heard how wise he was, so she put together a huge caravan, loaded the camels down with spices and four and a half tons of gold, and rode 1,300 miles north to Israel. Once she got there, she peppered Solomon with hard questions and he answered them all. A thousand years later, Jesus praised the Queen of Sheba. (See: 1 Kings 9:26–28; 10:1–13; Matthew 12:42.)

FUN FACTS!
How rich was King Solomon? Every year his income was 666 "talents" of gold. That's 25 tons of gold! (See: 1 Kings 10:14.)

People in Bible times didn't like dogs. Would you like dogs if they all looked like this?

Six Verses about Dirty Dogs of Canaan

1. Dogs lapped up the blood of King Ahab, after he died.
2. Dogs ate most of Queen Jezebel, after she fell out a window.
3. Dogs prowled around cities, snarling and looking for food.
4. Some dogs are so lazy they can't be bothered to bark.
5. Dogs licked the oozing sores of a beggar.
6. Dogs vomit on the ground, then slurp it back up.

(See: 1 Kings 22:35–38; 2 Kings 9:34–36; Psalm 59:6; Isaiah 56:10–11; Luke 16:21; 2 Peter 2:22.)

HEBRON

Hebron is a mountain city in the south of Israel. Abraham and Isaac lived there, and David ruled as king there for seven and a half years. (See: Genesis 13:18; 35:27; 2 Samuel 2:11.)

FUN FACTS!
David once sent some officials to Ammon, but the Ammonites shaved off half of every man's beard. David's men were so embarrassed that they didn't return to Jerusalem till their beards grew out. (See: 2 Samuel 10:1–5.)

Bars of gold sit on shelves in a heavily-guarded bank vault.

Job

A very wealthy, righteous man who lived in the land of Uz. God allowed Satan to take away all of Job's riches—and even his health—to test Job's love for God. (See: Job 1:1–2:10.)

Job gets bad news—he's lost all of his animals, and even worse, his children!

Joel

A prophet who wrote the book of Joel. We know nothing about Joel, his life, or even when he lived. Joel is famous for writing about an astonishing locust plague. (See: Joel 1:1–12; 2:1–11.)

John

One of Jesus' 12 apostles and the brother of James. John outran Peter to Jesus' tomb and later wrote the Gospel of John, the book of Revelation, and three other biblical letters. (See: Mark 1:19–20; John 20:1–9.)

STRANGE BUT TRUE!
Have you ever seen a beast with two curling ram's horns, coming up out of the ground? John did! And it gets stranger still! This monster sounded like a dragon! (See: Revelation 13:11.)

Demons

Also called evil spirits or devils, demons follow the devil and seek to do evil to humans. In the beginning, demons were angels who joined Satan in a rebellion against God and fell with him. Demons don't have physical bodies but are spiritual forces of evil who live in the spiritual realms. (See: Matthew 8:16; Ephesians 6:12; Revelation 12:7–10.)

Judah and Israel—the Nation Divides

When King Solomon was old, he foolishly worshipped other gods, and this angered God. One day Jeroboam, one of Solomon's officials, was walking down the road out of Jerusalem when who should meet him but the prophet Ahijah wearing a new wool cloak! While Jeroboam watched in surprise, Ahijah ripped his cloak into 12 strips—he was strong—then told Jeroboam to take ten pieces. He explained that God would make Jeroboam king over the ten northern tribes of Israel and only leave Judah and parts of some other tribes for Solomon's descendants to rule over. Sure enough, that's what happened. (See: 1 Kings 11:26–37; 12:1–17.)

Jerusalem

Jerusalem was once named Jebus, but King David made it the capital of Israel and called it Jerusalem, the City of David. Later on, King Solomon built God's temple there. (See: 2 Samuel 5:6–9; 1 Kings 6:1.)

Five Cases of the Most Animals Sacrificed at Once—Listed from Most to Least

1. King Solomon: so many sheep and cattle that they couldn't be counted
2. King Solomon: 22,000 cattle and 120,000 sheep and goats
3. King Josiah and his officials: 37,600 sheep and goats and 3,800 cattle
4. King Hezekiah: 600 bulls and 3,000 sheep and goats
5. Governor Tattenai: 100 bulls, 200 rams, 400 lambs, 12 goats

(See: 1 Kings 8:5, 63; 2 Chronicles 29:31–33; 35:7–9; Ezra 6:13, 17.)

STRANGE BUT TRUE!

The Bible talks about an astonishing, fire-breathing swamp monster called *leviathan*. Read all about it in Job 41. Was it real or symbolic? No one knows for sure.

THE NAME GAME!

In the Bible, a man's sons were almost always named, but his daughters usually weren't. But Job's three daughters *were* named and his seven sons *weren't*. (See: Job 42:13–14.)

FUN FACTS!

Where do locusts hide out on a cold day? The King James Bible says they hide inside hedges. The New International Version says they crawl into holes in walls. They actually do both. (See: Nahum 3:17.)

John the Baptist

The prophet who prepared the way for Jesus. John had an amazing birth, baptized Jesus, and was later imprisoned and beheaded. (See: Luke 1:5–25, 80; John 1:19–34; Mark 6:17–29.)

Jonah

A prophet of northern Israel. God told him to warn Nineveh, but Jonah ran away instead, got caught in a storm, and ended up in the belly of a great fish for three days. (See: Jonah 1.)

Jonathan

The son of King Saul. Prince Jonathan was a brave, godly warrior and David's closest friend. He stepped aside so that David could be king instead of him. (See: 1 Samuel 14; 18:1–4; 23:16–18.)

Baptism, Baptize

John the Baptist baptized sinners who repented. Jesus' disciples also told people, "Repent, and be baptized" (Acts 2:38 KJV). New Christians were baptized soon after they accepted Jesus. Being baptized doesn't save us, but it's an important way of showing publicly that we have had an inward change. (See: Matthew 3:5–6; Acts 2:41; 1 Peter 3:21.)

Shishak's Shattering Invasion

Egypt had a peace treaty with Israel—after all, David's son, King Solomon, had married Pharaoh's daughter—but then there was a dynasty change and a new pharaoh, Shishak, came to the throne. Shishak thought a *lot* about the 25 tons of gold that Solomon collected every year, so after Solomon died and Rehoboam was king, Shishak launched a surprise attack. The Israelites were disobeying God big time so He didn't protect them, and next thing you know, the Egyptian army was parked outside Jerusalem. Rehoboam repented, so God spared him, but he *did* have to hand over all the gold to Shishak. (See: 1 Kings 3:1; 10:14–16; 14:21–26; 2 Chronicles 12:1–13.)

FUN FACTS!
Hundreds of years after the Israelites left Egypt, the Egyptians invaded Israel, ruled it, and made Israel pay them huge amounts of gold. They did this *twice*! (See: 2 Chronicles 12:1–9; 36:1–4.)

Assyria (Assyrians)

Assyria was a giant empire that conquered most of the Middle East, including Israel. Their capital, Nineveh, was a huge city. The Assyrians were very cruel. (See: 2 Kings 17:1–6; Jonah 1:2; 4:11.)

A bird-like god of the Assyrians.

Seven Hebrews Who Married Egyptians

God commanded His people not to marry Canaanites but *didn't* say not to marry Egyptians:

1. Abraham took Hagar the Egyptian as a wife.
2. Hagar found an Egyptian wife for her son, Ishmael.
3. Joseph married Asenath, the daughter of an Egyptian priest.
4. An Israelite woman married an Egyptian.
5. Solomon married Pharaoh's daughter.
6. Sheshan let his daughter marry their Egyptian servant, Jarha.
7. Mered married Bithia, Pharaoh's daughter.

(See: Genesis 16:1–4; 21:21; 41:45; Leviticus 24:10; 1 Kings 3:1; 1 Chronicles 2:34–35; 4:18.)

FUN FACTS!
Jacob and his sons were shepherds, but when they moved to Egypt that was a bit of a problem, since the Egyptians *hated* shepherds. (See: Genesis 46:31–34.)

FUN FACTS!
The Israelites really enjoyed the melons of Egypt. When they arrived in Canaan they grew watermelons, cantaloupes, and honeydew melons. (See: Numbers 11:5.)

JORAM

The son of King Ahab and Queen Jezebel, and an evil king of Israel. Joram was killed by a well-aimed arrow when he was fleeing in his chariot from Jehu. (See: 2 Kings 3:1–3; 9:14–24.)

JOSEPH OF ARIMATHEA

A wealthy disciple of Jesus and a friend of Nicodemus. After Jesus died, Joseph asked Pilate for His body, then buried Jesus in his own tomb. (See: Luke 23:50–53; John 19:38–42.)

JOSEPH

Jacob's favorite son. Joseph's jealous brothers sold him as a slave into Egypt, and Joseph suffered injustices there. Then God made Joseph the ruler of all Egypt. (See: Genesis 37, 39–41.)

FUN FACTS!
Joseph was the governor of Egypt. Everyone bowed down to him. Yet when he visited his father Jacob, he bowed down to *him*, his face down to the ground. (See: Genesis 41:40; 48:12.)

Joseph receives a report on food supplies in Egypt. God gave Joseph wisdom to prepare Egypt for a terrible famine.

RESURRECTION

To raise someone back to life after they have died and decayed—not in the same weak, mortal body, but in a changed, powerful new body that will live forever. Jesus was the first one to rise from the dead, and all Christians will be resurrected one day. This will happen at the Rapture, when Jesus comes back for us. (See: *Rapture*—below; see also: 1 Corinthians 15:20–21, 35–44, 51–52.)

RAPTURE

Also known as our "gathering together" (2 Thessalonians 2:1 KJV) to be with Christ. When Jesus returns in the clouds of heaven, Christians who have died will be resurrected first. Then we who are still alive will be "caught up together with them in the clouds" (1 Thessalonians 4:17 KJV). Angels will fly around the world, gathering us up. (See: *Resurrection*—above; see also: Matthew 24:31.)

Hiding in Kerith Creek
STRANGE BUT TRUE!

When King Ahab of Israel married Jezebel, an evil Canaanite, the prophet Elijah stomped into the palace, told Ahab that there would be no rain for three years, then left before the guards could stop him. God told Elijah to hide out in the valley of Kerith Creek, east of the Jordan River. Elijah drank from the brook until it ran dry, and ravens snatched food off people's tables and flew it to him twice a day. Meanwhile, Ahab was desperately searching for Elijah. He sent men to nations around Israel, making them swear that they couldn't find Elijah and weren't hiding him. They weren't. *God* was hiding him. (See: 1 Kings 17:1–6; 18:10–11.)

STRANGE BUT TRUE!
One time, in Elijah's day, a gully-washer of a heavy rainstorm began with a cloud as small as a man's hand, rising out of the sea. (See: 1 Kings 18:44–45.)

Four Raven Stories: the Good, the Bad, and the Ugly

1. Noah sent a raven out of the ark to see if the Flood had ended.
2. God commanded ravens to fly food to Elijah in a secret ravine.
3. Ravens peck out the eyes of disrespectful sons. Ouch!
4. God feeds the ravens, so we should trust God like they do.

(See: Genesis 8:6–7; 1 Kings 17:4–6; Proverbs 30:17; Luke 12

A jet-black raven on desert rocks.

Places & People

Phoenicia (Phoenicians)

This land was on the sea coast north of Israel, and its most famous cities were Tyre and Sidon. Jezebel's father was a king of Phoenicia. Both Elijah and Jesus visited Phoenicia. (See: 1 Kings 16:31–17:24; Mark 7:24–30.)

FUN FACTS!
Jacob arrived in Egypt and saw Joseph again when he was 130, but he never saw Joseph's two sons until 17 years later when he was dying. (See: Genesis 47:7–9, 28; 48:8–11.)

FUN FACTS!
When Joseph was young, he was a strongman, ruling Egypt with an iron hand. When he was old, he sat around cuddling newborn babies on his knees. (See: Genesis 50:22–23.)

JOSEPH

A carpenter of Nazareth and the husband of Mary. When King Herod wanted to kill baby Jesus, God warned Joseph in a dream to flee with Him to Egypt. (See: Matthew 1:18–2:23; 13:55.)

Young Jesus holds a candle for his carpenter father, Joseph, in this painting from the 1600s.

JOSHUA

The army commander under Moses. Joshua became leader of Israel after Moses died, and his great faith helped him to conquer Canaan. (See: Exodus 17:8–13; Deuteronomy 31:1–8; Joshua 11:18–23.)

JOSIAH

The last great, good king of Judah. When the Assyrian empire fell, Josiah reconquered northern Israel and rid the land of idols. He died in a battle against the Egyptians. (See: 2 Kings 22–23.)

FUN FACTS!
Amon was such an idol-worshipping king that when godly Josiah became king, it was a major cleanup job to get rid of all the idols Amon had set up. (See: 2 Kings 23:4–14.)

GRACE

The kindness and favor of God toward man. Mary " 'found favor with God' " (Luke 1:30 NIV). *Grace* also means receiving God's favor and kindness when we don't deserve it. Paul talks a great deal about grace in the book of Galatians, and tells us that we are saved by God's grace—undeserved mercy—not by our own good works. (See: Ephesians 2:7–9.)

MERCY

Justice is when someone has offended you or has broken a law, and you punish them. *Mercy* is when you decided not to punish them. Jesus said, "Blessed are the merciful, for they shall obtain mercy" (Matthew 5:7 RSV). We were once spiritually dead, "but God, who is rich in mercy," (Ephesians 2:4 NKJV) has forgiven us and given us life. (See: Ephesians 2:4–5.)

GOAT-FLOCK ARMY ATTACKS

One time the king of Aram and his allies—32 kings and their armies—surrounded the city of Samaria. King Ahab had only 7,232 men, but a prophet of God told him to march out and attack, so he did, and defeated the monster army. (Even a bad king can do something right!) Next year the Arameans returned. They waited in the plains, basically saying, "Israel's gods are gods of the hills. That's why they defeated us last time." But God said that He would teach the Arameans that He was God of the plains, too. The Aramean army was so huge it covered the countryside, but the Israelites marched out "like two small flocks of goats" (1 Kings 20:27 NIV)—and defeated them again! (See: 1 Kings 20:1–30.)

STRANGE BUT TRUE!
Once Aramean and Israelite armies stared and glared at each other seven days before fighting. But the record goes to two armies who stood and stared at each other for 40 days. (See: 1 Kings 20:29; 1 Samuel 17:1–3, 16.)

Ten Times People Built Altars to God

1. Noah built an altar after leaving the ark.
2. Abraham built an altar at Shechem.
3. Abraham built an altar near Bethel.
4. Abraham built an altar at Mamre near Hebron.
5. Abraham built an altar on Mount Moriah.
6. Isaac built an altar at Beersheba.
7. Joshua built an altar on Mount Ebal.
8. Samuel built an altar at Ramah.
9. David built an altar on Mount Moriah.
10. Elijah rebuilt an altar on Mount Carmel during King Ahab's day.

(See: Genesis 8:20; 12:6–8; 13:3–4, 18; 22:2, 9; 26:23–25; Joshua 8:30; 1 Samuel 7:15, 17; 2 Samuel 24:24–25; 1 Kings 18:20, 30–31; 2 Chronicles 3:1.)

AWESOME FEAT!
Once, the king of Aram got 32 other kings and their armies together and attacked Israel. But God helped Israel and all 33 kings lost! (See: 1 Kings 20:1, 19–21.)

FUN FACTS!
King Josiah hated idol worship so much that he dug up skeletons and burned the bones on pagan altars to make sure the altars were never used again. (See: 2 Kings 23:16.)

JOTHAM

A good king of Judah. God made him powerful because he faithfully walked close to God. Jotham was a great builder. (See: 2 Kings 15:32–38; 2 Chronicles 27.)

STRANGE BUT TRUE!

When Tamar was giving birth to twin boys fathered by Judah, one baby stuck his hand out, then for some reason backed up and let his brother be born first. (See: Genesis 38:27–30.)

JUDAH

One of the 12 sons of Jacob and the ancestor of the tribe of Judah. Judah gave Tamar his signet as a pledge. Their son, Perez, is an ancestor of both King David and Jesus. (See: Genesis 35:23; 38; Matthew 1:1–16.)

JUDAS ISCARIOT

One of Jesus' 12 apostles. Judas betrayed Jesus for 30 pieces of silver and led His enemies to Him. Judas later hanged himself. (See: Matthew 26:14–16, 47–50; 27:1–10; John 13:18–30.)

Judas kisses Jesus, to show the armed crowd behind Him who to arrest.

CROWN OF LIFE

Not a heavy crown like a king or queen's crown, but a laurel leaf "crown" that was given to the winner of ancient Greek Olympic competitions. Some people believe that the *crown of life* is eternal life given to those who remain faithful. Others believe that the crown is the reward that believers will receive for the good they have done. (See: James 1:12; Revelation 2:10.)

AHAB GOES DOWN WITH AN ARROW

Talk about tricky! Before heading into a battle, King Ahab asked a prophet of God for advice. The prophet said that because Ahab had done evil, he'd die in battle. Ahab threw the prophet in prison and rode his chariot out to battle. But he was worried that the prophet's words might come true so he took off his crown and royal robes and dressed like a common soldier. When they were in the battle—*whunk*!—a stray arrow hit him right between the spaces of his armor. Ahab was wounded but thought he'd survive, so he watched the battle all day. . .but by evening he was dead. (See: 1 Kings 22:1–40.)

JEWS

Jew originally meant Israelites of the tribe of Judah. After the Babylonians carried them away to Babylon, *Jew* came to mean *any* Israelite, whether they were from Judah or not. For example, Mordecai was "a Jew of the tribe of Benjamin" (Esther 2:5 NIV).

FUN FACTS!
Men once "signed" documents using signets—cylinder seals with drawings carved on them. When they rolled it across a moist clay tablet it printed the drawing there. (See: Genesis 38:18.)

FUN FACTS!
When Joseph was ruling Egypt, and his father Jacob still lived in Canaan, Joseph sent his dad ten donkeys loaded down with the best Egyptian presents. (See: Genesis 45:23.)

A donkey awaits a tourist rider in the middle eastern country of Jordan.

FUN FACTS!
When Pharaoh asked Jacob how old he was, Jacob replied that he was 130—then complained that he hadn't lived a very long life at all. (See: Genesis 47:7–9.)

Seven Unusual Things That Happened on Mountaintops

1. Abraham nearly sacrificed his son on Mount Moriah.
2. Moses met God on top of Mount Sinai.
3. Aaron, Moses' brother, died on Mount Hor.
4. Moses saw Canaan from Mount Nebo, then died there.
5. Joshua built an altar and read the Law on Mount Ebal.
6. Jotham shouted out a fable on top of Mount Gerizim.
7. Elijah called down fire on Mount Carmel during Ahab's reign.

(See: Genesis 22:1–14; Exodus 19:16–20; Numbers 20:23–28; Deuteronomy 34:1–5; Joshua 8:30–35; Judges 9:7–20; 1 Kings 18:20, 36–38.)

JUDE

Also known as *Judah* (Hebrew) and *Judas* (Greek). A brother of Jesus and James. At first, Jude didn't believe in Jesus. Later, he became a believer and wrote the book of Jude. (See: Matthew 13:55; John 7:5; Jude 1:1.)

KETURAH

Abraham's second concubine—or lesser wife. (Hagar was Abraham's first concubine.) Keturah bore Abraham six sons, the ancestors of Arabian tribes. (See: Genesis 25:1–6.)

KORAH

A Levite who led a rebellion against Moses in the Sinai wilderness. God judged Korah by having the earth open up to swallow him alive. (See: Numbers 16:1–34).

FUN FACTS!
Hebrews 1:10–12 says that though God lives forever, the heavens and the earth will grow old. They will wear out like old clothes, and God will roll them up like a worn-out robe.

THE NAME GAME!
One guy in Israel was named Becher (Genesis 46:21 KJV), which means "young camel." You can be sure Becher didn't name his son "Gemalli" (Numbers 13:12). *Gemalli* means "camel driver."

FUN FACTS!
The Israelites celebrated a feast at the beginning of every month when the moon was "new" (blacked out). They called it the New Moon Festival. (See: Numbers 10:10; 28:11; 1 Samuel 20:18).

THE NAME GAME!
In ancient Israel, if a girl owned a pony, chances are she'd name it *Susi*. Why? Because in Hebrew *Susi* means "my horse." There was once a *man* named "Susi" (Numbers 13:11).

BELIEVE

To *believe* in God doesn't mean to simply agree that He exists. Even the devils do that. When the Old Testament says people *believe* in God, the Hebrew word used is *aman*, which means "to remain faithful." When the New Testament says to *believe* in Jesus, the Greek word used is *pisteuō*, which means "to stick to, trust, rely on." (See: Genesis 15:6; John 3:16; Acts 4:4; James 2:19).

INHERITANCE

In the Bible, an *inheritance* is property and belongings that sons (and sometimes daughters) received when their father died. God promised the land of Canaan to Abraham, so it was the inheritance of Abraham's children. Jesus promised that we would inherit eternal life in the Kingdom of God, and Peter said that we have an inheritance waiting in heaven for us. (See: Psalm 105:8–11; Matthew 25:34; 1 Peter 1:3–4.)

A crowd gathers in New York City to support Bobby Sands, an Irish soldier on a "hunger strike." In 1981, he went without food for 66 days before he died.

Three Men Who Went 40 Days without Eating Food

1. Moses
2. Elijah
3. Jesus

(See: Exodus 24:18; 34:28; 1 Kings 19:3–8; Matthew 4:1–2.)

102 Soldiers Fried by Falling Fire

When King Ahaziah of Israel was injured, he sent messengers to the Philistines to ask their god, Baal-Zebub, if he'd recover. Elijah sent this message to Ahaziah: "You will surely die!" Ahaziah sent a captain and 50 soldiers to arrest Elijah. They found him sitting on a hill. The captain ordered, "Man of God, the king has said, 'Come down!' " (2 Kings 1:9 NKJV). Instead, the soldiers were burned up by fire from heaven. The king sent a captain and 50 more soldiers. They were burned alive, too. Ahaziah sent another 50 soldiers. This time the captain begged for his men's lives, so Elijah went with him and told the king his message personally. (See: 2 Kings 1:1–17.)

Places & People

Mount Sinai

Also called Mount Horeb, it rises in the deserts of the southern Sinai Peninsula. Moses saw the burning bush and received the Ten Commandments from God there. (See: Exodus 3:1–2; 31:18.)

Laban

Brother of Rebekah. Laban was tricky and greedy. He cheated his nephew Jacob by making him work seven years for Rachel, then giving him Leah instead. (See: Genesis 24:29–59; 29:13–30.)

FUN FACTS!
"Are we there yet?" When the Israelites moved to Egypt, little kids like Hezron, Hamul, and Heber—Jacob's great-grandchildren—rode all the way there in carts. (See: Genesis 46:5, 12, 17.)

Lazarus

Brother of Mary and Martha. Lazarus became sick and died. After he'd been buried for four days, Jesus came to his village and raised him from the dead. (See: John 11:1–44; 12:1–2.)

Leah

Daughter of Laban and sister of Rachel. Laban tricked Jacob by giving him Leah as his wife instead of Rachel. Leah bore Jacob six sons. (See: Genesis 29:15–35; 35:23.)

THE NAME GAME!
Jacob had a wife named *Leah*. Her name means "wild cow." Other women had names like that, too—David's wife *Eglah*, for example. Her name means "calf." (See: Genesis 29:32; 2 Samuel 3:5.)

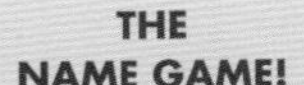

Tola—now *there's* a guy's name you don't hear every day! Tola was Leah and Jacob's grandson, and his name means "worm" or "scarlet (the juice produced by worms)." Imagine your dad calling you Red Worm Juice. (See: Genesis 46:13.)

Signs and Wonders

Miracles that God does to draw attention to the gospel and the power of Jesus. The apostles performed "many signs and wonders" (Acts 5:12 NKJV) among the people. Philip performed many miraculous signs in Samaria. (See: Acts 8:5–7.)

A Tale of Two Robes

When Jesus died on the cross, the Roman soldiers gambled for His robe. There's a famous movie called *The Robe*, telling of the miracles that Jesus' robe did. The Bible doesn't actually talk about those, but hundreds of years earlier when Elijah needed to cross the Jordan River, he rolled up his cloak (robe), hit the water with it, and the river divided and they crossed on dry land. When Elijah was caught up to heaven, Elisha inherited his cloak. Elisha walked up to the Jordan River and struck the water with his robe, and lo and behold, the water parted again and Elisha crossed back over. (See: John 19:23–24; 2 Kings 2:1–14.)

Red Sea

The Red Sea lies to the east of Egypt, and one branch of it separates Egypt from the Sinai Peninsula. Through Moses, God parted the Red Sea to let the Israelites cross through it. (See: Exodus 14.)

Sunset over the Red Sea.

Six Gravity-Defying Miracles

1. Moses divided the Red Sea and it became two walls of water.
2. Elijah and Elisha caused the Jordan River to part "to the one side and to the other" (2 Kings 2:8 RSV).
3. Elisha made an iron axhead float on top of the water.
4. Jesus walked on top of the storm-tossed waves.
5. Peter also walked on the waves—for a little while.
6. Jesus ascended (rose up) into the sky.

(See: Exodus 14:21–22, 29; 2 Kings 6:5–7; Matthew 14:25–26, 28–29; Luke 24:50–51.)

LEVI

One of the 12 sons of Jacob and ancestor of the Levites (priests whose rules are covered in the book of Leviticus) of the tribe of Levi. Levi and his brother Simeon attacked and killed every man in Shechem. (See: Genesis 34.)

REALLY GROSS!
God warned the Israelites twice that if they didn't obey Him, the very land of Israel would "vomit" (Leviticus 18:28; 20:22 NKJV) them out.

STRANGE BUT TRUE!
Weasels, rats, geckos, and chameleons were considered unclean. If one of them dropped dead on an Israelite's oven, she had to break her oven in pieces. (See: Leviticus 11:29–30, 35.)

LOT

Abraham's nephew Lot traveled with Abraham to Canaan. When they separated, Lot moved to Sodom. Abraham rescued him once; angels rescued him again. (See: Genesis 12:4–5; 13–14; 19.)

LUKE

A Greek doctor. Luke was a faithful friend of Paul, who often traveled with him. Luke wrote the Gospel of Luke and the book of Acts. (See: Colossians 4:14; 2 Timothy 4:9–11.)

FUN FACTS!
The apostle Paul wrote that he had been shipwrecked three times. After he wrote that, he was shipwrecked for the *fourth* time! (See: Acts 27:41–44; 2 Corinthians 11:25.)

TITHING

Tithing means giving God one-tenth of your earnings. In the Old Testament, the Law required the Jews to bring their tithes to the Levites in the temple. God promised to bless them if they tithed. Some people believe that Christians today must tithe. Others believe that the "one-tenth" law no longer applies, but that Christians should give generously. (See: Malachi 3:8–10; 2 Corinthians 9:6–8.)

Elisha and the Poisonous Stew

When Elisha was staying at Gilgal (near Jericho) some prophets gathered to learn from him. Elisha told his servant, "Put on the large pot and cook some stew." One clueless guy wandered through a nearby field, gathering herbs for flavoring, and stumbled upon some gourds. They *looked* good, so he cut them up and stirred them into the stew. When the prophets began to eat, they realized that the stew was poisoned! Elisha threw some flour in the pot and said, "Pour out for the men, that they may eat" (2 Kings 4:41 RSV). It took huge faith for them to try again, but God did a miracle and they were fine. (See: 2 Kings 4:38–41.)

You wouldn't want to put these pretty, but poisonous, toadstools in your soup!

Three Times People Moved to New Lands because of Their Animals

1. Abraham and Lot separated because they had too much livestock.
2. Jacob and Esau had so many flocks and herds they had to live in separate lands.
3. The sons of Simeon had to move to Gedor to find pasture for their flocks.

(See: Genesis 13:5–12; 36:6–7; 1 Chronicles 4:34–40.)

Lydia

A Jewish woman who lived in Philippi, Greece. Lydia imported purple cloth from Thyatira and resold it. She became a Christian and took Paul and Silas into her home, where they fellowshipped. (See: Acts 16:12–15; 40.)

Malachi

A prophet who wrote the book of Malachi, the last book in the Old Testament. He lived in the days of Nehemiah, after the Jews had returned from Babylon to Judah. (See: Malachi 1:1.)

FUN FACTS!
When the Israelites offered blind and lame animals to God, God replied through Malachi, "Try offering them to your governor! Would he be pleased with you?" (Malachi 1:8 NIV).

Mark

Also called John Mark. Mark joined his cousin Barnabas and Paul on their first missionary trip, then deserted them. Later he worked with Paul again. He wrote the Gospel of Mark. (See: Acts 12:25; 13:13; Colossians 4:10; 2 Timothy 4:11.)

Fellowship

Fellowship means "partnership." Christians have fellowship with Jesus. When believers work together to do God's will, encourage one another, or gather to worship God and study His Word, this is also called fellowship. The Bible tells us that it's important for Christians to fellowship regularly with each other. (See: Acts 2:42; 1 Corinthians 1:9; Hebrews 10:25.)

Reducing a Temple to Rubble

When Jehu became the new king of Israel, he had a huge problem. He had wiped out the old Baal-worshipping king and queen, but there were still hundreds of prophets and ministers and priests of Baal in Israel, teaching people to worship Baal. Jehu was quite crafty, however, and he called them all together to a special festival for Baal. When they filled the temple of Baal, he had them all killed. He then took out the "sacred pillar of Baal" (2 Kings 10:27 NKJV) and smashed it to bits. After that, he had the temple of Baal torn down. For hundreds of years afterwards, people used the ruins as a public toilet. (See: 2 Kings 10:18–28.)

FUN FACTS!
Job made it clear that he was not one of those weird sun-worshippers who blew kisses to the sun and the moon. (See: Job 31:26–28.)

What drought does to the landscape. This scene is from Africa.

Seven Deadly, Dry Droughts and Fierce Famines

1. The drought and severe famine in Abraham and Lot's day
2. The drought and famine in Isaac's day
3. The drought and famine in Joseph's day
4. The drought and famine in Ruth's day
5. The three-year famine in King David's day
6. The drought and famine in Nehemiah's day
7. The severe drought and famine in Claudius's day

(See: Genesis 12:10; 26:1; 41:53–55;Ruth 1:1; 2 Samuel 21:1; Nehemiah 5:3; Acts11:28.)

Moab (Moabites)

Moab was a son of Lot, and Moab's descendants, the Moabites, lived in the land of Moab east of the Dead Sea. Eglon, king of Moab, invaded Israel. (See: Genesis 19:36–37; Judges 3:12–30.)

STRANGE BUT TRUE!

When Ehud killed the dictator Eglon, Eglon's servants waited and waited *and waited* before entering the room. They thought Eglon was on the toilet the whole time. (See: Judges 3:20–25.)

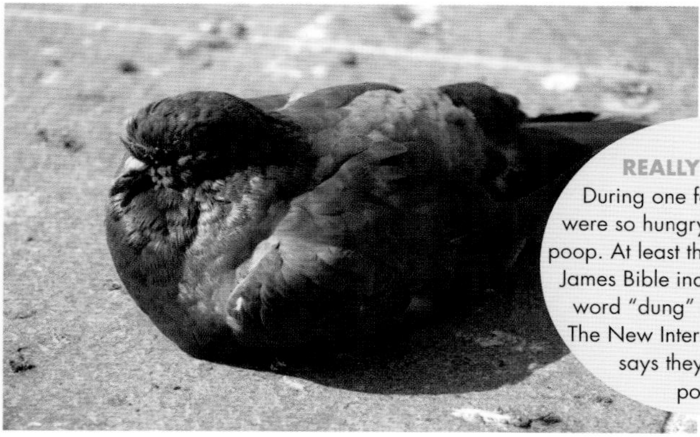

REALLY GROSS!

During one famine, people were so hungry they ate dove's poop. At least that's what the King James Bible indicates, using the word "dung" (2 Kings 6:25). The New International Version says they ate "seed pods."

Martha

The sister of Mary and Lazarus, of the village of Bethany. Martha worked hard—sometimes too hard—but she loved Jesus and had great faith in Him. (See: Luke 10:38–42; John 11.)

Martha (left), busy with work, looks angrily at her sister, Mary, spending quiet time with Jesus.

Mary Magdalene

A devoted believer who gave money to support Jesus. She bravely stood at His cross when He died and was the first one to see Him after His resurrection. (See: Luke 8:1–3; John 19:25; 20:1–18.)

Mary

The mother of Jesus and the wife of Joseph. The angel Gabriel told Mary that she would give birth to the Son of God, and she believed him. (See: Luke 1:26–38; 2:1–7, 21.)

Second Coming

After Jesus was crucified, He was resurrected and went to heaven to be with His Father. One day, He will return in the clouds of heaven and rapture all believers. He will then judge the world and set up His kingdom on earth. Jesus came the first time as a baby, but when He appears the second time, He will come to save and resurrect us! (See: Matthew 24:29–31; Hebrews 9:28.)

Witness

A witness is someone who testifies (speaks publicly) about the things he knows to be true. Peter refused to stop talking about Jesus and His resurrection, saying, "We cannot help speaking about what we have seen and heard" (Acts 4:20 NIV). Christians today are also commanded to witness to others that the gospel is true. (See Preach, page 124; see also: Mark 16:15.)

Feature

The Princess and the Witch Queen

After King Ahaziah of Judah died, one of his sons should've become king, but Ahaziah's evil mother, Athaliah, decided that *she* wanted to be queen. To be sure that no one would challenge her, she sent soldiers from room to room throughout the palace, killing all her grandsons! Ahaziah's sister, however, got wind of the plot and—just in time—grabbed baby prince Joash and his nanny and hid them in another room. Then when it was safe, she smuggled them out of the palace and into God's temple. Joash was hidden there for six years until it was time for him to be declared the rightful king. (See: 2 Kings 11.)

FUN FACTS!
Digging a well was hard work and was usually done by servants. When some nobles and princes dug a well, a song was made up to remember the rare event. (See: Numbers 21:17–18.)

Places & People

Bethany

Bethany was a Jewish village less than two miles east of Jerusalem, on the other side of the Mount of Olives. Jesus' friends Lazarus, Mary, and Martha lived there. (See: John 11:1–2, 18.)

FUN FACTS!
One time Elah, king of Israel, was getting drunk in a friend's house when Zimri, one of his army officers, walked in and killed him. Then Zimri became king. (See: 1 Kings 16:8–10.)

THE NAME GAME!
There's a famous book and movie called *Ben-Hur* about a man who lived in Jesus' day. The real Ben-Hur lived in King Solomon's day, 900 years earlier. (See: 1 Kings 4:8.)

Three Kings Who Were Killed in Their Beds

1. King Ish-Bosheth
2. King Ben-Hadad
3. King Joash

(See: 2 Samuel 4:5–7; 2 Kings 8:14–15; 2 Chronicles 24:25.)

MARY

The sister of Martha and Lazarus of Bethany. Mary sat at Jesus' feet, listening to Him teach, and later poured expensive perfume on His feet. (See: Luke 10:38–42; John 12:1–7.)

MATTHEW

One of Jesus' twelve apostles. Matthew was a tax collector and was also known as Levi. He wrote the Gospel of Matthew. (See: Matthew 9:9–13; Mark 2:13–17.)

MELCHIZEDEK

The king of Jerusalem in Abraham's day. Melchizedek was also a priest of God. The book of Hebrews says that Jesus is a high priest like Melchizedek. (See: Genesis 14:17–20; Hebrews 7:1–17.)

FUN FACTS!
Biggest tithe in the Bible: Abraham once gave Melchizedek, the king (and priest) of Jerusalem, one-tenth of the riches of two wealthy cities. (See: Genesis 14:11–16, 20.)

PHARISEE

Pharisees means "the separate ones." The Pharisees were a group of Jews who tried very had to be righteous by following all of God's commandments and keeping separate from sinners. Some Pharisees were self-righteous hypocrites. Many Pharisees, however, were good people. They believed in God, in angels, and in the resurrection from the dead (Matthew 23; Acts 23:6–9).

HYPOCRITE

The Greek word *hypokritēs* meant "someone who acts a part in a play." Jesus used this word to describe religious people who were just acting, pretending to be godly when they really weren't. Paul described it as "having a form of godliness but denying its power" (2 Timothy 3:5 NIV) and talked about people who say they know God, but live ungodly lives. (See: Matthew 23:13–15; Titus 1:16.)

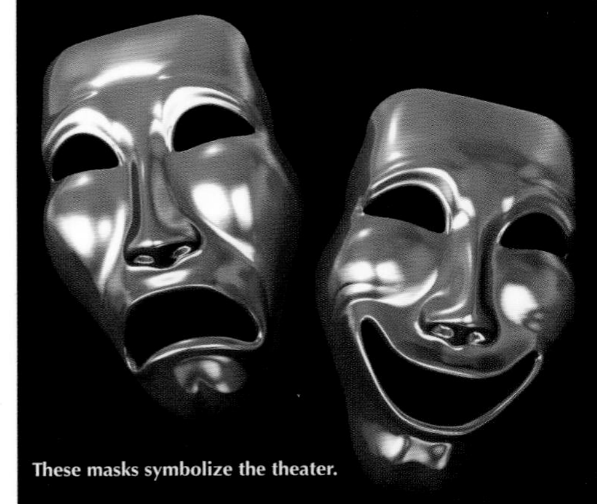
These masks symbolize the theater.

Two "Arrow Prophecies"

When Elisha was old, he became sick. One day Jehoash, king of Israel, visited him. Elisha told Jehoash to grab a bow and some arrows, then Elisha put his hands over the king's hands, and together they shot an arrow out the window. "The arrow of the Lord's victory over Aram!" Elisha shouted. Then Elisha told the king to smack the other arrows on the ground. Jehoash struck three times and stopped, but Elisha said, "You should have struck the ground five or six times; then you would have defeated Aram and completely destroyed it. But now you will defeat it only three times" (2 Kings 13:19 NIV). And that's what happened. (See: 2 Kings 13:14–19, 25.)

FUN FACTS!
The Pharisees in Jesus' day gave God one-tenth of their tiny garden spices—mint, dill, and cummin—but missed out on more important stuff, like loving their fellow man. (See: Matthew 23:23.)

Eight Times All the Treasure in the Temple Was Taken

1. Pharaoh Shishak stripped the temple in King Rehoboam's day.
2. King Joash gave Hazael, king of Aram, all the temple gold.
3. King Jehoash took all the gold in King Amaziah's day.
4. King Ahaz sent the Assyrian king all the temple's silver and gold.
5. Sennacherib, king of Assyria, took all the temple's silver and gold in King Hezekiah's day.
6. Nebuchadnezzar, king of Babylon, took the temple treasure in Jehoiachin's day.
7. The Babylonians melted and took the gold, along with silver and bronze items from the temple, in Zedekiah's day.
8. King Asa gave Aramean king Ben-Hadad all the silver and gold in the temple's treasury.

(See: 1 Kings 14:25–26; 2 Kings 12:17–18; 14:11–14; 16:7–8; 18:14–16; 24:12–13; 25:13–17; 2 Chronicles 16:2–4.)

Mephibosheth

The son of Prince Jonathan, David's best friend. Years after Jonathan had died, David showed great kindness to Mephibosheth. (See: 1 Samuel 20:42; 2 Samuel 9.)

Meshach

Nebuchadnezzar threw Shadrach, Meshach, and Abednego into a fiery furnace for refusing to worship his idol, but God protected them. The king then made them officials of Babylon. (See: Daniel 3.)

Micah

The prophet who wrote the book of Micah. He prophesied against Jerusalem in King Hezekiah's day, but the king repented, so God put off the judgment. (See: Micah 1:1; Jeremiah 26:18–19.)

FUN FACTS!
Once the people of Jerusalem were so rotten that God said, "I will wipe Jerusalem as one wipes a dish, wiping it and turning it upside down" (2 Kings 21:13 NKJV).

If you were asked to choose a real fruit—apples, oranges, cherries, and so on—for each of the nine fruits of the spirit, which would you choose? Why?

Fruit of the Spirit

The *fruits of the Spirit* are the virtues (good qualities) that we should have when God's Holy Spirit lives in our lives. These virtues are love, joy, peace, patience, kindness, goodness, faithfulness, gentleness, and self-control. (See: Galatians 5:22–23.)

Blaspheme, Blasphemy

To *blaspheme* does not simply mean to say a swear word. To *blaspheme* is to "take God's name in vain," to either say His name disrespectfully, mock God, or to say things about Him that aren't true. The high priests accused Jesus of blasphemy when He said that He was God's Son. Jesus wasn't blaspheming, however. He really *was* God's Son. (See: Exodus 20:7; Matthew 26:63–65.)

Hezekiah and an Angel against Assyria

King Hezekiah of Judah paid the Assyrians 11 tons of silver and a ton of gold to leave him alone. That satisfied them for a while, but soon they were back. Their armies surrounded Jerusalem and they shouted to the soldiers of Jerusalem, "Do not let Hezekiah persuade you to trust in the LORD" (2 Kings 18:30 NIV)! The Assyrians boasted about all the other "gods" they had defeated and boasted that they would defeat Israel's God, too. Hezekiah prayed and reminded God that the Assyrians had ridiculed and blasphemed Him. God answered. That night He sent an angel into the Assyrian army camp and slaughtered 185,000 soldiers. (See: 2 Kings 18:13–19:37.)

STRANGE BUT TRUE!
When the Israelites were carried away captive, the king of Assyria moved foreigners into their land. But because they didn't worship God, He sent lions to kill some of them. (See: 2 Kings 17:24–25.)

Six Battles Where the Most People Died at Once—Listed from Most to Least

1. The army of Judah killed 500,000 men of Israel.
2. An angel of God killed 185,000 Assyrian soldiers.
3. The army of Israel killed 120,000 men from Judah.
4. David and the Israelites killed 40,700 Aramean invaders.
5. David and the Israelites killed 22,000 Arameans of Damascus.
6. The Israelites killed 25,100 Benjamite warriors.

(See: Judges 20:35; 2 Samuel 8:5; 10:18; 2 Kings 19:35; 2 Chronicles 13:17; 28:6.)

Four Leopard Spottings in Israel

Leopards once lived in Israel and were even more dangerous than lions.

1. Leopards often lived in the mountains.
2. Once, leopards waited near cities to maul anyone who came out the gates.
3. Leopards can't change their spots. Not that they *want* to.
4. Leopards sometimes lurked in ambush by the sides of roads.

(See: Song of Solomon 4:8; Jeremiah 5:6; 13:23; Hosea 13:7.)

MICAIAH

A true prophet of God who lived in Samaria. When King Ahab asked Micaiah about his plans to go to battle, Micaiah predicted disaster—and it happened. (See: 1 Kings 22:1–38.)

MICHAEL

An archangel ("the great prince") whose job is to watch over the Jewish people. Michael overcame a demon that was influencing Persia and also had an argument with Satan over the body of Moses. (See: Daniel 10:13; 12:1; Jude 1:9.)

Michael the archangel kills a demon with a sword in this illustration from a book of the 1400s.

MICHAL

Daughter of Saul and first wife of David. They were separated for many years. Michal had no children because she mocked David. (See: 1 Samuel 18:20–27; 25:44; 2 Samuel 3:12–16; 6:16–23.)

FUN FACTS!
Once King Saul sent men to arrest David, but David's wife Michal said that he was sick in bed. Saul answered, "Bring him up to me in the bed, that I may kill him" (1 Samuel 19:15 NKJV).

EDIFY, EDIFICATION

A term used often in the King James version of the Bible. To *edify* means to "build up" or to strengthen. Believers were often told to "build each other up" (1 Thessalonians 5:11 NIV) spiritually by speaking wise and loving things. Paul said that just having knowledge simply "puffs up," while having love actually "builds up" (1 Corinthians 8:1 NIV).

FUN FACTS!
The people of Samaria used to sift the chaff from the grain on a threshing floor right in front of the city gate, and sometimes Kings Ahab and Jehoshaphat would sit on their thrones there. (See: 1 Kings 22:10.)

BROKEN-DOWN CITY UNDER SIEGE

Nehemiah asked the king of Persia to let him go back to Jerusalem to rebuild its broken-down walls and its gates, which had burned down, and the king agreed. However, enemies like Sanballat did everything in their power to stop the Jews' work—so Nehemiah had guards watch the city day and night. Sanballat didn't give up. He threatened to mount a sudden attack and kill all the workers. After that, Nehemiah's builders carried tools in one hand and weapons in the other. They worked from dawn till sunset and slept in their clothes so they'd be ready to fight all the time. Finally they finished rebuilding the walls! (See: Nehemiah 2, 4.)

FUN FACTS!
In Nehemiah's day, some of the gates leading out of Jerusalem had odd names such as the Horse Gate, the Fish Gate, the Sheep Gate, and the Dung (or "Poop") Gate. (See: Nehemiah 3:14, 28; 12:39.).

Places & People

PERSIA (PERSIANS)

Persia, now called Iran, once had an empire that ruled much of the Middle East. A Jewish woman named Esther was the queen of the Persian king, Xerxes. (See: Esther 1:1; 2:5–7, 17.)

Colorful mosques—Muslim houses of worship—are among the well-known images of modern Iran.

Six Innocent People Who Were Lied About

1. Joseph's brothers lied that he had been killed.
2. Potiphar's wife lied that Joseph had tried to hurt her.
3. False witnesses lied that Naboth had cursed God and the king of Persia.
4. Sanballat lied that Nehemiah was rebelling against the king.
5. Jesus' enemies lied that He told the Jews not to pay taxes.
6. Paul's enemies made many serious false charges against him.

(See: Genesis 37:19–20, 31–33; 39:11–20; 1 Kings 21:7–13; Nehemiah 6:5–8; Luke 23:1–2; Acts 25:7.)

FUN FACTS!
When Nehemiah and the Jews returned to Jerusalem, most of the houses in the huge city were in ruins and empty. Must've been fun for kids to play hide-and-seek there. (See: Nehemiah 7:4.)

MIRIAM

The older sister of Moses and Aaron, who looked out for baby Moses when his mother put him in a basket in Egypt's Nile River. Miriam was a prophetess but made the mistake of criticizing Moses. (See: Exodus 2:1–10; 15:20; Numbers 12.)

MORDECAI

Esther's cousin. Haman, King Xerxes's right-hand man, tried to kill Mordecai, but Haman was killed instead, and Mordecai took over his position. (See: Esther 2:5–7; 5:9–14; 7:9–8:2.)

MOSES

Moses, a Levite, was raised as a prince of Egypt but had to flee into the desert. He heard from God, came back as a miracle-working prophet, and freed the Israelite slaves. He then received the Law from God. (See: Exodus 2–3; 12:31–41; 32:15–16.)

AWESOME FEAT!
Moses sent 12,000 men to battle the Midianites, and they won. Not one Israelite died! The warriors were so impressed that they offered God 420 pounds of gold. (See: Numbers 31:5; 48–54.)

Moses holds a stone tablet, containing the Ten Commandments, in this painting from the 1600s.

FUN FACTS!
The record for the most people becoming Jews at once goes to the Midianites. After one battle—in which no Israelites were killed—32,000 young Midianite women joined the nation of Israel. (See: Numbers 31:9, 32–35.)

SABBATH

God commanded the Jews to rest from their work one day a week, just as He himself had rested on the seventh day after creating the world. This day was called the Sabbath, which means "to cease working, to rest." Jews rest every Saturday. Most Christians rest on Sunday, however, because that's the day that God raised Jesus from the dead. (See Lord's Day, page 138; see also: Exodus 20:8–11.)

REALLY GROSS!
When God sent the plague of frogs on Egypt, they crawled and croaked all over the Egyptian people's houses, beds, ovens, and bread-making containers. (See: Exodus 8:2–4.)

Fixing a Messed-up Royal Decree

Haman was the right-hand man of Xerxes, king of Persia, so when Haman told the king that there were some terrible, lawless people in his realm (he meant the Jews), Xerxes let Haman write a royal decree that all the Jews should be killed on a certain day. This law was sent to the entire empire. Then Queen Esther told the king that she herself was Jewish and asked King Xerxes to change his decree. The king wanted to, but no royal law could be changed. But he had an idea: Why didn't she write a *new* royal decree telling the Jews to defend themselves against their enemies? So she did, and they did! (See: Esther 3:8–15; 7:3–4; 8:1–17.)

Nile River

The longest river in Africa, it flows from Ethiopia (see Cush, page 45) north to Egypt. The civilization of ancient Egypt depended on its waters. God turned the Nile River into blood. (See: Exodus 7:14–20.)

21 of the Most Outstanding Lepers

1–2. Moses and Miriam were temporarily lepers.
3. God healed Naaman the Aramean from leprosy.
4. Gehazi received Naaman's leprosy for being greedy.
5–8. Four lepers outside Samaria announced great, good news.
9. King Azariah became a leper because of his pride.
10. Jesus had compassion on a leper and healed him.
11. Jesus stayed in the home of Simon the leper.
12–21. Jesus miraculously healed 10 lepers at once.

(See: Exodus 4:6–7; Numbers 12:9–15; 2 Kings 5:1–14, 20–27; 7:1–11; 15:1–5; 2 Chronicles 26; Matthew 8:1–3; 26:6; Luke 17:11–19.)

NAAMAN

The top commander of the army of Aram. The Arameans were Israel's enemies, but Naaman came to Israel to Elisha to be healed of leprosy. (See: 2 Kings 5:1–19; Luke 4:27.)

NABOTH

Naboth owned a vineyard near the palace of King Ahab. Ahab coveted Naboth's vineyard, so his wife Jezebel had Naboth falsely accused and killed so that Ahab could get it. (See: 1 Kings 21.)

FUN FACTS!
Once 200 warriors crouched and hid in the vineyards. When maidens came out to dance there at a festival, they jumped out and caught 200 of them for their wives. (See: Judges 20:47; 21:12–23.)

NAHUM

The prophet who wrote the book of Nahum. The Assyrians had destroyed northern Israel, but Nahum prophesied that God would destroy Nineveh, Assyria's capitol. (See: Nahum 1:1, 14; 2:1–10.)

FUN FACTS!
When the Israelites harvested their grapes, they couldn't check under the leaves twice for grapes they'd missed or pick up fallen grapes. They had to leave those for the poor. (See: Leviticus 19:10.)

A vineyard in Ontario, Canada.

And that Definition Means...

COVET, COVETOUS

To *covet* means to want something so bad that you can't stop thinking about it. To covet can be a good thing. Paul tells us to "covet" (1 Corinthians 12:31 KJV) or eagerly desire the gifts of God's Spirit. Usually, however, *covet* means to lust after something greedily. That's why Paul says that Christians shouldn't even have a tiny bit of covetousness. (See: Ephesians 5:3.)

YAHWEH

The personal name of God. Sometimes it's also pronounced "Jehovah" (Exodus 6:3 KJV; Psalm 83:18 KJV). To avoid accidentally speaking blasphemy against God, the Jews never pronounced this name, but whenever the name Yahweh appeared in the Bible, they read *Adonai* (Lord) instead. In most English Bibles, LORD (printed in what is called "capital and small capital letters") is written and used instead of God's actual name.

SATAN GETS TO PLAGUE JOB

Job was the wealthiest and godliest man in the land of Uz, but Satan insisted that Job only loved God because God had blessed him. Satan said that if Job lost everything he owned, Job would curse God—so God allowed Job to be tested. Next thing you know, Job's family was dead. His huge flocks and herds were gone. Job was devastated but he still praised God. Satan insisted that one final test would do it, so God allowed him to cover Job's body with painful, disgusting-looking sores. Job *still* refused to curse God. After Job had suffered awhile, God restored both his health and his wealth and blessed him more than ever before! (See: Job 1:1–2:10; 42:10–17.)

FUN FACTS!
Job said that he had often helped poor people and shared his food with them. He said that if this wasn't the truth he wanted his arm to fall off his shoulder. (See: Job 31:16–22.)

Six Amazing Women—with No Names!

1. Pharaoh's daughter who adopted Moses
2. Manoah's wife, the mother of Samson
3. The Queen of Sheba
4–5. Naaman's wife and (5) her Israelite slave girl
6. Isaiah's wife

(See: Exodus 2:1–10; Judges 13; 1 Kings 10:1; 2 Kings 5:2–3; Isaiah 8:3.)

MIDDLE EAST

All the lands from northern Africa in the west to Pakistan in the east. All the important Bible lands are here, including Egypt, Israel, Syria, and Persia (Iran).

STRANGE BUT TRUE!
In the book of Job, God talks about a monstrous beast named *behemoth* and says that "his tail sways like a cedar" (Job 40:17 NIV). What was *that*? Who knows? It sounds like an Ultrasaurus! (See: Job 40:15–24.)

A man stands underneath the skeleton of an Apatosaurus.

NAOMI

The mother-in-law of Ruth. During a famine, Naomi left Israel for Moab, where her husband and two sons died. Naomi returned to Israel with Ruth, and God blessed them both. (See: Ruth 1, 4.)

NATHAN

When King David asked if he should build a temple for God, the prophet Nathan said, "No." Nathan later rebuked David for killing Uriah and stealing his wife. (See: 2 Samuel 7:1–13; 12:1–25.)

THE NAME GAME!
"Hagab" (Ezra 2:46) and "Hagaba" (Nehemiah 7:48) were two men. Both of them were temple servants, and both their names meant "locust," a grasshopper-like bug.

NEBUCHADNEZZAR

The greatest king of Babylon. Nebuchadnezzar conquered Jerusalem and took the Jews as captives to Babylon. Daniel later interpreted his amazing dream. (See: 2 Kings 24–25; Daniel 1–4.)

King Nebuchadnezzar goes crazy, living like an animal for seven years, for his pride. See the whole story in Daniel 4.

And that Definition Means...

LOVE

The two most important commandments are to love God with all our heart and soul and mind and to love our fellow man as ourselves. To *love* others means to treat them with the same kindness that we ourselves wish to be treated with. Paul said that we are fulfilling all the laws of God when we love others. (See: Matthew 7:12; 22:35–40; Galatians 5:14.)

IMPORTANT IDEA!
Too often people are prejudiced against foreigners, immigrants from foreign countries with different customs. But God told His people to *love* them. (See: Leviticus 19:34.)

FUN FACTS!
Israel was a fertile, rich land most of the time, and at times so many foreigners came there to find work and settled there that they grew into families and clans. (See: Leviticus 25:45.)

Baruch and the Burning Scroll

A scribe named Baruch wrote down all the prophet Jeremiah's warnings in a scroll, then went to the temple and read them. Some of King Jehoiakim's officials heard him reading and told him that he and Jeremiah had better hide—so they did. Then the officials read the scroll to the king while he was sitting keeping warm in front of a fire pot. Every time they read a section, Jehoiakim, the servant king of Nebuchadnezzar of Babylon, cut it off with his knife and threw it in the fire. In the end, he had burned Jeremiah's entire scroll. God told Jeremiah not to worry. God gave him the warning prophecies again, and Baruch wrote them down again. (See: Jeremiah 36.)

Dead Sea

This large lake, also called the Salt Sea, is the lowest point on earth and is found on the western border of Moab. The Jordan River flows into the north end of it. The water is so salty that no fish can live there. (See: Genesis 14:3.)

Crusty salt collects on the shore of the Dead Sea.

Three Times Writings Were Destroyed or Lost

1. The long-lost Book of the Law was found.
2. King Jehoiakim burned the book of Jeremiah.
3. King Cyrus's decree about the Jews was found in Babylon.

(See: 2 Kings 22:8, 10; Jeremiah 36:21–23, 27–28; Ezra 5:17; 6:1–2.)

Three Unusual Bible Customs and Laws

1. The high priest sometimes dabbed ram's blood on his right ear lobe, on his big toe on the right foot, and on the thumb of his right hand.
2. If a man suspected his wife was sinning against him, she had to go to the temple and drink some holy water mixed with dust from the temple floor.
3. When buying someone's property, the sale wasn't legal until one person took off one of his sandals and gave it to the other person, which is how Boaz acquired Ruth and her land.

(See: Exodus 29:19–20; Numbers 5:11–31; Ruth 4:7.)

Nehemiah

A Jew and the official cupbearer (wine taster) for King Artaxerxes of Persia. The king made him the governor of Judah and sent him to rebuild the walls of Jerusalem. (See: Nehemiah 1:1–2:8; 5:14.)

FUN FACTS!
When he was governor of Judah, Nehemiah fed 150 guests and officials (not counting foreign visitors) a feast at his table *every day*—all at his own expense! (See: Nehemiah 5:17–18.)

Nero

Nero started out as a wise Caesar, which is why Paul chose to stand trial before him. Later Nero went insane and killed many Christians, including Peter and Paul. (See: Acts 25:9–11.)

This Roman coin, called a *denarius*, shows a picture of Nero.

FUN FACTS!
Where does the Bible talk about lots of children at the beach? In Acts 21:5—their families went to the harbor to say good-bye to Paul, and they all knelt on the beach and prayed.

Nicodemus

A leading Pharisee who talked with Jesus about being born again. Nicodemus spoke up for Jesus and, after Jesus died, helped bury Him. (See: John 3:1–21; 7:47–52; 19:38–42.)

Born Again

When Jesus talked with Nicodemus one night He told him, "You must be born again" (John 3:7 NIV). Jesus said that this was the same as being "born of the Spirit" (John 3:8 NIV). When we repent of our sins, put our faith in Jesus, and confess that Jesus is our Lord, the Spirit of Christ comes to live within our hearts. The Spirit gives us life and we are "born again" or "saved." (See: Romans 8:9–11; 10:9–10.)

GODLY GUY IN THE GOOEY MUD

When the Babylonians surrounded Jerusalem, Jeremiah told the Jews to make peace and surrender. This made some of King Zedekiah's advisers furious. King Zedekiah's son had a *cistern* (a huge water storage pit in the ground), but all the water was gone, and there was only mud in the bottom. The officials lowered Jeremiah into the mud and he would've died there except that a royal official, Ebed-Melech, got permission from the king to rescue him. Ebed lowered some old clothes down to Jeremiah, had him pad the ropes under his arms with them, then pulled the prophet back up out of the mud. (See: Jeremiah 38:1–13.)

Visitors to Israel today smear mud from the Dead Sea over their bodies—they think it's good for their health. Jeremiah's mud was a different thing entirely!

Six Times the Early Christians Were Beaten or Stoned

1. All 12 apostles were flogged (beaten with whips) in Jerusalem.
2. Stephen was stoned to death with rocks in Jerusalem.
3. Paul was stoned with rocks in Lystra and nearly died.
4. Paul and Silas were severely flogged in Philippi.
5. Paul was nearly beaten to death in Jerusalem.
6. Paul was beaten and suffered many times—see the full list in 2 Corinthians 11:23–26.

(See: Acts 5:27, 40; 7:57–60; 14:8–20; 16:12, 22–23; 21:30–32.)

72 Men Who Were Chucked into Cisterns

Israel was a dry land, so the Israelites carved cisterns (huge water-storage pits) in the ground. They were not meant for storing *people*, but—

1. Joseph's jealous brothers threw him into a cistern.
2. The evil princes of Judah dropped Jeremiah into a cistern.

3–72. Seventy men from Israel were killed and thrown into a cistern.

(See: Genesis 37:23–24; Jeremiah 38:6; 41:4–8.)

NIMROD

A descendant of Noah's son Ham and the world's first empire-builder after the Flood. Nimrod was a "mighty warrior" (Genesis 10:8 NIV) and founded many cities. (See: Genesis 10:6–12.)

FUN FACTS!
Noah's ark *was* actually huge enough to hold all those thousands of animals the Bible says it did. The ark was "450 feet long, 75 feet wide and 45 feet high" (Genesis 6:15 NIV).

NOAH

Long ago, mankind was so wicked that God decided to flood the earth. He chose godly Noah to build an ark to save his family and animals of every species. (See: Genesis 5:28–32; 6–9.)

What's wrong with this picture of Noah's ark? The Bible says it only had one window! (See Genesis 6:16.)

OBADIAH

A prophet who lived in Jeremiah's day and wrote a short prophecy against Edom. In fact, Obadiah 1:1–9 sounds *very* much like what Jeremiah wrote in Jeremiah 49:14–22.

STRANGE BUT TRUE!
Some years after the Flood, a man named Arphaxad died 403 years after his first son, Shelah, was born—and Shelah died exactly 403 years after *his* first son was born! (See: Genesis 11:13, 15.)

FUN FACTS!
You know those bizarre fish that live in the bottom of the ocean, that have shiny eyes and are *all mouth*? God made them. He created every living thing in the seas. (See: Genesis 1:20–21.)

COVENANT

An agreement between two people or two nations, or between God and people. A covenant between nations is also called a treaty. A covenant between God and people is also called an agreement or a contract. God made a covenant with Noah. He also made a covenant with the nation of Israel. (See: Genesis 9:8–17; Exodus 24:3–8.)

SIN

Also known as *iniquity* or *transgression*. Anything that displeases God, anything that is unloving, anything that breaks God's laws. In the New Testament, *hamartia*, which is the Greek word for *sin*, means "to miss the mark." Since none of us are perfect, we have all missed the mark and sinned. (See: Romans 3:23.)

The Perilous Adventures of the Royal Princesses

The Babylonians destroyed Jerusalem, burned the royal palace, then took King Zedekiah to Babylon and killed all his sons. Only his daughters were left, and they lived with the poor people in the town of Mizpah. Things were going fine until their cousin Ishmael came with ten men and kidnapped the princesses and everyone there. They were on their way to Ammon with them when Johanan and some Israelite soldiers caught up to Ishmael, drove him off, and then took the princesses and people and headed down to Egypt. Zedekiah's daughters were later part of the remnant of Judah that Johanan and the Israelite soldiers led into Egypt, where Jeremiah warned them of God's judgment. (See: Jeremiah 39:6–7; 40–41; 43:5–7.)

Mountains of Ararat

Noah's ark landed on "the mountains of Ararat" (Genesis 8:4 KJV). These mountains are on the border of Turkey and Armenia.

Seven Facts about Israelite Cities

1. Each city had a well, often just outside the city.
2. City gates were closed and locked at night.
3. Cities had watchmen (lookouts) watching from the tops of walls.
4. Most cities sat on hilltops (mounds) for better defense.
5. Half-wild dogs hung around cities, eating garbage.
6. Cities had walls around them for protection.
7. Children played in the city streets.

(See: Genesis 24:13; Joshua 2:5; 1 Samuel 9:11; 2 Samuel 18:24; 1 Kings 16:24; 2 Kings 9:34–36; 2 Chronicles 14:7; Psalm 59:6; Zechariah 8:5.)

Mount Ararat rises above the city of Yerevan, Armenia.

Og

The giant king of Bashan (east of the Sea of Galilee). He's famous for having a monster-sized bed. The Israelites conquered Og's armies and took over his land. (See: Deuteronomy 3:1–11.)

FUN FACTS!
Don't confuse Gog of Magog with Og of Argob. Gog is the chief prince of Magog—way up north.. Og was the giant king of Argob, near Israel. (See: Deuteronomy 3:4; Ezekiel 38:1–2.)

Omri

A king of Israel, the northern kingdom. Omri fought a civil war against King Zimri, defeated him, and became king and the father of Ahab. Omri built a new capital city, Samaria, on a hill. (See: 1 Kings 16:15–28.)

Onesimus

A runaway slave who became a Christian. Paul wrote a letter to Philemon, Onesimus's master. He asked him to forgive Onesimus and to not treat him as a slave any longer. (See: Philemon 1.)

STRANGE BUT TRUE!
How big was the giant Og? When the Israelites entered his bedroom, they measured his bed and found it was 13½ feet long and 6 feet wide! Og was heavy, too! The bed was made of iron to support all his weight. (See: Deuteronomy 3:11.)

Statues of slaves in Stonetown, Zanzibar—a center of the slave trade in Africa. Little wonder that Onesimus ran away!

Salvation, Saved

In the Old Testament, when the Jews prayed for God to save them or thanked Him for His salvation, they were usually talking about being saved from their enemies. In the New Testament, salvation means being saved from the fires of hell and being given eternal life. We are saved by believing in Jesus. (See: Psalm 44:6–7; Matthew 25:31–34, 41; Luke 1:71; John 3:16.)

Unity

Having *unity* means agreeing on the important things of the Christian faith and having enough love to agree to disagree on other minor issues. We can only have real unity when we treat each other with love and forgive each other. (See: 1 Corinthians 1:10; Romans 14:1–13; 1 Corinthians 12:25–26; Ephesians 4:32.)

Robbers are nothing new—they go way back to Bible times, too.

Four Cases of Missing Money

1. A man named Micah stole his mom's money and finally returned it.
2. Jesus talked about a dishonest manager who stole his master's wealth.
3. Judas kept the disciples' money bag and stole money from it.
4. Onesimus, a slave, stole money from his master.

(See: Judges 17:1–2; Luke 16:1; John 12:4–6; Philemon 1:18.)

Five Times Jesus Had Mercy on Despised Samaritans

1. Jesus talked with the Samaritan woman.
2. Jesus refused to take revenge on the Samaritans.
3. Jesus told the parable of the Good Samaritan.
4. Jesus healed and praised the Samaritan leper.
5. Jesus allowed Samaritans to receive salvation.

(See: John 4:7–9; Luke 9:51–56; 10:30–37; 17:11–19; Acts 1:8; 8:4–17.)

Handwriting on the Palace Wall

In the days of King Belshazzar, God had had enough of the cruel Babylonian Empire. So one night when Belshazzar and all his court were having a big drunken feast—drinking wine out of the holy vessels of God's temple—a hand (just a hand!) appeared and wrote a message on the wall: MENE, MENE, TEKEL, PARSIN. Belshazzar was so scared that his face went pale and his knees knocked together. The prophet Daniel was brought in, and he interpreted the mysterious message. God was about to judge Babylon! Sure enough, that very night, an enemy army slipped into the city, killed King Belshazzar, and took over his kingdom. (See: Daniel 5.)

FUN FACTS!
When the Israelites were rebuilding the temple of God, they wouldn't let the Samaritans help them, so the Samaritans built their *own* temple. (See: Ezra 4:1–3; John 4:20.)

Magog

This northern nation will lead an invasion of Israel someday. Some people believe that Magog is Russia; others say that it's a place in Turkey or somewhere else. (See: Ezekiel 38:1–2; 39:1–2.)

Othniel

A nephew of Caleb from the tribe of Judah. Othniel conquered Debir, a city of giants, in order to marry Caleb's daughter. Othniel later led the Israelites to drive out foreign invaders. (See: Judges 1:11–13; 3:7–11.)

THE NAME GAME!
One Israelite girl from the tribe of Judah was named "Hazzelelponi" (1 Chronicles 4:3). Unfortunately, it *doesn't* mean "a hazel-colored pony." It means "coming shadows."

Paul

The apostle Paul (first called Saul) started out by persecuting Christians, then had a vision of Jesus and became a Christian. He preached the gospel all over the Roman Empire and wrote half the letters in the New Testament. (See: Acts 8:1–3; 9:1–22; 13:9.)

Peter

Peter (also called Simon) was a fisherman who became one of Jesus' 12 apostles. He was a top leader of the church and performed many miracles. He wrote two letters, 1 Peter and 2 Peter. (See: Matthew 4:18–20; Acts 2:14; 5:12–15.)

STRANGE BUT TRUE!
One time Peter needed some money to pay taxes. So he went fishing, caught a fish, and opened its mouth—and there was a coin in its mouth. (See: Matthew 17:24–27.)

Jesus, walking on the water, rescues Peter—who walked on the water, too, for awhile. The picture is from a church window in Harrisburg, Pennsylvania.

And that Definition Means...

Preach

In Acts 8:25, the term to *preach the gospel* means to tell or to announce the good news about Jesus. *Preach* also has a special, colorful meaning in Romans 10:8. There *kērussō*, the Greek word for *preach*, means to call out or to proclaim news like a herald of the king. To *preach* can also mean to teach and explain to people how to live godly lives. (See: Romans 2:21; Acts 5:20.)

Gospel

Gospel comes from the old Anglo-Saxon word godspell, which means "good news." The gospel is the good news that Jesus has come, that He died to save us and was raised to eternal life. Christians are commanded to preach the gospel. Gospel also means the full story of Jesus' life, all the details that are told in the four Gospels—Matthew, Mark, Luke, and John. (See: Mark 16:15; Romans 1:15–16.)

When Locust Armies Come

Locusts are like huge, dark grasshoppers, and a monstrous locust swarm is a terrifying thing. When God was judging Egypt, He sent so many locusts that they made the sky turn dark, covered the entire land so the ground couldn't be seen, and ate everything in sight. It was the worst locust plague in history. But hundreds of years later, the Israelites were disobeying God, so He sent a locust plague on *Israel*! He sent four swarms of locusts—one right after another! They were so destructive and so unstoppable that God compared them to a foreign army invading the land. (See: Exodus 10:4–6, 13–15; Joel 1:1–7; 2:1–11.)

FUN FACTS!
When God sent the plague of locusts on Egypt, they not only covered the entire ground, but they also *filled* the Egyptians' houses. Imagine trying to clean house! (See: Exodus 10:4–6.)

Ten Jobs of Bible Times

1. Farmer
2. Carpenter
3. Potter
4. Barber
5. Scribe or letter writer
6. Fisherman
7. Tax collector
8. Fuller or clothes washer
9. Shepherd
10. Tanner or leather maker

(See: Ruth 2:2–4; 1 Kings 19:19; 2 Chronicles 24:12; Jeremiah 18:1–4; Ezekiel 5:1; 9:2; Matthew 4:18–22; 9:9; 27:7; Mark 6:3; 9:3; Luke 2:8; 19:1–8; Acts 9:43.)

Locusts swarming.

Pharaoh

All the kings of Egypt were called Pharaoh. Moses ordered one Pharaoh to let the Israelites go. Hundreds of years later, another Pharaoh named Shishak invaded Israel. (See: Exodus 6:1–13; 1 Kings 14:25–26.)

Philemon

A wealthy Christian who lived in Colosse. He was a close friend of the apostle Paul. Paul wrote him a letter asking him to forgive his runaway slave, Onesimus. (See: Philemon 1.)

Philip

A deacon of the early church who boldly preached the gospel and performed miracles, and was called "Philip the evangelist" (Acts 21:8 NIV). Years later, Philip had four daughters who were prophetesses. (See: Acts 6:3–5; 8:4–8, 26–40; 21:8–9.)

Evangelize

(See: Preach, page 124, and Witness, page 104.)

Gifts, Spiritual

Any ability that God's Spirit gives a person as a special gift. In 1 Corinthians 12:1–11, Paul lists some spiritual gifts: wisdom, knowledge, faith, healing, miraculous powers, prophecy, distinguishing between spirits, and speaking in tongues. There are, of course, other spiritual gifts.

Tongues, Gift of

When God poured His Holy Spirit upon the first Christians, they "began to speak with other tongues [foreign languages]" (Acts 2:4 NKJV) that they had never learned. This was a miracle of God. After this, almost every time Christians received the Holy Spirit, they spoke in tongues. Some Christians believe that God still gives the "gift of tongues" today. Others believe that was just for the days of the early church. (See: Acts 2:1–11; 10:44–46.)

LET'S GET BUILDING!

King Cyrus of Persia gave the Jews permission to rebuild their destroyed temple, but the enemies of the Jews got the next Persian king to stop them. The Jews thought, *Oh well, there's nothing we can do,* so for many years they went about their own business, built their own houses, and left the temple standing half-built. But God sent a drought on their crops, and no matter how hard they worked, they never had enough. The prophet Haggai said that if the people wanted God's blessing, they needed to finish building *His* house first—so they did, and God blessed them. (See: Haggai 1; Ezra 4:1–5:2; 6:13–15.)

STRANGE BUT TRUE!
A lawn on your roof? In Israel, roofs were flat and covered with clay. When it rained, grass sprouted and grew up there. It didn't last long, though. (See: 2 Kings 19:26; Psalm 129:6.)

Four Smelly Situations:

1. The Nile River "stank" (Exodus 7:21 NKJV) when its waters turned to blood.
2. Egypt "reeked" (Exodus 8:14 NIV) with the stench of rotting heaps of frogs.
3. Some manna was "full of maggots and began to smell" (Exodus 16:20 NIV).
4. Martha said that her brother, dead four days, had begun to "stinketh" (John 11:39 KJV).

ATHENS

Athens was—and still is—an important city of Greece, and was the home of many wise Greek philosophers. The city was also full of statues and idols. Paul preached the gospel there. (See: Acts 17:16–34.)

FUN FACTS!
Sometimes Paul quoted popular poets and playwrights. In a letter to Corinth, he quoted a line from a funny play, *Thais*, written by a Greek named Menander. (See: 1 Corinthians 15:33.)

FUN FACTS!
When Paul spoke on Mars' Hill, he was not standing on a mountain on the planet Mars. He was on the *Areopagus* (Hill of Ares) in Athens, dedicated to the Greek god of war named Ares, who was the same as the Roman God named Mars. (See: Acts 17:19.)

FUN FACTS!
In ancient days, most nations had fancy altars made of bronze or metal for their gods, but God said that His altars should be made of dirt or rough stones. (See: Exodus 20:24–25.)

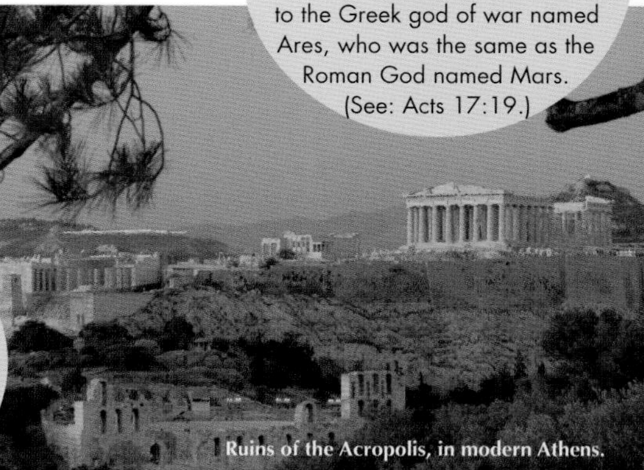
Ruins of the Acropolis, in modern Athens.

Phinehas

A grandson of the high priest, Aaron. Phinehas, a Levite, is famous for killing two sinners—an act that turned away God's wrath and stopped a plague. (See: Exodus 6:25; Numbers 25:1–15.)

FUN FACTS!
If the Israelites ate road kill, they had to bathe, wash their clothes, and be ceremonially unclean until evening. (See: Leviticus 17:15.)

Phoebe

A female servant (deaconess) of the early church. She had helped many people, and when she went to Rome, Paul urged the Romans to give her all the help she needed. (See: Romans 16:1–2.)

Pilate

The weak Roman governor of Judea. Pilate believed that Jesus was innocent and tried to set Him free, but finally gave in to Jesus' enemies and had Him crucified. (See: Matthew 27:11–26.)

THE NAME GAME!
Gallio was the tough, powerful Roman governor of the city of Corinth, and his word was law. His name, however, wasn't so tough. *Gallio* means "one who lives on milk." (See: Acts 18:12.)

FUN FACTS!
There wasn't just forbidden fruit in Eden. When the Israelites planted fruit trees in Israel, they were forbidden to eat the fruit of it for the first three years. (See: Leviticus 19:23–25.)

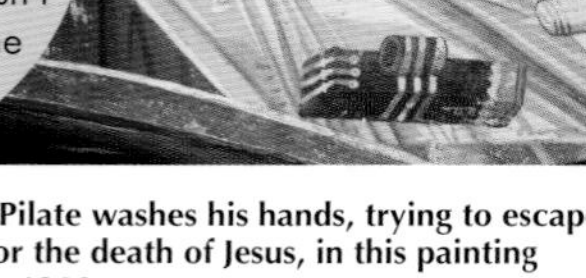

Pontius Pilate washes his hands, trying to escape blame for the death of Jesus, in this painting from the 1300s.

Crucifixion

When the Romans wanted to make examples of criminals and rebels, they nailed them to a wooden cross in a public place and let them hang there. Crucifixion was a very slow and painful death: Sometimes the crucified person lasted several hours, sometimes for days. Jesus was crucified on a hill called Golgotha near Jerusalem. (See: Mark 15:22–24.)

Deacon

In the New Testament, a *deacon* was a person who took care of the practical business matters of the church, such as making sure that the poor and widows were fed. Deacons had to be honest and faithful. Most of the deacons of the early church were men, but one lady named Phoebe was a servant of the church—that is, a deaconess. (See: Acts 6:1–6; 1 Timothy 3:8–13; Romans 16:1.)

Dead Believers Return to Life as Jesus Dies!

One of the weirdest stories in the Bible only gets a single, brief mention. When Jesus died on the cross, a lot of other people came back to life. Here's how Matthew described it: "When Jesus had cried out again in a loud voice, he gave up his spirit. At that moment. . .tombs broke open and the bodies of many holy people who had died were raised to life. They came out of the tombs, and after Jesus' resurrection they went into the holy city and appeared to many people" (Matthew 27:50–53 NIV). Why? The Bible doesn't say. But it sure proves how powerful God is!

Gethsemane, Garden of

Gethsemane was an olive orchard just east of Jerusalem, on the Mount of Olives. Jesus often went there with His disciples to pray. (See: Mark 14:26, 32; Luke 22:39.)

The Garden of Gethsemane today.

Four Times That Walking Sticks Did Incredible Stuff

1. Moses' staff turned into a snake and later parted the Red Sea.
2. The staffs of Pharaoh's magicians also turned into snakes, which were then swallowed up by Aaron's staff.
3. Aaron's staff blossomed and produced almonds.
4. An angel's staff started a fire.

(See: Exodus 4:2–4; 7:11–12; 14:15–22; Numbers 17:8; Judges 6:21.)

FUN FACTS!
God said that Israelites couldn't eat blood. He added, "nor may an alien living among you eat blood" (Leviticus 17:12 NIV). These "aliens" weren't Martians. *Alien* simply means "foreigner."

POTIPHAR

Captain of the guard for Pharaoh, king of Egypt. Joseph was his faithful slave, but Potiphar's wife falsely accused him, so Potiphar threw Joseph into prison. (See: Genesis 39.)

FUN FACTS!
When Joseph told his long-lost brothers who he was, he got so emotional and cried so loud that people standing outside his mansion heard him bawling. (See: Genesis 45:1–2.)

PRISCILLA

The wife of Aquila. They were tentmakers and important leaders in the early church. They worked closely with the apostle Paul for many years. (See: Acts 18:1–3, 18–26; Romans 16:3–5.)

PRODIGAL SON

Jesus told a parable about a wealthy man with two sons. The younger son wasted his part of the inheritance but came to his senses, went home to his father, and was forgiven. (See: Luke 15:11–32.)

Loving father forgives foolish son, in a painting from the 1600s.

BODY OF CHRIST

Paul called the Church the Body of Christ. Jesus has His own immortal body, of course, but symbolically He is called the head, and we, the Church—the millions of believers worldwide—are called the body. (See: 1 Corinthians 12:12–27; Ephesians 4:15–16.)

PARABLE

A story that is told to teach a lesson. Jesus' parables were often about common, everyday things—such as a farmer planting grain in his field—but also contained spiritual truths. Jesus told many parables. (See: Matthew 13.)

THE NAME GAME!
Here are two names that only a dad would give his son: *Abinadab*, meaning "my father is generous," and *Abitub*, meaning "my father is good." (See: 1 Samuel 7:1; 1 Chronicles 8:11.)

THE NAME GAME!
Some boys in ancient Israel had the best possible "brother" names: *Ahban* means "brother of intelligence" and *Ahitub* means "brother is good." (See: 1 Chronicles 2:29; 6:11.)

Two oxen wear a wooden yoke.

Seven Famous Farm Tools

1. Sickles—for cutting down grain
2. Ox goads—long sticks to poke oxen and make them move
3. Plows
4. Oxen yokes
5. Axes—for chopping wood
6. Pruning hooks (pruning knives)—for cutting off extra branches
7. Shovels—for tossing grain into the air so wind could blow away the chaff

(See: Deuteronomy 16:9; Judges 3:31; 1 Kings 19:19, 21; 2 Kings 6:4–5; Isaiah 18:5; 30:24; Jeremiah 27:2; Mark 4:29; Luke 9:62.)

Feature

Jesus Gets Lost. . .Kind Of

When Jesus was 12, His family went to Jerusalem for the Passover Feast, as they did every year. Jesus walked with the other boys from Nazareth, talking with them. When they headed home, Joseph and Mary thought Jesus was once again with His cousins and friends in the crowd, but when they looked for Him that night, they couldn't find Him! They hurried back to Jerusalem and on the third day found Him in the temple, talking to the teachers of the Law. Whew! God was Jesus' Father, so Jesus told Joseph and Mary that He was there doing His "Father's business" (Luke 2:49 KJV.) (See also: Luke 2:41–51.)

Places & People

Corinth (Corinthians)

Corinth was a large, wicked city in southern Greece, where Paul met Aquila and Priscilla, preached the gospel for a year and a half, and later wrote two long letters to the churches. (See: Acts 18:1–18.)

RACHEL

Jacob's beautiful second wife. Jacob worked for Rachel's father, Laban, for seven years so he could marry her. Rachel bore Jacob two sons, Joseph and Benjamin. (See: Genesis 29:15–30; 35:24.)

THE NAME GAME!
In the Bible, sometimes even trees were given personal names. Jacob once named a tree *Allon Bacuth*, which means "oak of weeping," marking the spot where Rebekah's nurse was buried. (See: Genesis 35:8.)

RAHAB

A woman living in the city of Jericho who had a bad reputation. Yet Rahab feared God and hid two Israelite spies, so Joshua spared her life when he conquered Jericho. She ended up being an ancestor of Jesus! (See: Joshua 2:1–21; 6:20–25; Matthew 1:5.)

REBEKAH

Sister of Laban, wife of Isaac, and mother of Esau and Jacob. God told Rebekah that Esau would serve his younger brother, Jacob, so she deceived Isaac to make sure that Jacob became heir. (See: Genesis 24; 25:20–26; 27.)

STRANGE BUT TRUE!
When Esau was born, his whole body was covered with hair like a hairy garment. It's no surprise that they called him *Esau*, which means "hairy." (See: Genesis 25:25.)

FUN FACTS!
Rebekah was a hard-working young lady! She volunteered to fetch enough jugs full of water for ten camels—and camels can drink a *lot* when they're thirsty. (See: Genesis 24:10, 19–20.)

ANTICHRIST

John said that "you have heard that the Antichrist is coming" (1 John 2:18 NKJV). Many people believe that the antichrist will appear on earth soon and that he will be a demon-possessed world leader called the beast and the man of sin (the lawless one). He will persecute Christians and demand to be worshipped as God. (See: 2 Thessalonians 2:3–8; Revelation 13.)

SINFUL NATURE

The natural, sinful nature that all people on earth are born with. Paul said, "I know that nothing good lives in me, that is, in my sinful nature" (Romans 7:18 NIV). The King James Version of the Bible calls this the "flesh" (Romans 7:18) or the "old man" (Romans 6:6). It came about as a result of the Fall. When we receive Christ as our Savior, we are set free from having to obey our sinful nature. (See: Romans 7:5–6, 24–25.)

Jesus Sends a Swarm of Demons Packing

One time Jesus crossed the Sea of Galilee and His boat beached near a graveyard. No sooner had He stepped onto land when a berserk, demon-possessed man came rushing out of the tombs. The guy was possessed by a legion of demons. (A legion was a group of Roman soldiers, 6,000 men strong!) He was so strong that every time he was bound with iron chains, he snapped them! Now he dropped to his knees and began shouting at the top of his lungs—right in front of Jesus. Jesus commanded, "Come out of the man!" (Mark 5:8 NKJV), and immediately the demons swarmed into a herd of 2,000 pigs. Squealing wildly, the porkers stampeded down a steep slope into the sea and drowned. (See: Mark 5:1–14.)

Jesus, wearing a white robe, sends demons from a possessed man into a herd of pigs—which rush over a cliff into the sea. This painting is from 1890.

Jericho

Jericho is an ancient city north of the Dead Sea, near the Jordan River. Its walls fell down in Joshua's day. It was rebuilt, however, and many years later Jesus visited it. (See: Joshua 6:1, 20; Luke 19:1–2.)

Five Verses about Stinking Swine

1. The pig is an "unclean" animal.
2. Boars from the forest lunched on vineyards.
3. A beautiful but foolish woman is like a pig with a gold ring in its snotty snout.
4. Pigs trample priceless pearls in the mud.
5. A freshly washed pig wallows in the mud.

(See: Leviticus 11:7; Psalm 80:8–13; Proverbs 11:22; Matthew 7:6; 2 Peter 2:22.)

Nine Times People Hugged, Kissed, and Wept

1. When Jacob met Rachel he kissed her and wept out loud.
2. Esau embraced his long-lost brother Jacob, kissed him, and wept.
3. Joseph wept as he hugged and kissed his 11 brothers.

4–5. Joseph hugged his father twice, weeping and kissing him.

6. Orpah and Ruth wept aloud when Naomi kissed them good-bye.
7. David and Jonathan wept as they kissed each other good-bye.
8. A sinful woman kissed Jesus' feet and washed them with her tears.
9. The elders of Ephesus wept as they kissed and hugged Paul good-bye.

(See: Genesis 29:11; 33:4; 45:14–15; 46:29; 50:1; Ruth 1:4, 8–9; 1 Samuel 20:41; Luke 7:37–38; Acts 20:17–18, 36–38.)

Rehoboam

Son of Solomon. Because he listened to bad advice, Rehoboam lost the entire northern kingdom (Israel) and was only left with the kingdom of Judah in the south. (See: 1 Kings 12:1–19.)

FUN FACTS!
King Rehoboam was attacked by an angry mob of Israelites, quickly jumped in his chariot, and escaped just in time. (See: 1 Kings 12:18.)

Rizpah

King Saul's concubine (lesser wife). Saul's son Ishbosheth fought with Abner over her. Rizpah later stood guard over the corpses of her dead sons. (See: 2 Samuel 3:7–12; 21:1–14.)

FUN FACTS!
Back in Old Testament days when guys wanted to insult each other, they said someone was a "dog's head" (like Abner in 2 Samuel 3:8 NIV) or a "dead dog" (like Abishai in 2 Samuel 16:9 NIV).

Ruth

A Moabite woman who loved God. When her husband died, Ruth returned to Israel with her mother-in-law, Naomi, and married Naomi's husband's wealthy cousin Boaz. (See: Ruth 1–4.)

Ruth "gleans," gathering grain dropped by the harvesters, in a field owned by Boaz.

Redeem, Redemption

To redeem means to buy back something that once belonged to you. For example, Boaz redeemed the field that belonged to his family. Also, we were slaves of sin but Jesus redeemed us. *Agorazō*, which is the Greek word for redeem, means "to buy at the public market." That's where people back then bought slaves. Jesus purchased us with His blood when He died on the cross. (See: Ruth 4:1–9; 1 Peter 1:18–19; Revelation 5:9.)

FUN FACTS!
Ever gone to school and forgotten your lunch at home? Once Jesus' disciples sailed across a lake but forgot to bring bread with them. It happens to us all. (See: Matthew 16:5.)

Walking on Wild, Windy Waves

One evening Jesus sent His disciples across the Sea of Galilee in a boat, while He stayed behind and prayed on a hilltop. In the dead of the night the boat was way out at sea, far from land, being tossed around by wind and waves. Already the disciples were worried! But when they saw what they thought was a ghost walking on top of the water, that's when they were completely terrified! They began shouting out in fear, "It is a ghost!" (Matthew 14:26 RSV). But it was just Jesus—walking on top of the wild waves, mind you—and He told them, "It is I; have no fear" (Matthew 14:27 RSV). When He got in the boat, the wind immediately died down. (See: Matthew 14:22–33.)

Capernaum

In Jesus' day, Capernaum was a city on the north shore of the Sea of Galilee. Fishermen such as Peter lived there, and Jesus often preached there. (See: Mark 1:21, 29.)

Six of the Richest People in the Bible

1. Abraham was "very wealthy" (Genesis 13:2 NIV).
2. Barzillai was "a very wealthy man" (2 Samuel 19:32 RSV).
3. King Solomon was the richest man on earth.
4. Xerxes, king of Persia, had "vast wealth" (Esther 1:4–7 NIV).
5. Job was the greatest man of the East, and very rich.
6. The rich young ruler had "great possessions" (Matthew 19:22 KJV).

(See: Genesis 24:34–35; 1 Kings 3:13; 10:14–27; Job 1:1–3.)

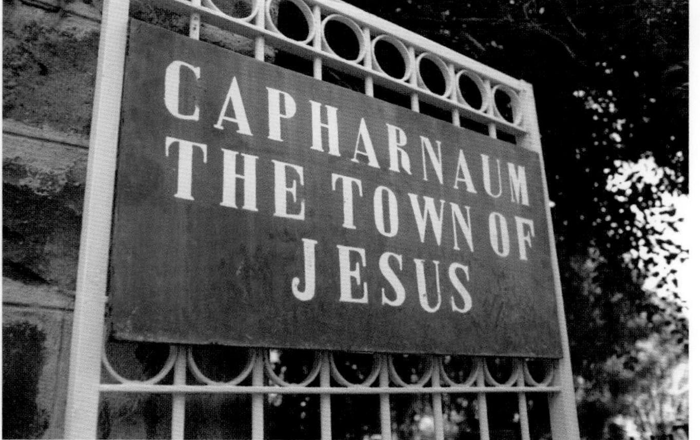

This sign welcomes tourists to modern Capernaum.

Salome

Daughter of Herodias. The Bible doesn't name her, but historians do. Salome danced for Herod Antipas (her stepfather) then, as a reward, asked for John the Baptist's head on a platter. (See: Matthew 14:3–11.)

Gross! Salome gets John the Baptist's head on a platter. Her mother, who hated John, told her to ask the king to kill the prophet.

Samson

An amazingly strong Israelite who fought the Philistines. The secret of Samson's strength was his long hair. He was betrayed by the Philistine woman Delilah. (See: Judges 13–16.)

FUN FACTS!
Long-haired Samson burned the Philistines' grainfields, and many years later, long-haired Absalom burned General Joab's grainfield. (See: Judges 15:4–5; 2 Samuel 14:28–30.)

Samuel

A great prophet and the last judge of Israel. Samuel anointed Saul as king of Israel, but Saul disobeyed God. Samuel then anointed David as the new king. (See: 1 Samuel 3; 9:27–10:1; 16:1–13.)

Anoint, Anointing

To put oil on a person, often by pouring it on his or her head. Oil symbolized the Holy Spirit, and anointing someone set him apart for a special job. Samuel anointed both Saul and David as kings and they became "the Lord's anointed" (1 Samuel 26:9 NKJV). Christians are anointed with the Holy Spirit. (See: 1 Samuel 10:1; 16:13; 2 Corinthians 1:21–22.)

FUN FACTS!
One of the early Christians was named Manaen. He was famous because he was the foster brother of Herod Antipas, wicked ruler of Galilee. As kids they'd grown up together. (See: Acts 13:1.)

Firstfruits

In Israel, the very first figs and grapes and other fruits to ripen were called *firstfruits*. The Israelites were told to give these firstfruits to God to show that they depended upon Him for the rest of the harvest (Exodus 23:19). It also was a way of showing that they were thankful. Jesus was the "firstfruits" (1 Corinthians 15:20, 23 KJV) of the dead. His resurrection shows that God will also raise all of *us* back to life one day, too. (See: 1 Corinthians 15:20–23.)

Dead Man Walks Out of Grave

Jesus had a good friend named Lazarus in the village of Bethany. One day when Jesus was away in Galilee, Lazarus's sisters sent a message saying that Lazarus was very sick. Instead of hurrying there, Jesus stayed two more days in Galilee. By the time He walked all the way to Bethany, Lazarus had been dead for four days, and his sisters and other Jews were mourning him. Jesus had them roll away the stone blocking the tomb, then shouted, "Lazarus, come forth!" (John 11:43 NKJV). To everyone's amazement, the dead man came back to life and walked out of the tomb, wrapped in strips of linen. (See: John 11:1–44.)

FUN FACTS!
The Israelites made a curly "ram's horn" (Exodus 19:13 NIV) into a musical instrument called a *shofar*, and used ram's horns as containers for olive oil to anoint kings. (See: 1 Samuel 16:13.)

Gaza

One of the five cities of the Philistines. Samson once visited Gaza and tore the city gates right off their hinges. (See: 1 Samuel 6:17; Judges 16:1–3.)

THE NAME GAME!
Have you heard of the corny cartoon superheroes Heman and Sheerah? They were both named after real-life Bible characters. (See: 1 Chronicles 6:33; 7:24.)

Eight—No, Nine!—Strongman Stunts by Samson

1. Samson tore a lion apart with his bare hands.
2. Samson killed 30 Philistines.
3. Samson attacked the Philistines and killed "many of them" (Judges 15:8 NIV).

4–5. *Twice* Samson ripped apart new ropes that tied him.

6. Samson killed 1,000 Philistines with a donkey's jawbone.
7. Samson ripped off the city gates and left them on top of a hill.
8. Samson ripped seven strong thongs (bowstrings) binding his hands.
9. Samson collapsed a stone temple, killing 3,000 Philistines.

(See: Judges 14:5–6, 19; 15:8, 13–15; 16:3, 6–9, 11–12, 27–30.)

Sanballat

The godless governor of Samaria in Nehemiah's day. Sanballat constantly tried to stop the Jews from rebuilding Jerusalem's walls. (See: Nehemiah 4:1–2; 6:5–14.)

Sarah

The wife of Abraham. Sarah had no children for many years, but when she was 90, God did a miracle and allowed her to get pregnant and have a son, Isaac. (See: Genesis 17:17; 18:1–15; 21:1–7.)

Satan

A powerful evil spirit, also called the devil or dragon. Satan rules over demons, hates and accuses good men, leads people astray, and fights God's will. (See: Job 1 – 2; Zechariah 3:1–2; Revelation 12:3, 7–11.)

STRANGE BUT TRUE!
The most bizarre-looking beast in the Bible is a flaming red dragon with seven heads and ten horns. Each of the heads was wearing a crown. (See: Revelation 12:3.)

Ascension

After Jesus was raised from the dead, He ascended (went up) to heaven from the Mount of Olives. He was "taken up" from the top of the hill and went straight up until He disappeared in the clouds. This event is called the *ascension*. When Jesus reached heaven, He sat down at the right hand of the throne of God. (See: Mark 16:19; Acts 1:9–12.)

The ascension of Jesus, as painted by the classic artist Rembrandt

Lord's Day

Sunday, the first day of the week, was very important to the early Christians because that was the day that God raised Jesus back to life. Jesus' resurrection was proof that He was the Messiah and Lord, so Christians called Sunday the *Lord's day*. (See: Matthew 28:1–7; Acts 2:32–36; Revelation 1:10.)

Jesus' Death-Conquering Resurrection

Jesus was mercilessly whipped with a cat-o'-nine-tails, then nailed to a cross. Finally, He had a spear thrust through His heart to make sure He was dead. He was then wrapped in linen and buried in a tomb. He lay there dead that day and the whole next day, but early Sunday morning there was a mighty earthquake, and God's Spirit brought Jesus' corpse back to life—and transformed it into a superpowerful body! When some women came to His tomb that morning, Jesus was gone. Only His graveclothes were left. Then Jesus began appearing to His astonished disciples, alive again! Through Jesus' death and resurrection, He rendered Satan powerless against all who are saved! (See: Matthew 27:26–28:10; John 20; Hebrews 2:14.)

FUN FACTS!
In Israel, certain godly, very intelligent women were famous for their advice. Everyone went to them to find out what to do. Each of these ladies was called a "wise woman" (2 Samuel 14:2; 20:16 KJV).

Samaria (Samaritans)

Many non-Jewish foreigners lived in Samaria (central Israel), and the Jews of Judea didn't like them. Jesus, however, showed kindness and love to the Samaritans. (See: John 4:1–42.)

THE NAME GAME!
One Israelite lady had the unusual name of "Hoglah" (Numbers 26:33). It doesn't mean Miss Piggy, though. *Hoglah* actually means "partridge." Wonder if she had a pear tree. . .

Seven Memorable Husband-Wife Conversations

1. Lamech explained to his two wives why he killed someone.
2. Job's wife told her sad, sick husband to "Curse God and die!"
2. Sarah convinced Abraham to take a second wife.
3. Manoah's wife convinced him that he wouldn't die.
4. Samson's wife got him to tell her the answer to his riddle.
5. Jezebel convinced Ahab he deserved to have Naboth's land.
6. The Shunammite woman talked her husband into building a room for Elisha.

(See: Genesis 4:23–24; Job 2:9; Genesis 16:1–3; Judges 13:9–23; 14:1–19; 1 Kings 21:1–16; 2 Kings 4:8–11.)

SAUL

The first king of Israel. Saul started off humble, but after he repeatedly disobeyed God, the prophet Samuel rebuked him and found a new king. (See: 1 Samuel 10:17–24; 13; 15; 16:1.)

THE NAME GAME!
One fellow who lived in Israel was named "Gazzam" (Ezra 2:48). If *Gazzam* sounds a bit like *guzzle,* it almost works out to the same thing. It means "consuming."

SENNACHERIB

A powerful king of the Assyrian empire. Sennacherib conquered all Judah except for Jerusalem. Because Sennacherib mocked God, God wiped out his huge army. (See: 2 Kings 18:13–19:37.)

SHADRACH

King Nebuchadnezzar threw Shadrach, Meshach, and Abednego into a fiery furnace for refusing to worship his idol, but God protected them. The king then made them officials of Babylon. (See: Daniel 3.)

Shadrach and his two friends—with God's protecting angel—as shown in an English church window.

HELL

Gehenna, the Lake of Fire and Brimstone (the Lake of Burning Sulfur) where the unsaved are punished after they die. It's also called the second death. Some people think there will be actual fire in hell; others think it's symbolic, but whatever hell is, Jesus described it as a place of great suffering. (See: Mark 9:47–48; Revelation 20:11–15; 21:8.)

JUDGMENT SEAT OF CHRIST

God the Father has appointed Jesus to be judge of the world. There will be a separate judgment for the saved when we appear before the judgment seat of Christ. At that time we will be rewarded for the good we have done, and judged for the evil. All of our worthless, unloving deeds will be burned up. (See: Acts 17:31; 1 Corinthians 3:11–15; 2 Corinthians 5:10.)

Peter Does One Miracle after Another

Peter was the leader of the early church, and one day he met a lame man at the temple gate and commanded him, in Jesus' name, to rise up and walk. The man didn't just walk—he leaped and jumped. After that, Peter became so famous that people brought their sick out into the streets so that as Peter walked by, his shadow might fall on them and heal them. Peter later healed a paralyzed man in Lydda, and the man got up and walked, and when an elderly woman named Tabitha (known as Dorcas to the Greeks) died in the nearby town of Joppa, Peter said, "Tabitha, rise," (Acts 9:40 RSV), and she came back to life and got up. (See: Acts 3:1–10; 5:15; 9:32–42.)

Four of the Longest-Lasting Miracles

1. For 40 years the Israelites' clothes didn't wear out and their feet didn't swell.
2. The Israelites had manna every day for 40 years.
3. A pillar of cloud and fire hovered over the Israelite camp 40 years.
4. In Elijah's day, a widow's jars of flour and oil lasted for two or three years.

(See: Deuteronomy 8:4; Exodus 13:20–22; 16:35; 40:36–38; Joshua 5:11–12; 1 Kings 17: 14–16; 18:1.)

I Love Lists!

Mount Carmel

This mountain is in northern Israel and juts out over the Mediterranean Sea. Elijah called down fire from heaven there to prove that God was the one, true God. (See: 1 Kings 18:19–40.)

THE NAME GAME!

When an Israelite named Nobah conquered the city of Kenath, he decided to rename it. Kenath wouldn't do. "What to call it? Ah, I got it! Let's call it *Nobah*!" (See: Numbers 32:42.)

IMPORTANT IDEA!

Ponce de Leon searched Florida for the Fountain of Youth. There is no Fountain of Youth, but there is a fountain of life. It's with God. (See: Psalm 36:9; Revelation 22:1.)

Shem

One of Noah's three sons. Shem's brothers were Ham and Japheth. Shem was the ancestor of the Semites, which includes Jews and Arabs and many Asians. (See: Genesis 9:18; 11:10–27.)

STRANGE BUT TRUE!
Shem had his first son when he was 100 and lived 500 years and had more sons and daughters.. That was probably a whole *lot* of sons and daughters! (See: Genesis 11:10–11.)

Shemaiah

A prophet in King Rehoboam's days. He ordered Rehoboam not to go to war against Jeroboam. Shemaiah also caused Rehoboam to repent later. (See: 1 Kings 12:21–24; 2 Chronicles 12:1–12.)

Shiphrah

A Hebrew midwife (a woman who delivers babies). Pharaoh ordered Shiphrah and Puah to kill all newborn Hebrew boys, but they disobeyed him. God blessed them for that. (See: Exodus 1:15–21.)

FUN FACTS!
Only two Israelites that we know of were embalmed in Egypt and turned into mummies—Jacob and his son Joseph. (See: Genesis 50:2–3, 26.)

Persevere, Perseverance

To persevere means to endure, to keep on at something even when it's difficult. For Christians, it means to remain faithful and strong in the faith, no matter what happens. Jesus said, "He who endures to the end shall be saved" (Matthew 24:13 NKJV). (See: Faithfulness, page 154.)

Persecution

When believers are attacked or mocked because of their stand for the truth. Worldly people have persecuted God's people for thousands of years. Jesus was persecuted and promised His disciples that they would be persecuted, too. He advised us to be happy that we were counted worthy to suffer for His sake. (See: Luke 6:22–23; John 15:20; Acts 5:41; Galatians 4:28–29.)

Repent, Repentance

Peter told people to "Repent, then, and turn to God, so that your sins may be wiped out" (Acts 3:19 NIV). To *repent* doesn't simply mean to feel bad about wrongdoing. It means to stop doing wrong and to literally "have another mind." Paul said we should do things that prove that we have repented. (See: Acts 26:20.)

Spaced-out Rhoda

Mark's mother had a large house in Jerusalem, and when Herod Agrippa arrested Peter, many Christians gathered in her house to pray for him. That night, an angel appeared in prison. Peter's chains fell off and the prison doors opened up. Quickly, Peter made his way through the city to Mark's house and knocked on the gate. A girl named Rhoda asked who it was. When Peter said it was he, Rhoda was so overjoyed that she left him standing outside and ran inside with the news. Unfortunately, no one believed her. Meanwhile, Peter was left standing out in the street and, with great perseverance, Peter kept on knocking. . .and knocking. They finally let him in. (See: Acts 12:1–17.)

Mount of Olives

A long ridge (a hill) just east of Jerusalem. It was covered with olive trees for thousands of years. Jesus rode triumphantly down this mountain into Jerusalem. (See: Mark 11:1–10.)

The Mount of Olives rises behind the golden Dome of the Rock, a Muslim church, in modern Jerusalem.

Six-point Romans Road to Salvation:

1. "For all have sinned" (Romans 3:23 KJV).
2. "The wages of sin is death..." (Romans 6:23 KJV).
3. ". . .But the gift of God is eternal life" (Romans 6:23 KJV).
4. "While we were yet sinners Christ died for us" (Romans 5:8 RSV).
5. " 'Whoever calls on the name of the LORD shall be saved' " (Romans 10:13 NKJV).
6. "If you confess with your mouth, 'Jesus is Lord,' and believe in your heart that God raised him from the dead, you will be saved" (Romans 10:9–10 NIV).

THE NAME GAME!

Is God cuddly? An Israelite man named Mishma thought so. He named one of his sons *Hammuel*, which means "God's warmth." (See: 1 Chronicles 4:26.)

Silas

A Jewish Christian (also called Silvanus) who traveled around the Roman Empire with the apostle Paul, preaching the gospel. Later on, he was a scribe for Peter. (See: Acts 15:40–41; 16 –17; 1 Peter 5:12.)

Simon the Sorcerer

A Samaritan magician who was called "the Great Power" (Acts 8:10 NIV). Simon sort of believed the gospel but didn't really repent of his evil, power-hungry ways and was cursed. (See: Acts 8:4–25.)

Solomon

The son of David and author of three Bible books—Ecclesiastes, Song of Solomon, and most of Proverbs. Solomon was the wisest, richest king Israel ever had. He built a temple for God, but in the end he foolishly began worshipping idols. (See: 1 Kings 3; 4:29–34; 6:1; 11:1–13, 41.)

STRANGE BUT TRUE!
Solomon sent ships to Africa to bring back—among other things—"apes and baboons" (1 Kings 10:22 NIV). He did this every three years. Now, why on earth did he want *so many* baboons?

FUN FACTS!
King Solomon must've had a small army of *hunters* bringing wild meat to his table. Every single day, in addition to beef, Solomon's cooks prepared deer, gazelles, and roebucks. (See: 1 Kings 4:22–23.)

FUN FACTS!
King Solomon had 700 wives. But only one wife—Pharaoh's daughter—was important enough and special enough to get her own palace. (See: 1 Kings 7:8; 11:3; 2 Chronicles 8:11.)

Ambassadors of Christ

An ambassador is someone who represents a ruler, or who takes a leader's message to someone else. Paul said that when we witness our faith and urge people to make peace with God, we are acting as "ambassadors for Christ" (2 Corinthians 5:20 KJV).

Sanctify, Sanctification

To be set apart, to be completely given over to God and made holy. Paul said, "For this is the will of God, your sanctification" (1 Thessalonians 4:3 RSV). First Corinthians 6:9–11 gives a clear list of the kinds of unholy people who are not sanctified, compared to those who are. (See Dedicate, page 60.)

Four Wise Sayings (or Proverbs) about Insects

1. Ants have no rulers but store away food for winter.
2. Bloodsucking leeches are greedy.
3. Once again, ants have no one telling them what to do, but do it anyway.
4. Locusts have no king but advance together in ranks.

(See: Proverbs 6:6–8; 30:15, 25, 27.)

Seven Cool Things about the Land of Israel

1. It had springs, pools, and streams.
2. It was full of food—wheat, barley, grapes, figs, pomegranates, and olives. It was " 'a land flowing with milk and honey' " (Deuteronomy 8:8; 11:9 NKJV).
3. The hills were full of copper and iron.
4. God watched over the land all year long.
5. God sent rain in two main rainy seasons—spring and autumn.
6. It was so hot in summer that people took midday siestas.
7. It often rained in one village but not the next village over.

(See: Deuteronomy 8:7, 9; 11:12, 14; 2 Samuel 4:5; Amos 4:7.)

Sergius Paulus and the Magician

Sergius Paulus was the governor of Cyprus, but he was tired of the Roman gods and was looking for spiritual truth. He brought a sorcerer named Elymas into his court, but he still wasn't satisfied. Then one day he heard about Paul and Barnabas and invited them to his palace to preach the gospel. When Elymas argued and tried to turn the governor away from the faith, Paul said, "You son of the devil" (Acts 13:10 NKJV) and commanded, "You shall be blind" (Acts 13:11 NKJV)! At once Elymas became blind and couldn't even see the sun. Sergius Paulus was so amazed that he immediately believed the gospel! (See: Acts 13:4–12.)

STEPHEN

The first Christian martyr. Stephen was a deacon and handled church business matters. He also did miracles and preached the gospel. Religious enemies stoned him to death after he gave a speech that began with the call of Abraham. (See: Acts 6–7.)

Stephen sees heaven opened (Acts 7:56) as he's stoned to death for serving Jesus.

TABITHA

A Christian lady of Joppa. Tabitha (also called Dorcas) was a kind woman who often made clothing for others. When she died, Peter came and raised her back to life. (See: Acts 9:36–42.)

TERAH

The father of Abraham. God called Abraham to leave Ur to go to Canaan, but Terah decided the family should stop at Haran and settle down there instead. (See: Genesis 11:27–32; Acts 7:2.)

THE NAME GAME!

One Bible fellow was named "Pochereth-hazzebaim" (Ezra 2:57 RSV). His name means "gazelle hunter." He'd have liked a New Testament lady named "Tabitha" (Acts 9:36), whose name means "gazelle."

THE NAME GAME!

In ancient Israel, Idbash (1 Chronicles 4:3) was a man's name. Kinda sounds like a guy's name, right?—especially the *bash* part. Actually, *Idbash* means "honey sweet."

THE NAME GAME!

Talk about just being a *number*! Check out these New Testament names. *Secundus* means "second," *Tertius* means "third," and *Quartus* means "fourth." (See Acts 20:4; Romans 16:22–23.)

VISION

Having a vision was like receiving a prophetic dream from God—except that a vision happened when a believer was wide awake, sometimes even with his eyes wide open. Before being stoned, Stephen had a vision of God and Jesus. The apostle Peter once fell into a trance and saw a strange vision of a bed sheet full of animals. Paul had a vision of a man of Macedonia, calling to him to come and help. (See: Acts 7:54–59; 10:9–12; 16:9–10).

Paul and Barnabas Fight and Forgive

Paul and Barnabas were two godly men, and when God told them to go preach the gospel to distant cities, they brought along Barnabas's cousin Mark as their helper. Problem was, Mark deserted them after the first city and headed home. Some months later when they were heading out again, Barnabas wanted to take Mark. Paul disagreed, and he and Barnabas had such a heated argument over it that they parted ways. Fortunately, a few years later Paul and Barnabas were friends again, and Paul even worked together with Mark again. (See: Acts 13:13; 15:36–41; 1 Corinthians 9:6; Colossians 4:10; 2 Timothy 4:11.)

Five Men Who Had Visions of God Sitting on His Throne

1. Isaiah
2. Ezekiel
3. Daniel
4. Stephen
5. John

(See: Isaiah 6:1; Ezekiel 1:26–28; Daniel 7:9–10; Acts 7:55–56; Revelation 4:2–3.)

Places & People

Galatia (Galatians)

Galatia was a Roman province in what is now central Turkey. Paul preached the gospel in many Galatian cities and later wrote a letter to the Galatians. (See: Acts 16:6; Galatians 3:1.)

THOMAS

One of Jesus' 12 apostles. Thomas was very brave and loyal, but when Jesus was raised from the dead, Thomas doubted it. He wanted solid proof before he believed. (See: John 11:7–16; 20:19–29.)

FUN FACTS!
In Jesus' day, Jews often wore *phylacteries*—little boxes with scriptures inside—on their foreheads. Show-offs wore bigger boxes to show how "holy" they were. (See: Matthew 23:5.)

TIMOTHY

One of Paul's closest coworkers. Timothy was Paul's young helper, traveled with him for years, and ended up as the leader of the churches of Ephesus. (See: Acts 16:1–4; 1 Timothy 1:2–3.)

TITUS

One of Paul's fellow workers. Titus was caring and enthusiastic. Paul left him on the island of Crete to teach and organize the churches there. (See: 2 Corinthians 8:16–17; Titus 1:4–5.)

FUN FACTS!
Paul always started his letters with the *same* blessing! Check out Romans 1:7; 1 Corinthians 1:3; 2 Corinthians 1:2; Galatians 1:3; Ephesians 1:2; Philippians 1:2; etc.

A colorful town in modern Crete.

JUSTIFIED, JUSTIFICATION

To be justified means "to be declared free from sin and to be just (righteous)." Jesus lived a perfectly righteous life and died in our place to pay the price for our sins. When we have faith in His sacrifice for us, God justifies us. He looks at us and sees Christ's righteousness. (See: Imputation, page 156; see also: Romans 3:24–25, 28.)

FAITH

(See: Believe, page 96.)

FUN FACTS!
Paul used to persecute and beat Christians, and tried to get them to blaspheme Jesus' name. Then God blinded Paul, and he became a Christian himself! (Acts 8:3; 9:1–19; 26:9–11.)

A statue of Paul in front of an Italian church.

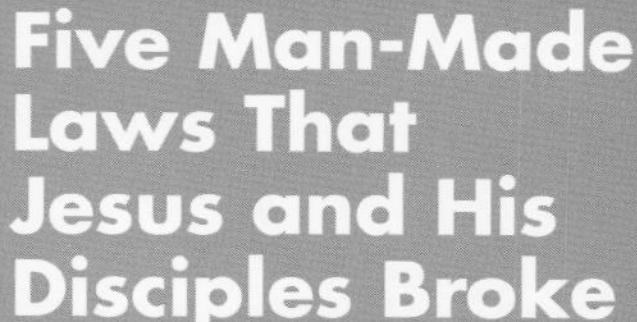

Five Man-Made Laws That Jesus and His Disciples Broke

1. Jesus associated with "unclean" tax collecters and sinners.
2. Jesus' disciples crushed wheat kernels on the Sabbath.
3. Jesus healed people on the Sabbath.
4. Jesus' disciples didn't ceremonially wash up to the elbows before they ate.
5. Jesus' disciples went into the home of "unclean" Gentiles.

(See: Matthew 9:10–12; 11:19; 12:1–6; Mark 3:1–5; 7:1–4; Luke 13:10–16; Acts 10:27–28; 11:2.)

Apostle Left for Dead

Paul was one of those guys who "took a lickin' and kept on tickin'." When he and Barnabas healed a lame man in Lystra, the people believed that they were the Greek gods Hermes and Zeus. Paul and Barnabas were barely able to persuade the crowds that they were just men. Then some enemies persuaded the crowds that Paul was an evil villain, so the people—talk about fickle!—dragged him outside the city gates, stoned him with rocks, and left him for dead. But when the Christians gathered around his battered, bleeding body, Paul got up—still alive! He even went back into the city. (See: Acts 14:8–20.)

Thessalonica (Thessalonians)

A city in Macedonia (northern Greece). Paul preached the gospel there and later wrote two letters to the persecuted Thessalonian Christians. (See: Acts 17:1–9; 1 Thessalonians 1:1; 2 Thessalonians 1:1.)

Trophimus

A Greek Christian from Ephesus. He traveled with Paul from Greece to Jerusalem, and while there was falsely accused of defiling God's temple. (See: Acts 20:4; 21:27–29.)

FUN FACTS!
Paul was a leader of the Christian church, but since Jesus was a Jew from Nazareth, some Jews called Christians the "sect of the Nazarenes" (Acts 24:5 KJV).

Tyrannus

A Greek teacher—probably a philosopher—in Ephesus. He let the apostle Paul preach the gospel in his lecture hall for two years, and this really helped spread the gospel. (See: Acts 19:8–10.)

Uriah

One of David's mightiest warriors. Uriah was a Hittite married to Bathsheba, a beautiful Israelite woman, but David had Uriah killed so that he could take his wife. (See: 2 Samuel 11; 23:8, 39.)

STRANGE BUT TRUE!
When Paul was persecuting Christians, God struck him blind. Years later, when Paul was preaching the gospel, he prayed and God struck a bad magician blind. (See: Acts 9:1–9; 13:6–11.)

Feast of Pentecost

This feast was called the Feast of Harvests because it happened at the end of the wheat harvest. It was also called the Feast of Weeks. *Pentecost* means "fifty," and this feast happened seven weeks after Passover, on the fiftieth day. God poured out His Holy Spirit on the church on the Day of Pentecost. (See: Deuteronomy 16:9–11; Acts 2:1–4.)

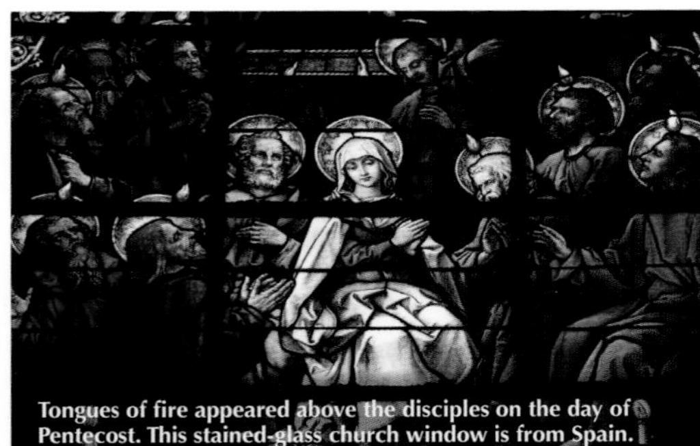

Tongues of fire appeared above the disciples on the day of Pentecost. This stained-glass church window is from Spain.

Infilling (of Holy Spirit)

To be completely filled with God's Holy Spirit. All Christians receive a measure of the Spirit when they are saved, and being "filled with the Spirit" often happened at the same time. Sometimes this happened a while after they were saved, however. (See: Acts 10:44–45; 19:1–6; Romans 8:9.)

STRANGE BUT TRUE!
God's altar in the temple had metal horns on its four corners, and when people were in trouble they ran in, grabbed hold of two horns, and were safe. (See: Exodus 27:1–2; 1 Kings 1:50–53.)

A British warship on the high seas.

Four Things Agur Simply Couldn't Understand

1. The way of an eagle in the sky
2. The way of a snake on a rock
3. The way of a ship on the high seas
4. The way of a man with a young woman

(See: Proverbs 30:1, 19.)

Idolatrous Mob Riots at Ephesus

The city of Ephesus worshipped the Roman goddess Diana (Artemis), and they built a magnificent temple for her. The city's silversmiths earned a good living making silver idols to sell. But Paul preached that man-made gods were no gods at all, and many Diana-worshippers became Christians. This angered a silversmith named Demetrius, and he got everyone so stirred up that soon the whole city was in an uproar, screaming how great Diana was. They seized some Christians and dragged them to the amphitheater. No telling what they would have done if a city official hadn't shown up and commanded them to stop rioting. (See: Acts 19.)

Hittites

In Joshua's day, the Hittites were an empire to the north in Turkey. There were also some Hittites (sometimes called sons of Heth) living down south in Canaan. (See: Genesis 23:1–4; Joshua 1:1–4; 9:1–2.)

Five Migrating Birds in the Bible

1. Stork
2. Dove
3. Swift
4. Thrush
5. Quail

(See: Jeremiah 8:7 NIV; Numbers 11:31.)

Six Different Kinds of Owls the Israelites Couldn't Eat

1. Horned owl
2. Screech owl
3. Little owl
4. Great owl
5. White owl
6. Desert owl

(See: Leviticus 11:13, 16–18 NIV)

Uzziah

A king of Judah. For most of his life, Uzziah sought God, and God helped him win many battles. In the end, Uzziah became a leper because of his pride. (See: 2 Chronicles 26.)

THE NAME GAME!
A Bible character named "Shaashgaz" (Esther 2:14) was the keeper of the Persian king's harem of gorgeous women. Wouldn't you know it?—*Shaashgaz* means "servant of the beautiful."

Vashti

The first wife of King Ahaseurus (Xerxes). When the king wanted her to show off her beauty to his nobles, Vashti refused, so he divorced her and picked a new queen Esther. (See: Esther 1; 2:17.)

Zacchaeus

A tax collector in Jericho. He was so short he had to climb a tree so that he could see Jesus. After he became a believer, Zacchaeus promised to pay back anyone whom he had cheated. (See: Luke 19:1–10.)

STRANGE BUT TRUE!
The custom of bells on horses' harnesses (like the kind they wear when pulling sleighs at Christmas) is an old one. Over 2,000 years ago in Israel, horses wore bells, too. (See: Zechariah 14:20.)

STRANGE BUT TRUE!
Elisha had a rare spiritual gift—he could see what was happening in places when he wasn't even there. Jesus had the same ability. (See: 2 Kings 5:19–26; John 1:47–48.)

And that Definition Means...

Restitution

To pay back, to return something that was stolen, or to make good something that was damaged. When Zacchaeus the tax collector repented, he offered to make restitution to (to pay back) any man whom he had cheated. Restitution also means restoring something to the way it originally was. For example, one day God will restore the world to the way it was before the Fall. (See: Luke 19:8; Acts 3:21.)

Paul Revere warns of the approach of the British army.

Paul's Midnight Ride

Seventeen hundred years before Paul Revere went on his famous midnight ride, another Paul rode a horse for freedom—the apostle Paul. He'd gone to Jerusalem to take money to the poor Christians when he was spotted by his enemies. They went wild and tried to kill Paul, but the Romans rescued him. These enemies then decided to tell the Romans that they wanted to have a "little talk" with Paul the next day—but they planned to ambush and kill him. Fortunately, Paul's nephew heard of the plot and told the Romans, who escorted Paul from Jerusalem at 9:00 that night with 200 soldiers, 70 horsemen, and 200 spearmen. (See: Acts 23:12–33.)

Six Earth-shaking, Ground-breaking Earthquakes

1. Mount Sinai "trembled violently" (Exodus 19:18 NIV) when God came down.
2. An earthquake shook Mount Horeb when Elijah was there.
3. A devastating earthquake hit in King Uzziah's day.
4. An earthquake struck when Jesus died.
5. A violent earthquake shook Jerusalem at Jesus' resurrection.
6. An earthquake hit Philippi, Greece, and destroyed the local jail where Paul and Silas were imprisoned.

(See: Exodus 19:16–18; 1 Kings 19:8, 11–12; Amos 1:1; Zechariah 14:5; Matthew 27:51, 54; 28:1–2; Acts 16:11–12; 25–26.)

ZADOK

A very godly priest. Abiathar the high priest was disloyal to Solomon, so he lost his job, but because Zadok was loyal, Solomon made him high priest instead. (See: 1 Kings 1:5–8; 2:27, 35.)

FUN FACTS!
King David built a palace in Jerusalem, but about 40 years later King Solomon built a bigger, fancier palace there. No telling what he used the old palace for. (See: 2 Samuel 5:11; 1 Kings 7:1.)

ZEBEDEE AND HIS WIFE

A fisherman and the father of James and John. Zebedee's wife traveled to Jerusalem with Jesus and His disciples and made a bold request. (See: Matthew 4:21–22; 20:20–21.)

ZECHARIAH (OF THE OLD TESTAMENT)

A prophet who lived in the days after the Jews returned from Babylon. God's temple had been destroyed, and Zechariah and Haggai encouraged the Jews to rebuild it. (See: Ezra 5:1–2; 6:14.)

REALLY GROSS!
You never saw a gross plague like *this*! Through Zechariah, God warned that some people's bodies—and their eyes and tongues—would rot while they were standing on their feet! (See: Zechariah 14:12.)

THE NAME GAME!
Zaham was a son of King Rehoboam and Mahalath, David's granddaughter. Some Bible experts say *Zaham* means "fatness." Others think it means "detest." Others say it means "disgusting fool." (See: 2 Chronicles 11:18–19.)

And that Definition Means...

FAITHFUL, FAITHFULNESS

To be reliable and trustworthy. God is faithful in keeping His promises, and that is why we can trust Him. God also calls us to be faithful, to follow Him consistently without giving up, to keep on doing what we're supposed to be doing. God wants us to "be faithful until death" (Revelation 2:10 NKJV). (See also: Hebrews 10:23; Luke 16:10–12.)

The apostle Paul described people who walked away from their Christian faith as "shipwrecks" (1 Timothy 1:9).

The Pleiades.

Seven Stars, Constellations, and Planets Mentioned in the Scriptures

1–2. Ursa Major *and* Ursa Minor the Bear and its cub
3. Pleiades—the Seven Sisters
4. Orion—the Hunter
5. The star of Bethlehem
6. Saturn—"Chiun" (Amos 5:26 KJV) or "Rephan" (Acts 7:43 NIV)
7. Venus—the Morning Star

(See: Job 9:9; 38:31–32; Amos 5:8, 26; Matthew 2:1–2, 9; Revelation 22:16.)

Six People Who Fled to Egypt for Safety

1. Hadad the Edomite fled from King Solomon.
2. Jeroboam fled from King Solomon.
3. The prophet Uriah fled from King Jehoiakim.
4–6. Joseph, Mary, and Jesus fled from King Herod.

(See: 1 Kings 11:14–19, 40; Jeremiah 26:20–21; Matthew 2:13–14.)

Savage Storm and Shipwreck

When Paul was sent as a prisoner to Rome, the soldiers booked passage on an Egyptian ship and set out. They were just south of Crete when a terrific hurricane struck and blew them off course. The storm raged for two weeks. For many days and nights, the clouds were so dark they couldn't see either the sun or the stars by which they navigated their ship. Everyone gave up hope of surviving. They were so sick that they stopped eating. Then the ship smashed into some rocks and began breaking apart in the fierce waves. By a miracle, everyone survived: They either swam to shore or hung on to pieces of wood. (See: Acts 27.)

ZECHARIAH (OF THE NEW TESTAMENT)

A priest and the father of John the Baptist. Zechariah saw the angel Gabriel in the temple but doubted his promise, so he was struck speechless for nine months. (See: Luke 1:5–25, 57–79.)

THE NAME GAME!
Sheerah was a granddaughter of Joseph, who oversaw the building of three cities—Lower Beth Horon, Upper Beth Horon, and Uzzen Sheerah. She named the last city after herself. (See: Genesis 46:20; 1 Chronicles 7:22–24.)

ZEDEKIAH

The last king of Judah. Zedekiah was a weak king who gave in to his nobles and imprisoned Jeremiah. The city and temple were destroyed because of his wrong decisions. (See: Jeremiah 38:1–6; 2 Kings 24:17–25:7.)

ZEPHANIAH

A prophet who wrote the book of Zephaniah. He was probably a cousin of the kings of Judah, and prophesied a lot about the royal court and Jerusalem's destruction. (See: Zephaniah 1:1.)

THE NAME GAME!
One Bible guy obviously had an older sister named Rachel, because his parents named him *Aharhel*, which means "brother of Rachel." Oh, how humbling! (See: 1 Chronicles 4:8.)

ZIPPORAH

A Midianite woman and the daughter of Jethro, the priest of Midian. Zipporah married Moses and bore him two sons, Gershom and Eliezer. (See: Exodus 2:15–25; 18:1–4.)

THE NAME GAME!
Canaan was such a dry land and wells were so important that people gave names to them. Isaac called his wells Esek, Sitnah, Rehoboth, and Shibah. (See: Genesis 26:20–22, 33.)

A middle eastern woman at an ancient well.

IMPUTE, IMPUTATION

To declare that something legally belongs to someone—to credit it to them. When we accept that Jesus died in our place, God "imputes" Jesus' righteousness to us. God then no longer counts (imputes) our sins against us. (See: Romans 4:6, 22–24; 2 Corinthians 5:19.)

Prisoner Rescues Thief

When Paul was under house arrest in Rome, he had a surprise visitor from a distant city—Onesimus, a slave of Paul's wealthy friend named Philemon. Even though Philemon had treated him well, Onesimus wanted to be free so badly that he stole money from his master, fled the city, and ended up in Rome. When his money ran out, Onesimus showed up at Paul's house. There he became a Christian. Paul sent him back to Philemon with a letter that asked Philemon to forgive Onesimus and not to treat him like a slave anymore, but as a brother in Christ. (See: Philemon 1.)

Prisons are places of punishment for people who've done bad things. But sometimes, innocent and godly people end up in prison, too. God has His own good reasons!

Seven Famous Shepherds and Shepherdesses

1) Abel, the son of Adam
2) Lot, Abraham's nephew
3) Rachel, Laban's daughter
4) Jacob (Genesis)
5) Zipporah, Jethro's daughter, future wife of Moses
6) Moses
7) David

(See: Genesis 4:2, 4; 13:5; 29:9–10; 31:36–40; Exodus 2:16, 21; 3:1; 1 Samuel 17:34–35.)

Nine Men of God Who Were in Prison

1. Joseph
2. Samson
3. Micaiah
4. Jeremiah
5. Jehoiachin
6. John the Baptist
7. Peter

8–9. Paul and Silas

(See: Genesis 39:20; Judges 16:20–21; 1 Kings 22:26–27; Jeremiah 37:15; 52:31; Mark 6:17; Acts 16:19–24.)

KEY TO INDEX:

Note: Only key entries are included. Many of these people, places, and things will also be referenced in other entries throughout the book. Colored numbers indicate a picture.

Art Resource/NY: Pages 14 (Scala), 24 (Snark), 72 (Cameraphoto Arte, Venice), 82 (Scala/ Ministero per i Beni e le Attività culturali), 94 (DeA Picture Library), 110 (HIP), 112 (Finsiel/Alinari), 116 (Tate, London), 120 (The Metropolitan Museum of Art), 130 (Alinari), 133 (HIP), 146 (National Gallery, London)

Bildarchiv Preussischer Kulturbesitz/Art Resource/NY: Pages 46, 86, 138

Bill Aron: Page 60

Corbis: Pages 9 (Jean Pierre Fizet/Sygma), 22 (Sunset Boulevard), 26 (John Springer Collection), 58 (William Whitehurst), 62 (Hanan Isachar), 74 (Brooklyn Museum), 76 (Sunset Boulevard), 113 (DLILLC), 115 (Louie Psihoyos), 135 (Brooks Kraft), 153 (PoodlesRock)

Erich Lessing/Art Resource/NY: Pages 12, 42, 49, 54, 78. 128

Flickr: Pages 16, 26, 34, 40, 50, 54 (photopolly), 140

Getty Images: Pages 7 (Hulton Archive), 10 (AFP), 19 (Hulton Archive), 29 (Michael Ochs Archives), 32 (FilmMagic), 53 (Michael Ochs Archives), 81 (AFP), 97 (Premium Archive), 151 (Getty Images News)

Google: Page 64

Gustave Dore: Page 52

iStock: Pages 7, 8, 11, 13, 15, 17, 18, 20, 21, 23, 25, 32, 35, 36, 37, 39, 41, 43, 44, 45, 48, 51, 56, 57, 61, 65, 66, 67, 69, 70, 71, 73, 75, 77, 79, 80, 83, 85, 87, 89, 91, 95, 96, 98, 99, 100, 101, 103, 106, 107, 108, 109, 111, 114, 117, 118, 119, 121, 122, 123, 124, 125, 127, 129, 131, 134, 142, 143, 145, 147, 148, 149, 150, 152, 154, 155, 156, 157

Réunion des Musées Nationaux/Art Resource/NY: Pages 92, 104, 136

Wikipedia: Page 38

KiDS'
Bible
Questions
&
Answers

CONTENTS

WHERE DID GOD COME FROM?

God didn't "come from" anywhere. God has always been around. He has been here forever and will continue to be here forever. This is hard for us to understand, because everything we see around us has a beginning and an ending—even the universe. The first verse in the Bible tells us that God already existed in the beginning, before He created the heavens and the earth (Genesis 1:1). One day, everything we see will come to an end, but God will never end (Psalm 102:27).

God's name in Hebrew is *Yahweh*, which simply means "to exist" or "the Existing One." In other words, God has always existed and He always will. Nobody created God, because no one was around before Him (Isaiah 43:10). King David writes, "Before. . .You had formed the earth and the world, even from everlasting to everlasting, You are God" (Psalm 90:2 NKJV).

The good news is that this means God will always be there for you (Isaiah 46:4)!

In the beginning God created the heaven and the earth.
GENESIS 1:1 KJV

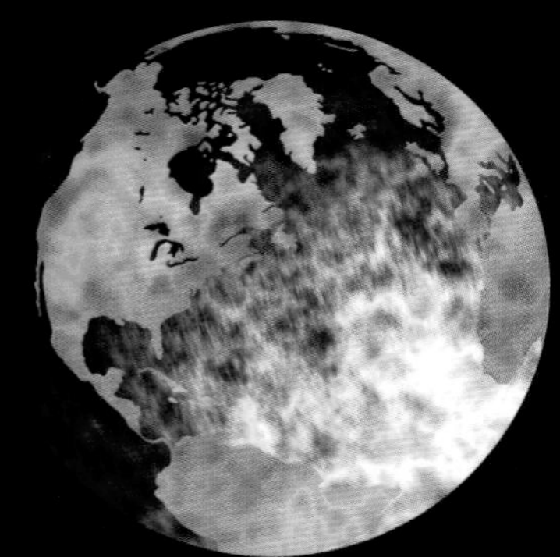

COULD GOD REALLY CREATE THE WORLD IN JUST SIX DAYS?

> *And God saw every thing that he had made, and, behold, it was very good. And the evening and the morning were the sixth day.*
>
> GENESIS 1:31 KJV

Yes! Absolutely! In fact, God's power and wisdom are *infinite* (Psalm 147:5)—meaning that they are totally unlimited—so He could have created everything in less time than it takes for you to blink an eye. Think about it: God knows everything that's happening on earth at once. He can concentrate on a billion people praying at one time, so it really would not have been difficult for Him to create all the animals and plants at high speed.

Scientists who don't even believe in God talk about the Big Bang theory, which says that the entire universe, with all the millions of galaxies and billions of stars, came into existence in a fraction of a second. If scientists are convinced that the universe could create *itself* in less than a heartbeat, it shouldn't be difficult to believe that an all-powerful God could create all the galaxies in one day (Genesis 1:14–19) and then create all life on earth in the other five days (Genesis 1–2).

HOW WERE HUMAN BEINGS CREATED?

For thousands of years, God's people have believed that God created human beings exactly the way the Bible describes it: On the sixth day of creation, God formed Adam from the dust of the earth and then created Eve from one of Adam's ribs. God could very easily have made men and women that way—and millions of Christians believe that's just how He did it.

Many scientists disagree with this viewpoint. They say that the earth and animals came into being millions and billions of years *before* people, in a process called "evolution."

But the Bible paints a picture of a God who is closely involved in both the creation and care of His people—first, Adam and Eve, and then all the people who came after them.

It's important to know that God is the one who created us, and that He loved us and created this world for us to live in (Isaiah 45:12, 18).

God breathes life into the dust-man Adam in this painting by William Blake.

And God said, Let us make man in our image, after our likeness: and let them have dominion over the fish of the sea, and over the fowl of the air, and over the cattle, and over all the earth, and over every creeping thing that creepeth upon the earth. So God created man in his own image, in the image of God created he him; male and female created he them. . . . And the LORD God said, It is not good that the man should be alone; I will make him an help meet for him. And out of the ground the LORD God formed every beast of the field, and every fowl of the air; and brought them unto Adam to see what he would call them: and whatsoever Adam called every living creature, that was the name thereof. And Adam gave names to all cattle, and to the fowl of the air, and to every beast of the field; but for Adam there was not found an help meet for him. And the LORD God caused a deep sleep to fall upon Adam, and he slept: and he took one of his ribs, and closed up the flesh instead thereof; And the rib, which the LORD God had taken from man, made he a woman, and brought her unto the man. And Adam said, This is now bone of my bones, and flesh of my flesh: she shall be called Woman, because she was taken out of Man.

GENESIS 1:26–27; 2:18–23 KJV

WHY DID GOD HAVE TO REST ON THE SEVENTH DAY?

God didn't *have* to rest the way we need to rest when we're exhausted after a hard day's work. He wasn't tired, because God never becomes weary (Isaiah 40:28).

The Bible says that "on the seventh day God ended His work which he had done, and He rested on the seventh day from all His work" (Genesis 2:2 NKJV). When it says that God "rested," it simply means that He stopped creating. In other words, God stopped working because He had created everything He planned to create. He was done.

Thus the heavens and the earth were finished, and all the host of them. And on the seventh day God ended his work which he had made; and he rested on the seventh day from all his work which he had made. And God blessed the seventh day, and sanctified it: because that in it he had rested from all his work which God created and made.

GENESIS 2:1–3 KJV

God also rested from His work as an example to us. We humans get tired every day and have to sleep at night, but even that isn't enough. We also need to rest one day a week from our schoolwork or jobs. It's fine for us to relax on that day, but God also wants us to use the Sabbath to spend time with Him, read His Word, and recharge our batteries (Exodus 20:8–11).

Doesn't he look tired? Animals and people can get very tired—but God never will!

WHERE EXACTLY WAS THE GARDEN OF EDEN?

The Garden of Eden was, of course, in the land of Eden. In ancient times, Eden was an actual place—but where was it? The Bible says, "The LORD God planted a garden eastward in Eden" (Genesis 2:8 KJV), so we know that Eden was somewhere in the east.

Our best clue is that the Bible says that four rivers came from different directions and joined into one big river, and this river flowed through the land of Eden. It names two of those rivers as the Tigris and the Euphrates (Genesis 2:14). We don't know the identity of the other two rivers, but today the Tigris and the Euphrates flow through the land of Iraq and nearly join before they empty into the Persian Gulf.

Bible scholars believe that, in ancient days, the Tigris and Euphrates actually joined into one river before flowing into the sea. Our best guess is that the Garden of Eden was located in the far southern region of what is today Iraq.

Now the LORD God had planted a garden in the east, in Eden; and there he put the man he had formed. And the LORD God made all kinds of trees grow out of the ground—trees that were pleasing to the eye and good for food. In the middle of the garden were the tree of life and the tree of the knowledge of good and evil. A river watering the garden flowed from Eden; from there it was separated into four headwaters. The name of the first is the Pishon; it winds through the entire land of Havilah, where there is gold. (The gold of that land is good; aromatic resin and onyx are also there.) The name of the second river is the Gihon; it winds through the entire land of Cush. The name of the third river is the Tigris; it runs along the east side of Asshur. And the fourth river is the Euphrates.

GENESIS 2:8–14 NIV

WHO WAS CAIN'S WIFE?...

So Cain went out from the LORD's presence and lived in the land of Nod, east of Eden. Cain lay with his wife, and she became pregnant and gave birth to Enoch. Cain was then building a city, and he named it after his son Enoch.

GENESIS 4:16–17 NIV

The Bible says that, at first, Adam and Eve had only two children—Cain and Abel—and Cain killed Abel. Yet after God drove Cain out of Eden and he went to live in Nod, Cain's wife became pregnant. So the question is, Who was Cain's wife if the only human beings on earth at the time were Adam, Eve, and Cain?

Eve was "the mother of all the living" (Genesis 3:20), so we know that there weren't any *other* humans on earth except for Eve's descendants. Obviously then, Cain's wife was a daughter of Adam and Eve. Back then, many thousands of years ago, humankind's DNA wasn't as damaged as it is today, so brothers and sisters could marry.

Also, the Bible lists descendants through the father. This is why sons are named in genealogies (family lists) but almost no daughters are mentioned. Daughters were born as often as sons, and were just as important, but because of the Bible's method of drawing up family trees, daughters (such as Cain's wife) were seldom included.

Most cultures today discourage close relatives from marrying. One of the United States' best-known presidents, Franklin D. Roosevelt, married a relative of his—Eleanor Roosevelt was a distant cousin.

DID PEOPLE IN ANCIENT TIMES ACTUALLY LIVE HUNDREDS OF YEARS?.....

So all the days that Adam lived were nine hundred and thirty years, and he died. . . .
So all the days of Seth were nine hundred and twelve years, and he died. . . .
So all the days of Enosh were nine hundred and five years, and he died. . . .
So all the days of Kenan were nine hundred and ten years, and he died. . . .
So all the days of Mahalalel were eight hundred and ninety-five years, and he died. . . .
So all the days of Jared were nine hundred and sixty-two years, and he died. . . .
So all the days of Methuselah were nine hundred and sixty-nine years, and he died.

GENESIS 5:5, 8, 11, 14, 17, 20, 27 NASB

Yes, they did. Before the flood of Noah's day, people lived for many centuries. For example, Adam lived to be 930 years of age, and Methuselah, the oldest man on record, died at age 969 (Genesis 5:5, 27). We shouldn't be surprised by this. Even today, Sequoia redwood trees can live 2,500 years. Since human beings were God's greatest creation, He wanted them to live a long time too.

But something happened after the Flood. Maybe it was changes in the earth, or perhaps sin had greatly damaged humankind's DNA, but gradually people began living shorter lives. After the Flood, Shem lived only 600 years, Arphaxad lived just 438 years, Peleg lived a mere 239 years, and Terah died of old age at 205. Abraham lived 175 years, Jacob lived 147 years, and Joseph lived 110 years (Genesis 11:10–32; 25:7; 47:28; 50:26).

By King David's day, three thousand years ago, people were living only seventy or eighty years (Psalm 90:10), just like today.

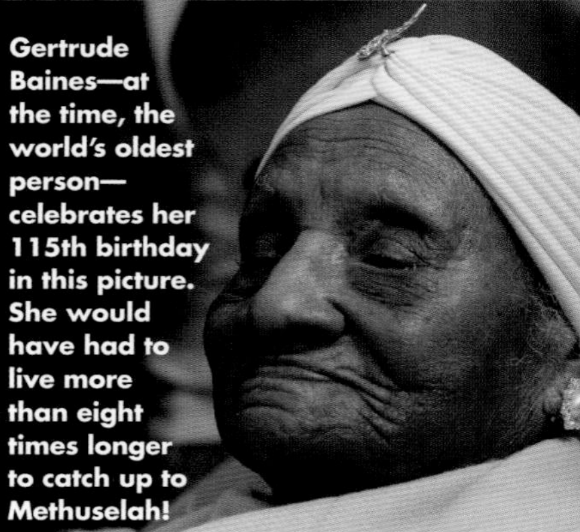

Gertrude Baines—at the time, the world's oldest person—celebrates her 115th birthday in this picture. She would have had to live more than eight times longer to catch up to Methuselah!

HOW COULD TWO OF EVERY SPECIES OF ANIMAL FIT INTO NOAH'S ARK?

First of all, the ark was not small. It was a massive ship—450 feet long, 75 feet wide, and 45 feet tall; and it had three decks (each one 15 feet high) to house all the animals (Genesis 6:15–16).

Second, God told Noah to bring two of every species of animal onto the ark (Genesis 6:19–20). All the hundreds of breeds of dogs in the world today are not separate species. All dogs are descended from a common ancestor—wolves—so Noah only needed to take two wolves on board. It was the same with cows, horses, and so on.

> *Then Noah and his sons and his wife and his sons' wives with him entered the ark because of the water of the flood. Of clean animals and animals that are not clean and birds and everything that creeps on the ground, there went into the ark to Noah by twos, male and female, as God had commanded Noah.*
>
> GENESIS 7:7–9 NASB

Third, while some animals, such as elephants and rhinos, are huge, most animals are smaller. The average animal is only about the size of a sheep. Birds and hamsters and butterflies are *very* small indeed.

Fourth, Noah didn't need to take any fish or sea creatures on board. They survived just fine out in the ocean.

This model of Noah's Ark gives a sense of how big it was—check out the elephants and giraffes lining up in front!

WHY DID GOD PROMISE THE LAND OF CANAAN TO ABRAHAM WHEN IT ALREADY BELONGED TO THE CANAANITES?

When Abraham (also called Abram) arrived in Canaan, the Bible says, "At that time the Canaanites were in the land. The LORD appeared to Abram and said, 'To your offspring I will give this land'" (Genesis 12:6–7 NIV).

The land didn't belong to the Canaanites. They were there, yes, but they'd moved in without permission. To whom did the land belong? It belonged to God; and because it was His, He could give it to the Israelites. Just the same, He made it clear even to Israel: "The land is Mine; for you are strangers and sojourners with Me" (Leviticus 25:23 NKJV).

Because it was God's land, only God's people had the right to live there. The Canaanites were a wicked people and had no business being there. God said that they "defiled the land" and that the land itself would "vomit them out" (Leviticus 18:24–28; Ezra 9:11) so that God's people could move in.

Abram passed through the land to the place of Shechem, as far as the terebinth tree of Moreh. And the Canaanites were then in the land. Then the LORD appeared to Abram and said, "To your descendants I will give this land." And there he built an altar to the LORD, who had appeared to him.

GENESIS 12:6–7 NKJV

Unlike the Middle East, where people have been fighting for land for thousands of years, the United States welcomes newcomers. A poem on a bronze plaque at the Statue of Liberty reads, "Give me your tired, your poor, your huddled masses yearning to breathe free. . . ."

IF ABRAHAM WAS SUCH A GREAT MAN, WHY DID HE LIE THAT HIS WIFE, SARAH, WAS ONLY HIS SISTER?

Abraham was a righteous man, and the most outstanding thing about Abraham was that he had such great faith. God promised Abraham that he would have as many descendants as the stars of the sky, and even though it seemed impossible, Abraham believed God (Genesis 15:2–6). Read Romans 4:18–22 to see just how strong his faith was!

Yet Abraham was only human, and he had weaknesses, too. His wife, Sarah, was so beautiful that Abraham was frightened that some ruthless king would kill him so he could take Sarah as a wife. That's why Abraham told Pharaoh that Sarah was just his sister (Genesis 12:10–20).

Later, God told him, "Do not be afraid, Abram. I am your shield." But the next time Abraham was faced with a dangerous situation, he gave in to his fears again and stopped trusting God (Genesis 15:1; 20:1–18). This is a lesson for all of us: Trust God and *keep* trusting God!

Now there was a famine in the land, and Abram went down to Egypt to dwell there, for the famine was severe in the land. And it came to pass, when he was close to entering Egypt, that he said to Sarai his wife, "Indeed I know that you are a woman of beautiful countenance. Therefore it will happen, when the Egyptians see you, that they will say, This is his wife'; and they will kill me, but they will let you live. Please say you are my sister, that it may be well with me for your sake, and that I may live because of you." So it was, when Abram came into Egypt, that the Egyptians saw the woman, that she was very beautiful. The princes of Pharaoh also saw her and commended her to Pharaoh. And the woman was taken to Pharaoh's house. He treated Abram well for her sake. He had sheep, oxen, male donkeys, male and female servants, female donkeys, and camels. But the LORD plagued Pharaoh and his house with great plagues because of Sarai, Abram's wife. And Pharaoh called Abram and said, "What is this you have done to me? Why did you not tell me that she was your wife? Why did you say, 'She is my sister'? I might have taken her as my wife. Now therefore, here is your wife; take her and go your way." So Pharaoh commanded his men concerning him; and they sent him away, with his wife and all that he had.

GENESIS 12:10–20 NKJV

We all get nervous and scared sometimes. . .but the Bible says that God didn't give us a spirit of fear, "but of power, and of love, and of a sound mind" (2 TIMOTHY 1:7 KJV).

WHY DID GOD TELL ABRAHAM TO SACRIFICE (KILL) HIS SON ISAAC?

Now it came to pass after these things that God tested Abraham, and said to him, "Abraham!" And he said, "Here I am." Then He said, "Take now your son, your only son Isaac, whom you love, and go to the land of Moriah, and offer him there as a burnt offering on one of the mountains of which I shall tell you."

GENESIS 22:1–2 NKJV

God had just done a miracle to give Abraham and Sarah a son in their old age, and Abraham loved Isaac dearly because he was his very own son. Also, he knew that this miracle child would now inherit all the promises that God had given to him. So you can imagine how shocked Abraham was when God asked him to sacrifice Isaac!

Abraham didn't know it at the time, but God had no intention of letting him kill his son. He wanted to test Abraham's love and obedience. Sure enough, when Abraham showed that he was willing to give his beloved son to God, God responded immediately. He called Abraham's name *twice* to make sure to stop him; then—to be certain that Abraham understood clearly—God told him *twice* not to harm his son. And then God blessed Abraham with three fantastic blessings at once.

When Abraham obeyed God, Isaac lived. If Abraham had disobeyed God, Isaac still would have lived, but both father and son would have missed the blessings that God intended for them. Either way, though, Isaac was in no danger of being killed by Abraham.

An angel stops Abraham from killing Isaac in this classic 1635 painting by Rembrandt.

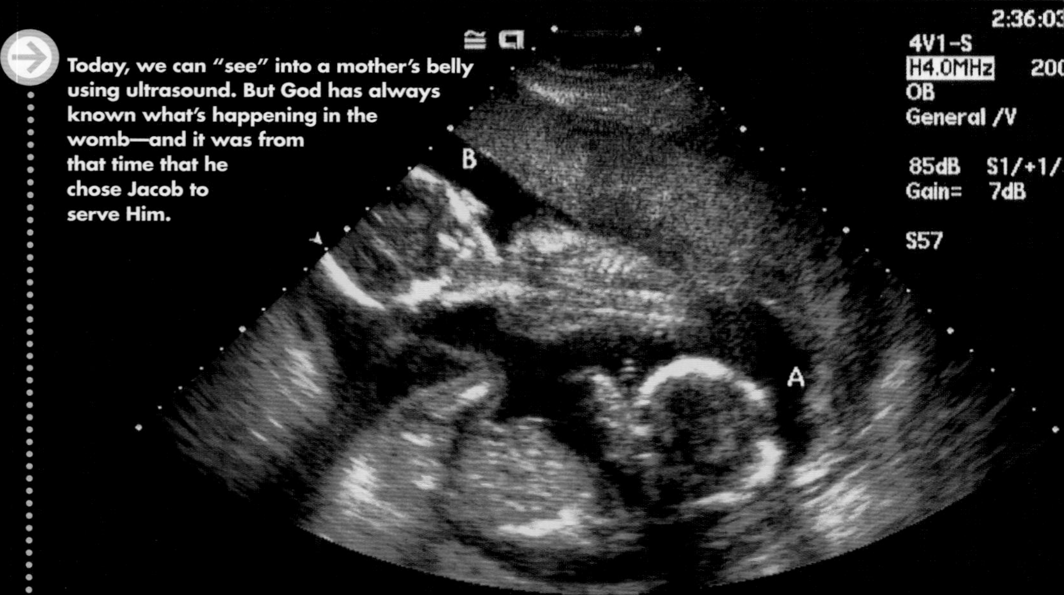

Today, we can "see" into a mother's belly using ultrasound. But God has always known what's happening in the womb—and it was from that time that he chose Jacob to serve Him.

WHY DID GOD CHOOSE JACOB OVER ESAU BEFORE EITHER SON WAS EVEN BORN?

Before Jacob and Esau were even born—before they had done anything good or evil—God told their mother, Rebekah, "The older shall serve the younger" (Genesis 25:23; Romans 9:10–12 NKJV). In other words, the youngest twin would inherit the promises God had made to Abraham and would be the father of God's people, Israel.

The LORD said to her, "Two nations are in your womb, and two peoples from within you will be separated; one people will be stronger than the other, and the older will serve the younger."

GENESIS 25:23 TNIV

Most Christians believe that because God knows everything—even the future—He knew exactly what kind of terrible, selfish choices Esau (the older son) would make. That's why He didn't choose Esau to inherit the promises.

Or perhaps Esau just wasn't the kind of person God was looking for. Esau was strong physically, headstrong, and warlike, whereas Jacob was weaker and meeker. Why on earth would God choose Jacob? Because He knew that Jacob would have to trust Him more than strong, able Esau—and thus God would get the credit for doing miracles. "God has chosen the weak things of the world to put to shame the things which are mighty. . .that no flesh should glory in His presence" (1 Corinthians 1:27, 29 NKJV).

WHY DID REBEKAH AND JACOB DECEIVE ISAAC? WAS IT RIGHT?

When Isaac's wife, Rebekah, became pregnant with twins, God told her, "The older shall serve the younger" (Genesis 25:23 NKJV). Isaac apparently didn't believe that God had spoken to his wife. Even after Esau sold his birthright to Jacob (Genesis 25:29–34), Isaac still favored Esau. For nearly 80 years, year after year, Rebekah probably reminded Isaac what God had said, but Isaac refused to change his mind.

Finally, the day came when Isaac prepared to bless Esau in the traditional manner—which was the *opposite* of what God had said would happen. Rebekah must have panicked, because she disguised Jacob as Esau and sent him into Isaac's tent pretending that he was Esau. Because Isaac was blind, the trick worked, and once Isaac had given Jacob his blessing, he couldn't take it back and give it to Esau.

After Isaac finished blessing him, and Jacob had scarcely left his father's presence, his brother Esau came in from hunting. He too prepared some tasty food and brought it to his father. Then he said to him, "My father, please sit up and eat some of my game, so that you may give me your blessing." His father Isaac asked him, "Who are you?" "I am your son," he answered, "your firstborn, Esau." Isaac trembled violently and said, "Who was it, then, that hunted game and brought it to me? I ate it just before you came and I blessed him—and indeed he will be blessed!"

GENESIS 27:30–33 TNIV

Isaac's stubborn disbelief was wrong, but Rebekah's deception was wrong also. God wanted Jacob to receive the blessing, but He could have worked out a different solution to the problem.

Jacob and his mother, Rebekah, trick old Isaac into giving his younger son the blessing his firstborn should have gotten. This painting is from 1638.

WHY DID JOSEPH'S BROTHERS HATE HIM AND SELL HIM AS A SLAVE?

God gave Jacob 12 sons but chose one of Jacob's youngest sons, Joseph, for great things. God then prepared Joseph for his future by giving him dreams that one day his older brothers would bow down to him. Joseph should have kept his dreams to himself, or perhaps told only his father, but he couldn't resist boasting to his brothers. That made them *so* mad! On top of it, Jacob spoiled Joseph by giving him—and *only* him—a beautiful, expensive coat. You can see why his brothers were jealous.

Still, this was no excuse for their wanting to kill Joseph. Fortunately, they spared his life and sold him as a slave into Egypt instead. Once there, Joseph became a powerful ruler and saved many countries from a great famine.

This is one of those amazing stories in which people act in anger and jealousy, but God—in His love and great power—turns a bad situation around and makes good come out of it (Genesis 45:4–8).

They spotted him off in the distance. By the time he got to them they had cooked up a plot to kill him. The brothers were saying, "Here comes that dreamer. Let's kill him and throw him into one of these old cisterns; we can say that a vicious animal ate him up. We'll see what his dreams amount to." Reuben heard the brothers talking and intervened to save him, "We're not going to kill him. No murder. Go ahead and throw him in this cistern out here in the wild, but don't hurt him." Reuben planned to go back later and get him out and take him back to his father. When Joseph reached his brothers, they ripped off the fancy coat he was wearing, grabbed him, and threw him into a cistern. The cistern was dry; there wasn't any water in it. Then they sat down to eat their supper. Looking up, they saw a caravan of Ishmaelites on their way from Gilead, their camels loaded with spices, ointments, and perfumes to sell in Egypt. Judah said, "Brothers, what are we going to get out of killing our brother and concealing the evidence? Let's sell him to the Ishmaelites, but let's not kill him—he is, after all, our brother, our own flesh and blood." His brothers agreed.

GENESIS 37:18–27 MSG

In a 1630 painting, Diego Velazquez didn't make Joseph's coat very colorful...but he shows how Joseph's brothers dipped the coat in animal blood to make their father, Jacob, believe his son had been killed by a wild animal. Read the story in Genesis 37:31–34.

Why Did God Appear as a Burning a Bush?

When Moses first saw a bush burning near Mount Horeb, he probably thought that someone had lit it or that perhaps lightning had started a fire. But as he kept watching, he noticed that the fire didn't burn out. The bush was still there! Moses then went over to investigate. So part of the reason God appeared that way was to get Moses' attention.

But why would God appear as fire? Why didn't He let Moses see what He actually looked like? God couldn't do that. Later on, when Moses begged God, "Please, show me Your glory," God replied, "You cannot see My face; for no man shall see Me, and live" (Exodus 33:18–23 NKJV). God is too glorious and awesome for human eyes to look upon. It would have been more devastating to Moses than staring at the sun.

This was the same reason that God appeared to the Israelites in a pillar of cloud and fire (Exodus 33:7–11).

Moses was shepherding the flock of Jethro, his father-in-law, the priest of Midian. He led the flock to the west end of the wilderness and came to the mountain of God, Horeb. The angel of God appeared to him in flames of fire blazing out of the middle of a bush. He looked. The bush was blazing away but it didn't burn up. Moses said, "What's going on here? I can't believe this! Amazing! Why doesn't the bush burn up?" God saw that he had stopped to look. God called to him from out of the bush, "Moses! Moses!" He said, "Yes? I'm right here!"

Exodus 3:1–4 MSG

This bright red plant is called a "burning bush"—but the one Moses saw was actually on fire with God's presence!

DOES GOD STILL SPEAK TO PEOPLE OUT LOUD AS HE DID TO MOSES?

God said to Moses, "I AM WHO I AM"; and He said, "Thus you shall say to the sons of Israel, 'I AM has sent me to you.'"

EXODUS 3:14 NASB

The Bible doesn't say that God always spoke to Moses in an audible (out loud) voice. Certainly He did at times. When the Israelites arrived at Mount Sinai, "Moses spoke, and God answered him by voice" (Exodus 19:19 NKJV). However God spoke to Moses, we know that God spoke to him clearly and in great detail.

God also spoke out loud to Jesus; but even though an entire crowd heard a voice from heaven, many thought it was an angel speaking. Some who weren't spiritually sensitive thought that it had simply thundered (John 12:28–29).

It would be very rare for God to speak to people out loud today. Instead, most Christians sense God speaking to them as they read the Bible. It is God's Word, after all. Sometimes a specific verse grabs their attention. Other times, God communicates with people through their conscience or intuition. Many Christians believe they have heard God speak in a "still small voice" in their minds (1 Kings 19:12 NKJV).

There's still something special about a family's first baby!

WHY WAS THE FIRST-BORN SON SO SPECIAL? . . .

Among the ancient Hebrews, the first signs of new life—whether plant, animal, or human—were seen as the beginning of God's creative power. They understood that this first new life belonged to God and should be given back to Him. Thus, the Hebrews always gave the best of the *firstfruits* (the first ripened fruit or crop) to God (Exodus 23:16). They also knew that the firstborn of their animals were God's, which is why they sacrificed them to Him (Exodus 34:19).

This was also true for a man and woman's first son: He belonged to God (Exodus 13:1–2). Of course, God didn't expect parents to sacrifice their sons, which is why He told them to redeem (buy back) their firstborn by sacrificing a lamb (Exodus 13:11–15; Leviticus 12:6–8). Even Jesus' parents redeemed Him (Luke 2:22–24).

In Israelite society, the firstborn son had special responsibilities and rights; after his father died, he was given twice as big an inheritance as his younger brothers and was expected to lead the family.

"Now when the LORD brings you to the land of the Canaanite, as He swore to you and to your fathers, and gives it to you, you shall devote to the LORD the first offspring of every womb, and the first offspring of every beast that you own; the males belong to the LORD. But every first offspring of a donkey you shall redeem with a lamb, but if you do not redeem it, then you shall break its neck; and every firstborn of man among your sons you shall redeem. And it shall be when your son asks you in time to come, saying, 'What is this?' then you shall say to him, 'With a powerful hand the LORD brought us out of Egypt, from the house of slavery. It came about, when Pharaoh was stubborn about letting us go, that the LORD killed every firstborn in the land of Egypt, both the firstborn of man and the firstborn of beast. Therefore, I sacrifice to the LORD the males, the first offspring of every womb, but every firstborn of my sons I redeem.'"

EXODUS 13:11–15 NASB

HOW DID GOD PART THE RED SEA?.......

The Bible says, "The LORD drove the sea back by a strong east wind all night," and when the Israelites crossed on the dry sea bed, the water was like a *wall* on their right and left hands (Exodus 14:21–22 RSV). Normally, a wind with enough force to part the seas would also have picked up the Israelites and hurled them through the air violently—so the wind couldn't have been *too* strong.

Then Moses stretched out his hand over the sea, and all that night the LORD drove the sea back with a strong east wind and turned it into dry land. The waters were divided, and the Israelites went through the sea on dry ground, with a wall of water on their right and on their left.

EXODUS 14:21–22 NIV

The key to understanding this mystery is found a few verses later, where Moses, an eyewitness to the miracle, says, "The floods stood upright like a heap; the depths congealed in the heart of the sea" (Exodus 15:8 NKJV). The word *congealed* means "hardened."

So the wind wasn't just blowing the sea apart; the water had been hardened and made solid, like walls. That doesn't mean the Red Sea was frozen like ice, but to say that the water "congealed" does mean that something very strange happened. The normal laws of nature were bent to the miracle-working power of God.

The bright coral reef and fish here were photographed in the waters of the Red Sea. . . . Do you think Moses and the people of Israel might have seen something like this through those walls of water they walked between?

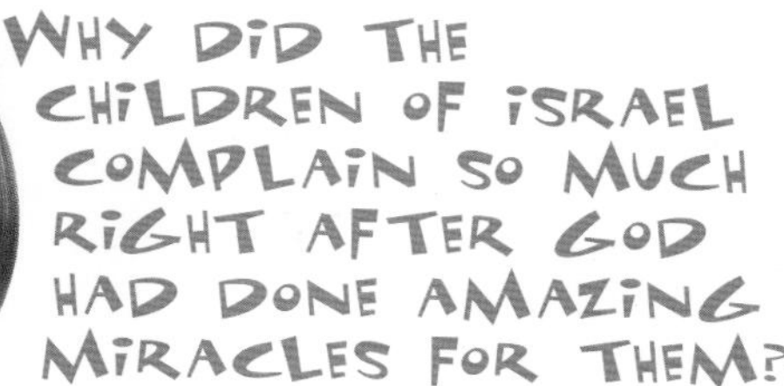

WHY DID THE CHILDREN OF ISRAEL COMPLAIN SO MUCH RIGHT AFTER GOD HAD DONE AMAZING MIRACLES FOR THEM?

God did a huge miracle by parting the Red Sea for the Israelites. Three days later, at Marah, God made bitter water drinkable (Exodus 14–15). But now the Israelites were in the desert and hungry and they complained that God had brought them out there just to let them starve. What a lack of trust! God promptly did a miracle and supplied them with manna for the next 40 years (Exodus 16:1–12).

When we look back at the whole story from beginning to end, it's easy to see that God was ready to do miracles for the Israelites and that they should have continued to trust Him and have patience. God loved them and was not about to abandon them.

Yet when we get in difficult situations ourselves, *our* faith gets tested, too. We remember that God has done good things for us, but when new difficulties arise, we can easily forget His past miracles and wonder whether God is powerful enough to take care of us *now*. We may even doubt whether He loves us enough to help us. Rather than judging the children of Israel, we should learn lessons from what they did.

Complaining is never pretty. . . and the Bible often warns against it!

And the whole congregation of the people of Israel murmured against Moses and Aaron in the wilderness, and said to them, "Would that we had died by the hand of the LORD in the land of Egypt, when we sat by the fleshpots and ate bread to the full; for you have brought us out into this wilderness to kill this whole assembly with hunger."

EXODUS 16:2–3 RSV

DO WE STILL NEED TO OBEY THE TEN COMMANDMENTS TODAY?

Yes, we should certainly obey the Ten Commandments. They instruct us to do good things, such as worshipping God only. What Christian would think that it's no longer important to love and worship God? And of course we should obey the commands not to lie, steal, or kill. All these are vitally important rules.

But much of the *rest* of the detailed Law of Moses no

longer applies. Since Jesus, the Lamb of God, died as the perfect sacrifice (John 1:29; 1 Peter 1:18–19), believers no longer need to sacrifice animals to take away their sins. We don't need to follow all the ceremonial laws or go through endless rituals to stay clean. But the Ten Commandments still apply.

Remember, however, that Jesus said that the most *important* commands are to love God with all our hearts and to love our neighbors as ourselves (Matthew 22:36–40). The good news is that if we keep these two commands, we're already fulfilling the Ten Commandments (Romans 13:8–10).

Moses carries the Ten Commandments down Mount Sinai in this classic engraving from the 1800s.

"Worship no god but me. Do not make for yourselves images of anything in heaven or on earth or in the water under the earth. Do not bow down to any idol or worship it, because I am the Lord your God and I tolerate no rivals. I bring punishment on those who hate me and on their descendants down to the third and fourth generation. But I show my love to thousands of generations of those who love me and obey my laws. Do not use my name for evil purposes, for I, the Lord your God, will punish anyone who misuses my name. Observe the Sabbath and keep it holy. You have six days in which to do your work, but the seventh day is a day of rest dedicated to me. On that day no one is to work—neither you, your children, your slaves, your animals, nor the foreigners who live in your country. In six days I, the Lord, made the earth, the sky, the seas, and everything in them, but on the seventh day I rested. That is why I, the Lord, blessed the Sabbath and made it holy. Respect your father and your mother, so that you may live a long time in the land that I am giving you. Do not commit murder. Do not commit adultery. Do not steal. Do not accuse anyone falsely. Do not desire another man's house; do not desire his wife, his slaves, his cattle, his donkeys, or anything else that he owns."

EXODUS 20:3–17 GNT

DOES GOD REALLY PUNISH CHILDREN FOR THEIR PARENTS' SINS?

"You shall not bow down to them nor serve them. For I, the LORD your God, am a jealous God, visiting the iniquity of the fathers upon the children to the third and fourth generations of those who hate Me, but showing mercy to thousands, to those who love Me and keep My commandments."

EXODUS 20:5–6 NKJV

In the Ten Commandments, the first command is to worship God only. The second command is also vitally important: The Israelites were not to make idols or worship other gods—which were actually demons (1 Corinthians 10:19–20). Idolatry was so damaging and evil that God added, "For I the LORD thy God am a jealous God, visiting the iniquity of the fathers upon the children unto the third and fourth generation of them that hate me" (Exodus 20:5 KJV).

When people hated God, worshipped demons, and taught their children to hate God and worship demons, it often affected families for generations. And as long as the children continued in their parents' sins, yes, God continued to judge them, too.

Later, some Israelites claimed that they were innocent but that God was judging them for their fathers' sins. God told them to stop saying that and explained that no matter how bad their fathers had been, if *they* would do what was right and not worship idols, He would bless them (Ezekiel 18:1–9).

"Be careful, little lips, what you say" is what an old Sunday school song warned. God is very particular about how His name is spoken!

WHAT DOES IT MEAN TO TAKE GOD'S NAME IN VAIN?

Thou shalt not take the name of the LORD thy God in vain; for the LORD will not hold him guiltless that taketh his name in vain.

EXODUS 20:7 KJV

The third commandment says, "You shall not take the name of the LORD your God in vain" (Exodus 20:7 NKJV). To use God's name "in vain" means to speak it in the wrong way or to carelessly say that God will do things that God would actually not do.

The NIV translation says, "You shall not misuse the name of the LORD your God." You hear a lot of people misuse God's name these days. Whenever they are hateful or angry, they use God's name to curse others, or want God to judge or damn somebody to hell.

People who do this are showing a great lack of respect and love for God and a lack of respect and love for other people. They are not only breaking the third commandment, but also breaking the two most important commands in the Bible: to love God with all their hearts and to love their neighbor as themselves (Matthew 22:36–40).

WHY DO SOME CHRISTIANS REST ON SATURDAY AND OTHERS REST ON SUNDAY?

When God said, "Remember the Sabbath day, to keep it holy" (Exodus 20:8 RSV), He explained that His people should do all their work during six days and rest on the seventh day. This was because God created the world in six days but ceased from work on the seventh day. Because Saturday was the last day of the week, the Jews celebrated Sabbath on Saturday—and still do.

For this reason, some Christians also rest on Saturday; but for two thousand years, most Christians have rested on Sunday. This is because Jesus was raised back to life on a Sunday, the first day of the week (John 20:1). Christians considered the Resurrection to be such an important event that they began to rest on Sundays instead. The early church gathered together to "break bread" (celebrate the Lord's Supper) and meet every Sunday (Acts 20:7; 1 Corinthians 16:2).

"Observe the Sabbath day, to keep it holy. Work six days and do everything you need to do. But the seventh day is a Sabbath to GOD, your God. Don't do any work—not you, nor your son, nor your daughter, nor your servant, nor your maid, nor your animals, not even the foreign guest visiting in your town. For in six days GOD made Heaven, Earth, and sea, and everything in them; he rested on the seventh day. Therefore GOD blessed the Sabbath day; he set it apart as a holy day."

EXODUS 20:8–10 MSG

"Day of rest" doesn't mean you have to sleep the whole time—but God does want you to slow down, rest, and think of Him more.

WHAT WAS THE ARK OF THE COVENANT, AND WHAT MADE IT SO SPECIAL?

The original ark disappeared centuries ago—but this model is based on the Bible's description of the special box. From under those cherubim angels' wings, God would actually speak to the high priest of Israel!

"Make a Box out of acacia wood, 45 inches long, 27 inches wide, and 27 inches high. Cover it with pure gold inside and out and put a gold border all around it."

Exodus 25:10–11 GNT

The ark of the covenant was a small chest made out of acacia wood and covered with gold, both inside and out. A golden lid, called the atonement cover, was placed on top of the ark, with two golden cherubim with outspread wings on top of that. The two stone tablets of the Law, a gold jar of manna, and Aaron's rod were stored inside the ark (Hebrews 9:4).

When the Israelites were in the wilderness, the ark was kept inside the Tent of Meeting. When Solomon built a permanent temple in Jerusalem, the ark was kept in the heart of the temple, in a special room called the Holy of Holies.

God did not live permanently in, or on, the ark, but He sometimes appeared between the two golden cherubim and spoke from there (Exodus 25:22). That's why the Israelites considered the ark to be a symbol of the presence of God and treated it as a holy object.

WHAT WAS THE TABERNACLE?

"Moreover you shall make the tabernacle. . . ."

Exodus 26:1 NASB

When the children of Israel wandered in the desert for 40 years, they needed a place where they could worship God and offer sacrifices to Him. And they had to be able to pack it up and carry it along with them when they moved. So instead of building a temple of stone, they built a large tent and surrounded it with a tall cloth wall. *Tabernacle* is an Old English word that means "tent" or "meeting-place tent," which is why some Bible translations call the tabernacle the Tent of Meeting.

The ark of the covenant and other holy articles were kept inside the tabernacle. The Israelites went to the tabernacle to ask God questions, and God often descended in a pillar of cloud and fire and met with Moses there (Exodus 33:7–11).

For hundreds of years after they settled in Canaan, the Israelites still worshipped at the Tent of Meeting. Finally, King Solomon built a permanent stone temple.

This sketch of the tabernacle shows the outer "walls" of cloth hung on poles, and the inner tent where the priest would meet with God. Sacrifices were made on the altar in front of the tent.

DOES GOD HAVE A BODY LIKE WE DO?....

God is a spirit (John 4:24), so He doesn't have a physical body like ours. A physical body can be in only one place at a time. That, of course, would limit God, and the Bible tells us that God has no limits. He is *omnipresent*, which means that He is everywhere at once (Psalm 139:7–10). God is so vast, in fact, that even the universe itself can't contain Him (2 Chronicles 2:6).

Nevertheless, if God so chooses, He *can* take on a form like a human body. When He appeared to Moses, God had a face, hands, and a back (Exodus 33:20–23). Mind you, God can *also* appear as the flame in a burning bush or a pillar of cloud and fire instead (Exodus 3:2–6; 13:20–21). God is simply not limited.

Many Christian scholars teach that each time God appeared in a human body, it was actually God's Son, Jesus, who appeared. God the Father, Jesus, and the Holy Spirit are all part of God, but Jesus is the only one who actually has a physical body. Jesus could do this because He is God, so He has always existed, even before He was born physically.

"Then I will remove my hand and you will see my back; but my face must not be seen."
EXODUS 33:23 NIV

You've probably seen pictures—like this classic painting by Michelangelo—of God as a stern, white-haired man. But that's just an artist's idea.

WHY DID GOD GIVE THE ISRAELITES SO MANY RULES AND LAWS TO FOLLOW?

God gave the Israelites many rules to teach them how to serve Him, how to come into His presence with respect, and how to sacrifice to Him the right way. Because God is all-powerful and holy, the Israelites needed to respect and worship Him. They could not afford to approach God flippantly and carelessly.

Also, many of the laws that God gave were practical laws about how to farm, how to settle unsolved murders, how to provide for the poor, how to treat foreigners, how to hold fair court cases, and how to give just punishments for crimes. Israel was a brand-new nation and needed rules to govern them, so God gave them many helpful laws. (We have many *more* laws in modern times.)

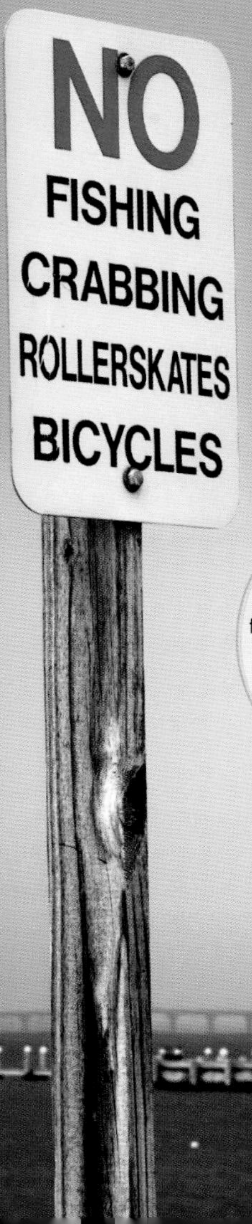

The Lord called to Moses from the Tent of the Lord's presence and gave him the following rules. . . .
LEVITICUS 1:1 GNT

NO
FISHING
CRABBING
ROLLERSKATES
BICYCLES

Does it ever seem like everyone's telling you "No"? Even the Bible can seem that way sometimes—but all those rules were designed to give people a better, happier life.

AFTER THEY HAD SINNED, WHY DID THE ISRAELITES HAVE TO SACRIFICE AN ANIMAL?

The Law of Moses said that anyone who sinned and broke the Lord's commands had to bring an animal (a bull or a goat) to the Lord's altar and sacrifice (kill) it. This was called a sin offering (Leviticus 4).

> *"He shall lay his hand on the head of the sin offering, and kill the sin offering in the place of burnt offering."*
>
> LEVITICUS 4:29 RSV

When a sin had been committed, the penalty for sin was death. The Bible says, "Blood, which is life, takes away sins," and "Sins are forgiven only if blood is poured out" (Leviticus 17:11; Hebrews 9:22 GNT). However, instead of dying for their sins, the people could repent and bring a bull or a goat to sacrifice instead.

Lambs—cute little guys like this—paid a high price for people's sin in Old Testament times. But animal sacrifices came to an end when Jesus—"the Lamb of God"—died on the cross. His sacrifice was enough to cover every sin, of every person, for all time!

God did the same thing when He told the Israelites to sacrifice a lamb at Passover and sprinkle its blood on their doorposts (Exodus 12). Finally, Jesus was the Lamb of God (John 1:29) who died at Passover for the sins of the world. After Jesus' blood was poured out to cover our sins once and for all, there was no longer any need for animal sacrifices.

WHY DID THE ISRAELITES HAVE SO MANY RULES ABOUT FOOD, AND WHY DON'T CHRISTIANS FOLLOW THESE DIETARY LAWS TODAY?

There were practical reasons for God's health laws. Most of the animals on God's do-not-eat list are scavengers—animals such as vultures and other carrion-eaters—and their meat is full of diseases. Pigs eat just about anything, too, and pork can make you sick if it's not cooked properly. Many kinds of (nonfish) sea creatures are scavengers, too.

Many Christians believe that the laws about clean and unclean foods are no longer in

> *"These are the regulations concerning animals, birds, every living thing that moves in the water and every creature that moves about on the ground. You must distinguish between the unclean and the clean, between living creatures that may be eaten and those that may not be eaten."*
>
> LEVITICUS 11:46–47 TNIV

Who'd want to eat that nasty vulture—especially when you know the gross stuff he's been feeding on? God's laws said "No" to eating vultures—but also to much tastier dishes, too.

effect, since God gave Peter a vision in Acts 10:9–16 (NIV) about a sheet full of all kinds of unclean animals and told him, "Get up, Peter. Kill and eat."

Other Christians say that Peter's vision wasn't actually about food, but that the unclean beasts symbolized the unclean Gentiles, whom God was now accepting (Acts 10:13–15, 28). They believe that God's food laws still apply.

Ultimately, what we choose to eat is a matter of conscience. Whatever you believe, remember, don't judge others because of what they eat or don't eat (Romans 14:1–3).

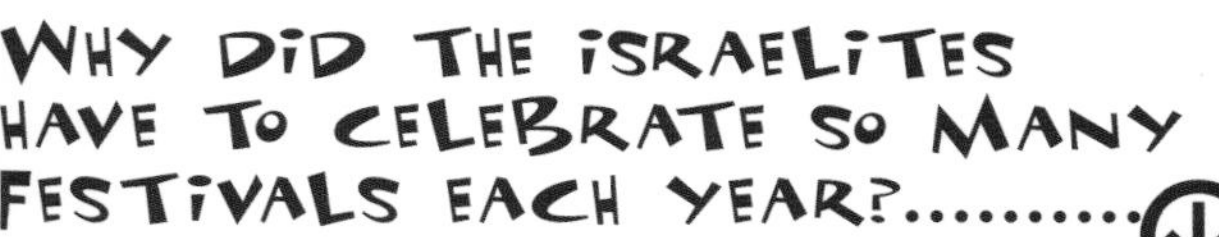

WHY DID THE ISRAELITES HAVE TO CELEBRATE SO MANY FESTIVALS EACH YEAR?

GOD spoke to Moses: "Tell the People of Israel, These are my appointed feasts, the appointed feasts of GOD which you are to decree as sacred assemblies. . . ."

LEVITICUS 23:1–2 MSG

Most of the Israelites' festivals were a time for the people to rest from their work, celebrate, and have feasts. They looked forward to these holidays.

For us today, Christmas and Easter are special dates when we pause to remember that God sent Jesus and raised Him from the dead. Just so, at the Passover feast, or seder, the Israelites remembered how God delivered them from slavery in Egypt. The Feast of Tabernacles reminded them how God had cared for them for 40 years in the wilderness.

A Jewish family celebrates Passover, as Jewish families have been doing for more than 3,000 years!

At Thanksgiving (after harvest), we thank God for providing for us during the past year. The Israelites had two harvest festivals—the Feast of Firstfruits and the Feast of Weeks, when people showed their thankfulness by giving God offerings from their crops and vineyards.

And just as we have a serious holiday, Memorial Day, to honor soldiers who have died in our nation's wars, the Jews had a serious festival called the Day of Atonement, when they remembered their sins and trusted God to forgive them.

WERE MEN WORTH MORE THAN WOMEN IN OLD TESTAMENT TIMES?....

"If your valuation is of a male from twenty years old up to sixty years old, then your valuation shall be fifty shekels of silver, according to the shekel of the sanctuary. If it is a female, then your valuation shall be thirty shekels; and if from five years old up to twenty years old, then your valuation for a male shall be twenty shekels."

LEVITICUS 27:3–5 NKJV

In ancient Israel, sometimes a man would dedicate certain family members to the Lord. Later on, however, they might be needed again to help support the family. In those cases, their family would have to redeem them (buy them back) from the Lord so they could work for the family again.

When that happened, the Israelites had to pay 50 shekels of silver to redeem a man and 30 shekels to redeem a woman. Men were not worth more than women in ancient times just because they were male. The reason was simple: Men were physically stronger than women and could do more work; thus, they could earn more money in their lifetime than most women.

Over 60 years of age, men were less able to do the hard, physical work in the fields, so it cost less to redeem them than a younger man or a woman. The Israelites still had to pay 30 shekels to redeem a 60-year-old woman, but that was *twice* as much as the 15 shekels needed to redeem a 61-year-old man.

In the United States, women have worked to obtain "equal rights" with men—including the right to vote. This postage stamp celebrates the 19th Amendment to the U.S. Constitution in 1920, granting women "suffrage."

And the LORD spake unto Moses in the wilderness of Sinai, in the tabernacle of the congregation, on the first day of the second month, in the second year after they were come out of the land of Egypt, saying, Take ye the sum of all the congregation of the children of Israel, after their families, by the house of their fathers, with the number of their names, every male by their polls. . . .

NUMBERS 1:1–2 KJV

The Bible's book of Numbers is about a "census"—a count of a nation's people. In the United States, that happens every ten years, in years ending in zero.

WHY DID GOD TELL MOSES TO COUNT ONLY THE MEN WHO CAME OUT OF EGYPT?

Two years after the children of Israel came out of Egypt, God told Moses to count every male "from twenty years old and above—all who are able to go to war" (Numbers 1:3 NKJV). The Israelites were about to invade the land of Canaan, so it was important to know how many fighting men they had. Because women and children wouldn't be going out to battle, they weren't counted. Even young men 18–19 years of age weren't counted.

Unfortunately, the Israelites were afraid to enter Canaan (Numbers 13–14), so God made them wander for 40 years in the wilderness until all the older generation who had been counted died. At the end of 40 years, when they had a whole new army ready to enter the Promised Land, God told Moses to conduct a second count of the fighting men (Numbers 26).

WHAT IS A NAZIRITE?

Priests and Levites were Israelites who were dedicated to the Lord their entire lives; they were set apart from the regular Israelites to serve God. But sometimes ordinary Israelites could also be dedicated to the Lord—either for their entire lives or for a short time. If a man or a woman felt that they should take some time to serve God, or to become closer to God, they could take a vow (promise) to become a Nazirite.

For as long as their vows lasted, they could not cut their hair, drink wine or vinegar or eat grapes, or come near a dead body (Numbers 6:1–8). Samson was a Nazirite his entire life (Judges 13:3–5).

The Lord said to Moses, "Speak to the Israelites and say to them: 'If a man or woman wants to make a special vow, a vow of dedication to the Lord as a Nazirite, they must abstain from wine and other fermented drink and must not drink vinegar made from wine or other fermented drink. They must not drink grape juice or eat grapes or raisins. As long as they remain under their Nazirite vow, they must not eat anything that comes from the grapevine, not even the seeds or skins. During the entire period of the Nazirite's vow, no razor may be used on their head. They must be holy until the period of their dedication to the Lord is over; they must let their hair grow long. Throughout the period of their dedication to the Lord, the Nazirite must not go near a dead body. Even if their own father or mother or brother or sister dies, they must not make themselves ceremonially unclean on account of them, because the symbol of their dedication to God is on their head. Throughout the period of their dedication, they are consecrated to the Lord.'"

Numbers 6:1–8 RSV

A long-haired lion is no match for the long-haired Samson, in this engraving from the 1800s. As a Nazirite, Samson was never supposed to cut his hair. When his enemies learned about that, they gave him a buzz cut—with disastrous results for Samson.

WHY DIDN'T GOD ALLOW MOSES TO ENTER THE PROMISED LAND JUST BECAUSE MOSES LOST HIS TEMPER ONE TIME?

When the Israelites were wandering thirsty in the desert, God told Moses to strike a rock with his staff and water would come out of it. Moses obeyed, and water gushed out (Exodus 17:1–7). Forty years later, the Israelites again needed water and complained. This time God commanded Moses to simply *speak* to a rock and water would flow out.

But the LORD said to Moses and Aaron, "Because you did not trust in me enough to honor me as holy in the sight of the Israelites, you will not bring this community into the land I give them."

NUMBERS 20:12 TNIV

But Moses was angry at the people for complaining, and he shouted, "Hear now, you rebels! Must we bring water for you out of this rock?" (Numbers 20:10 NKJV). On top of it, he didn't believe that just speaking to the rock would work. So he hit it with his staff. No water came out. He hit it again. This time water gushed out.

God did the miracle, but Moses had lacked faith and had lost his temper (Psalm 106:32–33). God said that because Moses didn't believe Him and didn't show proper respect to Him in front of the Israelites, Moses couldn't lead the people into the Promised Land (Deuteronomy 3:23–27).

Moses had a view like this of the Promised Land, from atop Mount Nebo. But his disobedience to God kept him from ever stepping into the land.

HOW WAS BALAAM'S DONKEY ABLE TO TALK?

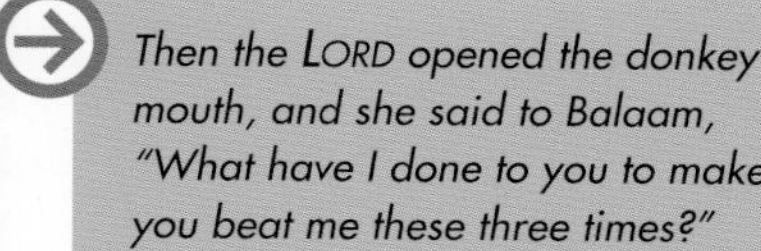

Then the LORD opened the donkey's mouth, and she said to Balaam, "What have I done to you to make you beat me these three times?"

NUMBERS 22:28 NIV

Normally, animals, including donkeys, can't talk. That's why they're called dumb beasts. (*Dumb* means "unable to speak.") God didn't design a donkey's vocal cords to speak human language; they can barely make donkey sounds. Obviously,

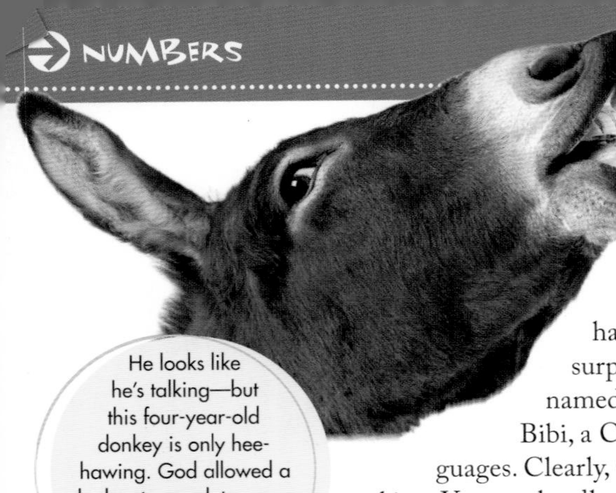

He looks like he's talking—but this four-year-old donkey is only hee-hawing. God allowed a donkey to speak to a man named Balaam, scolding him for being so foolish!

God did a miracle to enable Balaam's donkey to speak.

Some people doubt that God could have done such a miracle. The funny thing is, if Balaam had had a parrot and the parrot had started speaking, no one would have been surprised. After all, in modern times, a parakeet named Puck had a vocabulary of 1,728 words, and Bibi, a Congo African gray parrot, can speak 20 languages. Clearly, God designed their brains and vocal cords for speaking. You can hardly get them to keep quiet.

God did an astonishing miracle to allow Balaam's donkey to speak intelligently in human language.

WHAT ARE "HIGH PLACES," AND WHAT WAS SO BAD ABOUT THEM?

"Drive out all the inhabitants of the land before you. Destroy all their carved images and their cast idols, and demolish all their high places."

NUMBERS 33:52 NIV

When the Israelites prepared to drive out the Canaanites, God ordered, "Destroy all their carved images and their. . .idols, and demolish all their high places" (Numbers 33:52 NIV). The Israelites had to destroy the idols of the Canaanite gods Baal and Asherah because these gods were actually demons (1 Corinthians 10:19–20). If they left the idols standing, the Israelites might be tempted to worship them (Exodus 23:32–33).

The Canaanites often worshipped on top of mountains and hills, the "high places" where they felt closer to their gods. That's where the altars to their demon-gods were located, and that's where the Canaanites did their disgusting worship. So God told the Israelites to tear apart the Canaanite altars on the high places.

God wanted His people to have nothing to do with these defiled "high places." He wanted His people to worship Him at the temple on Mount Zion—the mountain He chose—not on whatever high place they chose themselves (Deuteronomy 12:2–14).

Jerusalem was the only "high place" where God wanted His people to worship.

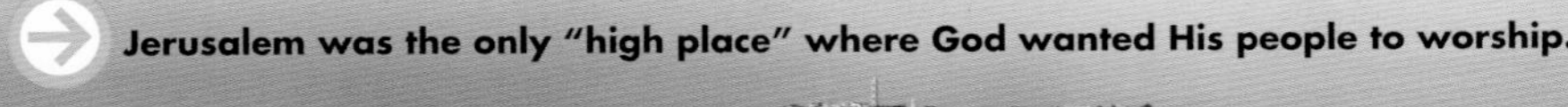

And he humbled thee, and suffered thee to hunger, and fed thee with manna, which thou knewest not, neither did thy fathers know; that he might make thee know that man doth not live by bread only, but by every word that proceedeth out of the mouth of the LORD doth man live. Thy raiment waxed not old upon thee, neither did thy foot swell, these forty years.
DEUTORONOMY 8:3–4 KJV

HOW DID THE ISRAELITES SURVIVE IN THE DESERT FOR 40 YEARS?

A few shepherds still live in the Sinai Desert today, and they scrounge around and find enough food and water, as well as pasture for their flocks. But there were so *many* Israelites—perhaps a couple of million—that there simply wasn't enough food for all of them to eat. God had to do huge miracles to supply them with food.

For example, for 40 years, He caused a delicious, nutritional food called manna to come down from heaven. He also sent vast flocks of quail flying into their camp—twice (Exodus 16; Numbers 11:4–9, 31–32)! God also did miracles to give them water to drink (Exodus 15:22–25; 17:1–7; Numbers 20:1–13).

God even did miracles to keep their feet from swelling with all their wandering in the desert, and kept their clothing from wearing out for 40 years (Deuteronomy 8:4). God did countless miracles to help His people survive. He had to, or they wouldn't have made it.

It would be hard to spend forty minutes—let alone forty years—in a place like the Sinai Desert. But God performed miracles to keep His people alive in the desert for four decades.

HOW DID THE ISRAELITES KEEP FROM GETTING SICK WHEN THEY KNEW NOTHING ABOUT GERMS AND DISEASE?

God knows everything there is to know about germs. However, if He had explained to the Israelites what causes sickness, they still wouldn't have understood. So God simply gave them practical rules to prevent them from getting sick in the first place.

For example, being careless with human waste is a major cause of a disease called dysentery, so God ordered the Israelites to keep their toilets away from their camps (Deuteronomy 23:12–14).

As recently as 200 years ago, most people didn't know enough to wash the germs off their hands, yet the Jews have been thoroughly washing their hands for thousands of years, in keeping with God's commands (Mark 7:3–4).

God also told the Israelites to quarantine anyone who had an infectious skin disease, and He explained how to get rid of mildew that caused asthma and other health problems (Leviticus 13; 14:33–57).

Aliens from outer space? No—the "swine flu" virus, magnified thousands of times. Many of God's rules for His people in the Old Testament were to protect them from sicknesses carried by germs and viruses like this.

Designate a place outside the camp where you can go to relieve yourself. As part of your equipment have something to dig with, and when you relieve yourself, dig a hole and cover up your excrement. For the LORD your God moves about in your camp to protect you and to deliver your enemies to you. Your camp must be holy, so that he will not see among you anything indecent and turn away from you.

DEUTERONOMY 23:12–14 TNIV

ARE CHRISTIANS TODAY SUPPOSED TO TITHE?

Different churches have different opinions about tithing. In Old Testament times, God commanded the Israelites to give 10 percent of all their earnings and flocks and crops to Him. This tithe was used to support the Levites and priests in the temple, and also provided food for the poor and the widows and orphans. God promised to bless and protect the Israelites if they tithed (Malachi 3:8–12). That was the law in Old Testament times.

Many churches believe that Christians today are also supposed to tithe; they say that most financial problems are caused by people failing to give one-tenth of their income to God.

Other churches point out that the New Testament doesn't tell Christians to tithe. However, Jesus did talk a lot about giving generously (Luke 6:38), and the apostle Paul urged believers to give as much as they were able (2 Corinthians 9:6–8). Whether you believe in tithing or not, part of being a Christian is giving to God and others.

Every third year, the year of the tithe, give a tenth of your produce to the Levite, the foreigner, the orphan, and the widow so that they may eat their fill in your cities. And then, in the Presence of GOD, your God, say this: I have brought the sacred share, I've given it to the Levite, foreigner, orphan, and widow. What you commanded, I've done. I haven't detoured around your commands, I haven't forgotten a single one.

DEUTERONOMY 26:12–13 MSG

"God Loves a cheerful giver" is what the Bible says (2 Corinthians 9:7). He doesn't need the money—but He knows it's good for us not to be too attached to the stuff!

WHY WAS CANAAN CALLED THE PROMISED LAND?

God promised Abraham that He would give the land of Canaan to him and to his descendants. In fact, God promised him the land again and again (Genesis 12:7; 13:14–17; 15:7; 17:8). God later made the same promise to Abraham's son Isaac (Genesis 26:2–4) and to Isaac's son Jacob (Genesis 28:13–14). No wonder Canaan was called the Promised Land.

When the older generation of Israelites were fearful and doubted that God could bring them into the land He had promised them, God let them all die in the wilderness. He then promised that, 40 years later, when their children were grown up, He would bring the younger generation into Canaan (Numbers 14:26–31). God declared that Joshua would be the one to lead the children of Israel into the Promised Land (Joshua 1:5–6). And he did!

"You shall give this people possession of the land which I swore to their fathers to give them."
JOSHUA 1:6 NASB

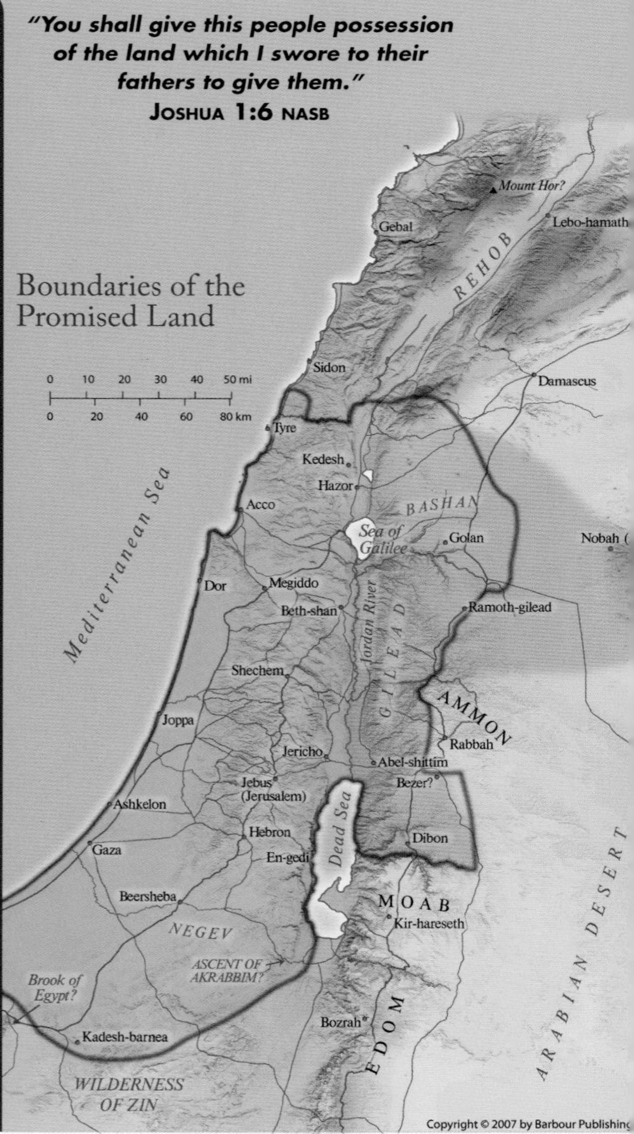

WHY DID GOD BLESS RAHAB THE PROSTITUTE EVEN THOUGH SHE TOLD A LIE?

But the woman had taken the two men and hidden them; and she said, "True, men came to me, but I did not know where they came from; and when the gate was to be closed, at dark, the men went out; where the men went I do not know; pursue them quickly, for you will overtake them." But she had brought them up to the roof, and hid them with the stalks of flax which she had laid in order on the roof.

JOSHUA 2:4–6 RSV

The Bible tells us, "Do not lie. Do not deceive one another" (Leviticus 19:11 NIV). Yet we also know that undercover police officers must pretend to be someone else to bring criminals to justice. They can't tell the truth about who they are, what they're doing, or where they're going. Also, when our country is at war, brave men and women who serve as spies must use deception. Citizens of enemy nations who help them must conceal the truth also.

Remember the story of Pinnochio, the wooden toy that came to life—but whose nose grew every time he told a lie? This drawing is from an early edition of the Pinnochio story.

Israel was at war with the nations that lived in Canaan, so the two Israelite spies tried to make the people of Jericho think they were ordinary travelers. Somehow their cover was blown, and when Rahab realized that, she hid them on her roof. Aiding the enemy was a crime for a loyal citizen of Jericho, but Rahab now believed in God (Joshua 2:8–11) and had new loyalties. She was like a secret agent operating a safe house—so yes, she lied to protect the spies when their lives were in danger.

For protecting God's people, Rahab and her family were spared and she was allowed to live in Israel the rest of her life (Joshua 6:25). Many Christians believe she was an ancestor of Jesus (Matthew 1:5).

HOW DID THE JORDAN RIVER PART?

"And as soon as the priests who carry the ark of the LORD—the Lord of all the earth—set foot in the Jordan, its waters flowing downstream will be cut off and stand up in a heap."

JOSHUA 3:13 TNIV

Normally, the Jordan River near Jericho is not wide, but it was springtime and the river was swollen with rain and melted snow. It overflowed its banks, filled the flood plains, and was nearly a mile wide. But as soon as the priests stepped into the river carrying the ark of the covenant, the water level fell until the riverbed was empty. Only after all the Israelites had crossed through did the river start flowing again.

How did God achieve this miracle? Well, "the waters which came down from upstream stood still, and rose in a heap very far away at Adam" (Joshua 3:16 NKJV). Adam was a town 20 miles upstream from Jericho. The river gorge is narrow there, and sometimes the cliffs collapse and a landslide dams the river. This happened in 1927, blocking the Jordan River for 20 hours.

The Jordan isn't normally a huge river. . .but when the Israelites crossed, it was at flood stage. Still, that's no match for a miracle-working God.

How did God cause the landslide in Joshua's day? It could have been the heavy spring rains. Or, very likely, God sent an earthquake to shake the hills (Psalm 114:3–7). Even if God used natural means, the *exact timing* of the river drying up was a huge miracle. And speaking of timing, as soon as the last Israelite walked out of the riverbed, the Jordan flooded back again.

HOW DID THE WALLS OF JERICHO FALL DOWN?

Jericho was the first city the Israelites came to when they entered Canaan. God could have simply allowed them to besiege it, but He wanted the Canaanites to fear His mighty power. He therefore had Joshua's army march silently around the city once a day for six days while the priests blew trumpets. On the seventh day, the army marched around Jericho seven times. When the priests gave a long blast on the trumpets, the entire army shouted and the city walls collapsed (Joshua 6).

When the trumpets sounded, the people shouted, and at the sound of the trumpet, when the people gave a loud shout, the wall collapsed; so every man charged straight in, and they took the city.

JOSHUA 6:20 NIV

How did this happen? Bible scholar Kenneth Kitchen believes that there may have been an earthquake at the precise moment that the Israelites shouted, and this brought the walls down. God sometimes sent earthquakes as a sign of His power (Isaiah 29:6; Ezekiel 38:18–20; Matthew 27:50–54; 28:2).

Some people guess that the shouting and the trumpet blast vibrated the walls and caused them to collapse, but that's not likely. Otherwise the Israelites would have done that to *every* Canaanite city.

The city of Ávila, in central Spain, is surrounded by walls just like the biblical Jericho was. Ávila's walls were built nearly a thousand years ago!

WHY DID GOD TELL THE ISRAELITES TO KILL THE CANAANITES—MEN, WOMEN, AND CHILDREN? WASN'T THAT TOTALLY CRUEL?

> *They put everything in the city under the holy curse, killing man and woman, young and old, ox and sheep and donkey.*
>
> JOSHUA 6:21 MSG

Canaanite society was so corrupt that God said that He was casting them out to make room for the Israelites; in fact, the Canaanites were so wicked that the land itself was *vomiting* them out (Leviticus 18:24–25).

God tried to strike such fear into the Canaanites that those who weren't totally corrupted would fear His power and flee the land. That's why He did such astonishing miracles—and the Canaanites did indeed fear God. Rahab told the spies, "Our hearts melted and no courage remained in any man" (Joshua 2:11 NASB).

God told the Israelites again and again to "drive them out" (Exodus 23:27–31; 34:11; Deuteronomy 7:1). The Canaanites simply could have fled south to Egypt. In the past, tens of thousands of Canaanites had migrated to Egypt—and at that time there was a huge need for workers because a couple of million Israelite slaves had moved out.

Sad to say, the evil Canaanites hardened their hearts and stayed—even though they knew that God Himself was fighting them; even though they knew that the Israelites were prepared to wipe them out (Joshua 9:24; 10:1–5). The Canaanites who dug in their heels to fight God brought destruction on themselves and their families.

DID THE SUN ACTUALLY STAND STILL WHEN JOSHUA PRAYED THAT IT WOULD?

One day, five Amorite kings surrounded the Israelites' allies at Gibeon, so the Israelites attacked the Amorites. Joshua wanted to finish the battle before sunset, so he prayed, "Sun, stand still over Gibeon." The Bible says, "The sun stood still in the middle of the sky and did not go down for a whole day" (Joshua 10:12–13 GNT).

> *Then Joshua spoke to the LORD in the day when the LORD delivered up the Amorites before the sons of Israel, and he said in the sight of Israel, "O sun, stand still at Gibeon, and O moon in the valley of Aijalon." So the sun stood still, and the moon stopped, until the nation avenged themselves of their enemies.*
>
> JOSHUA 10:12–13 NASB

We know that the sun doesn't move around the earth, but that the earth's rotation makes the sun appear to rise and set. So did the earth abruptly stop rotating? No. That would have caused global destruction, wiping out the Israelites, too. Perhaps God refracted the sun's light so that it appeared as if it were staying in the same spot for the rest of the day.

This story comes from the lost book of Jashar,

which describes the Israelites' wars in poetry. (See Joshua 10:13; 2 Samuel 1:18.) Some of the poetry is symbolic, such as when it describes Israel's rulers as "swifter than eagles" (2 Samuel 1:23), though, of course, no one can actually run 200 miles per hour.

We know that God did a miracle that day, but exactly what kind of miracle is a mystery.

Joshua asks God to stop the sun, in an 1816 painting by John Martin.

WHY WERE THERE SO MANY WARS AND KILLINGS IN THE OLD TESTAMENT? WHY DIDN'T THE ISRAELITES JUST LOVE THEIR ENEMIES LIKE JESUS SAID?

> *Joshua waged war against all these kings for a long time. Except for the Hitites living in Gibeon, not one city made a treaty of peace with the Israelites, who took them all in battle.*
>
> JOSHUA 11:18–19 TNIV

Jesus said, "Love your enemies" (Matthew 5:44 NIV), and "If someone strikes you on the right cheek, turn to him the other also" (Matthew 5:39 NIV). This may mean avoiding a fight by letting someone insult you or slap you. But there comes a point when even Christians have to use physical force to stop someone from beating them up or to defend their loved ones.

The apostle Paul said that the police and armed forces do not "bear the sword" for no reason. They are appointed by God Himself to "execute wrath on him who practices evil" (Romans 13:4 NKJV). So when an enemy nation attacks, it is the duty of Christian soldiers to use their weapons to defend their country.

Wars have been fought throughout human history, and since the days of the New Testament, Christians have had to fight. Sometimes wars can be avoided, but often they cannot.

Who Was Baal, and Why Did the Israelites Worship Him?

Canaan was a dry land that depended on rain to produce crops. The Canaanites had many gods, but they worshipped Baal most of all because they believed he controlled the weather and the rain. The Canaanites also thought Baal was the fertility god, who caused animals to bear their young and who blessed people with children. They gave Baal credit for everything that *God* was really doing.

As if that weren't bad enough, when people worshipped Baal, they cut themselves, ate unclean animals, and slept with prostitutes (1 Kings 18:28; Isaiah 65:2–4).

God had forbidden people to make idols of *Him*, yet there were often idols of Baal around. When the land went through a dry spell, the people were tempted to bow down to the idol of Baal, hoping that it could bring rain.

Then the Israelites did evil in the eyes of the Lord and served the Baals.
Judges 2:11 NIV

This figurine of Baal is more than 3,000 years old!

WHY DID GOD DO SUCH HUGE MIRACLES IN OLDEN DAYS BUT DOESN'T DO THEM TODAY?......

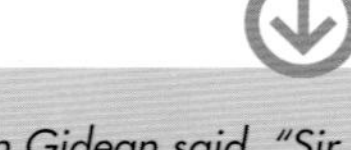

Then Gidean said, "Sir, if the Lord is with us, why are we having so much trouble? Where are the miracles our ancestors told us he did when the Lord brought them out of Egypt? But now he has left us and handed us over to the Midianites."

JUDGES 6:13 NCV

Gideon asked that very question nearly 3,500 years ago! When Israel was overrun by invaders, Gideon asked why God wasn't doing mighty miracles to rescue Israel as He had done many years earlier—such as when He sent plagues on Egypt and parted the Red Sea. Gideon knew that God still *could* do miracles if He chose to, but he complained that the Lord had abandoned them (Judges 6:13).

Gideon was partially right. A prophet had just finished telling Israel that because they had disobeyed and abandoned God, God was allowing them to suffer (Judges 6:7–10). But when they learned their lesson and turned back to God, He chose Gideon to lead Israel's armies and did miracles to deliver them.

Some people say the birth of a baby is a miracle—and though it is an amazing thing, it happens millions of times each year, all around the world. True miracles are really unusual, like when Moses parted the Red Sea or the walls of Jericho fell before the people of Israel.

At first Gideon had trouble believing that God could use him to rescue His people. Doubt is another reason why God sometimes doesn't do miracles. When Jesus returned to His hometown of Nazareth, the Bible says, "He did not do many mighty works there, because of their unbelief" (Matthew 13:58 RSV). We have to believe God (Mark 9:23).

IF GIDEON WAS SO FEARFUL AND DOUBTING, HOW DID HE BECOME SUCH A GREAT HERO?

"Pardon me, my lord," Gideon replied, "but how can I save Israel? My clan is the weakest in Manasseh, and I am the least in my family."

JUDGES 6:15 NIV

When an angel declared that God was going to use Gideon to rescue Israel, Gideon believed him but still had doubts. Nevertheless, he trusted God enough to obey. Even though he was afraid, he destroyed his father's idols. He then gathered an army and prepared for battle. Then Gideon got cold feet, so he asked God to do two small miracles to show that He was really with him. God did the miracles, and Gideon was reassured.

Gideon was facing a monster-sized army and had only 32,000 men—yet God told him to send almost his entire army home. What a test! Yet Gideon believed and obeyed. God then told Gideon that he would save Israel with only three hundred men. Gideon obeyed. God knew that Gideon was afraid, so to encourage him, God let him overhear an amazing dream. God then gave Gideon a crazy, wild battle plan—and it worked!

All of this should encourage us. Even though we struggle with fears and doubts, God can use us to do great things as long as we trust and obey Him.

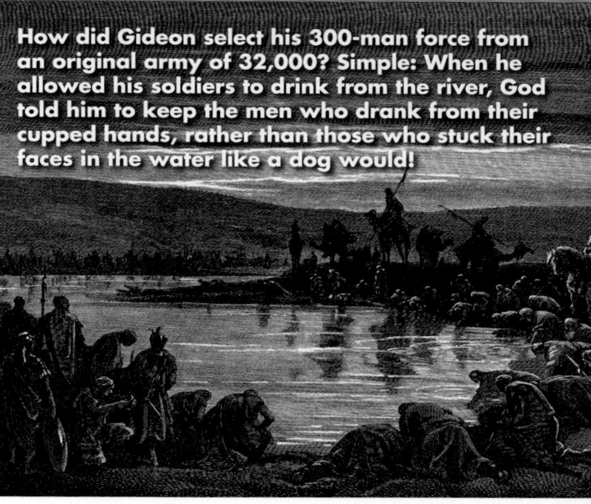

How did Gideon select his 300-man force from an original army of 32,000? Simple: When he allowed his soldiers to drink from the river, God told him to keep the men who drank from their cupped hands, rather than those who stuck their faces in the water like a dog would!

WHY DID JEPHTHAH HAVE TO KEEP HIS VOW TO SACRIFICE HIS DAUGHTER?

One time the Israelites chose a bandit chief named Jephthah to liberate them from their oppressors. As he marched out to battle, Jephthah vowed to the Lord that if God helped him win, when he returned home, he would sacrifice to God whatever came out of the door of his house to greet him.

Maybe Jephthah expected an animal to greet him at his front door. But whatever the case, his vow was a foolish one.

Jephthah was shocked when his only child, a daughter, came out the door—but what was he *hoping* would step out first? His wife? A servant? His dog? The family's goat? It was a very thoughtless vow to make.

> *Alas, my daughter! thou hast brought me very low, and thou art one of them that trouble me: for I have opened my mouth unto the LORD, and I cannot go back. And she said unto him, My father, if thou hast opened thy mouth unto the LORD, do to me according to that which hath proceeded out of thy mouth.*
>
> JUDGES 11:35–36 KJV

Jephthah knew that men were supposed to keep vows they made; otherwise they would be "guilty of sin" (Deuteronomy 23:21 NIV). So he sacrificed his daughter. But by doing so, he committed a much greater sin. When the Israelites foolishly sacrificed their sons and daughters, God called it a terrible sin and said, "I never commanded, nor did it enter my mind, that they should do such a detestable thing" (Jeremiah 32:35 NIV).

WHY DID SAMSON LOSE ALL HIS STRENGTH JUST BECAUSE OF A HAIRCUT?

When Delilah cut Samson's hair, he lost his supernatural strength and became as weak as any other man. But remember: Samson's great strength was not actually in his hair. It was a gift from God (Judges 14:6; 15:14), which he lost when "the LORD had departed from him" (Judges 16:20 NKJV).

The reason it was important that Samson's hair never be cut was because he was a Nazirite—someone specially dedicated to God. Among other things, Nazirites were not allowed to cut their hair (Judges 13:4–5). When Samson told Delilah that cutting his hair would make him lose his strength, he knew good and well that she would try to do it. (After all, the previous three times he told her something that would make him lose his strength, she had done precisely what he said.)

By telling Delilah to cut his hair, Samson broke the rules of a Nazirite. Once Samson was no longer dedicated to the Lord, God departed from him and removed the gift of strength.

She kept at it day after day, nagging and tormenting him. Finally, he was fed up—he couldn't take another minute of it. He spilled it. He told her, "A razor has never touched my head. I've been God's Nazirite from conception. If I were shaved, my strength would leave me; I would be as helpless as any other mortal." When Delilah realized that he had told her his secret, she sent for the Philistine tyrants, telling them, "Come quickly—this time he's told me the truth." They came, bringing the bribe money. When she got him to sleep, his head on her lap, she motioned to a man to cut off the seven braids of his hair. Immediately he began to grow weak. His strength drained from him. Then she said, "The Philistines are on you, Samson!" He woke up, thinking, "I'll go out, like always, and shake free." He didn't realize that GOD had abandoned him.

JUDGES 16:17–20 MSG

Does Samson's story teach us that haircuts are bad? No. . .Samson got in trouble with God for breaking his promise, not just for cutting his hair.

"Blessed are you of the Lord, my daughter! For you have shown more kindness at the end than at the beginning, in that you did not go after young men, whether poor or rich."
Ruth 3:10 NKJV

"Marrying for the money"? Some people do, but that wasn't Ruth's style.

WAS RUTH CONNIVING AND GREEDY FOR GOING AFTER A RICH, OLDER MAN?

Once in a while, you hear about a young woman marrying a rich, older man, and people say, "She just married him for his money!" Some women do that, but that is not what Ruth did—even though she followed Naomi's advice and offered herself in marriage to a wealthy, older man.

Ruth was a deeply spiritual widow from Moab, who had forsaken her family, her country, and her pagan gods to follow her mother-in-law, Naomi, back to Israel. Ruth knew that Naomi was desperately poor and had nothing to offer her, but she went with Naomi because she loved God and wanted to serve Him, and she loved Naomi and wanted to take care of her. Those two things are what made Boaz admire Ruth (Ruth 1:16–17; 2:10–12).

WHAT IS A KINSMAN REDEEMER?

> "Although it is true that I am near of kin, there is a kinsman-redeemer nearer than I."
>
> RUTH 3:12 NIV

Family was very important in ancient Israel, and brothers and sisters and close relatives looked out for one another. It was a law, in fact, that if a man became very poor and had to sell his land, his closest relative (kinsman) was to come and buy back (redeem) the land that the poor man had sold (Leviticus 25:25). That way the land stayed in the family. The relative who did this was called the kinsman redeemer. If the closest relative couldn't afford to buy the land—or refused to—then the responsibility passed to the next nearest relative.

A man named Elimelech had sold his land during a famine, and when his widow, Naomi, came back years later, she had no land and no money to buy it back. A kinsman said he would redeem her land, but Boaz reminded the man that when he bought the land, he also had to marry Ruth, the widow of Naomi's son. That was also according to the law. The relative then said that he couldn't redeem the land. Boaz then became the kinsman redeemer (Ruth 4).

A giant statue called Christ the Redeemer towers over Rio de Janeiro, Brazil. Boaz, by "buying back" Ruth, was an example of what Jesus would later do for everyone who believes in Him.

WHY WAS IT SO IMPORTANT IN OLD TESTAMENT DAYS TO HAVE CHILDREN?

> "May your house be like the house of Perez, whom Tamar bore to Judah, because of the children that the LORD will give you by this young woman."
>
> RUTH 4:12 RSV

In ancient Israel, as in the early days of America, there were several reasons why it was important for a husband and wife to have children—*several* children. First of all, there was always lots of work to do on the family farm, and the more sons and daughters there were, the more work could get done.

Second, parents cared for their children and provided for them when they were young, and it was expected that when the parents became old, their grown children would then care for them. The more children a couple had, the more certain it was that they would be cared for in their old age, and the more they felt blessed by God. Therefore, they looked forward to having seven or even ten sons (Psalm 127:3–5; Ruth 4:15; 1 Samuel 1:8).

A Dutch artist portrayed Hannah presenting her baby, Samuel, to Eli the priest, in 1665.

And she made a vow, saying, "O LORD Almighty, if you will only look upon your servant's misery and remember me, and not forget your servant but give her a son, then I will give him to the LORD for all the days of his life, and no razor will ever be used on his head."

1 SAMUEL 1:11 NIV

WHERE DID THE PRACTICE OF DEDICATING CHILDREN COME FROM?

Many churches have ceremonies in which parents bring their newborn baby to the front of the church to have a pastor pray over him or her. The parents promise to raise their child to serve God. This is called a baby dedication or dedicating a child to the Lord.

The practice is based on the story of Samuel. His mother, Hannah, couldn't have children, so she promised God that if He gave her a son, she would give him back to the Lord. Sure enough, she had a son, named Samuel, and when he was about three years old, she brought him to God's temple and gave him into the care of Eli the priest. Samuel grew up serving God there, and his mother visited him once a year (1 Samuel 1:24–28; 2:18–19). Samuel became a great man of God.

Today after parents "give their children to God," they raise them at home and teach them to dedicate their hearts and lives to God.

IF THE ARK OF THE COVENANT WAS SO SPECIAL, WHY DID GOD ALLOW THE PHILISTINES TO CAPTURE IT?

Here's the ark of the covenant, Hollywood-style, from the 1981 film *Raiders of the Lost Ark*. Nobody knows where the ark went after the Babylonians destroyed Jerusalem in 586 BC.

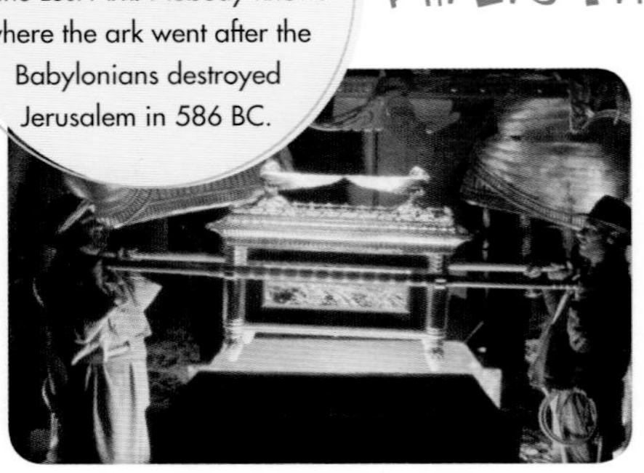

> *So the Philistines fought, and Israel was defeated, and they fled, every man to his home; and there was a very great slaughter, for there fell of Israel thirty thousand foot soldiers. And the ark of God was captured.*
>
> 1 Samuel 4:10–11 RSV

God didn't dwell in the ark, but He sometimes appeared there (Exodus 25:22). The Israelites, however, began to believe that God was *always* there, even when they disobeyed Him—and at this time they were very disobedient. They thought that the ark itself would help them. They said, "Let us bring the ark of the covenant. . .that when it comes among us it may save us from the hand of our enemies" (1 Samuel 4:3 NKJV).

God taught the Israelites a very good lesson when He allowed the Philistines to capture the ark: They needed to obey *Him*—not just depend on the ark—if they wanted Him to be with them.

God also showed that He was more than able to protect the ark from the Philistines. He sent so many plagues on the Philistines that they willingly sent the ark back to Israel (1 Samuel 5–6).

WHY DID THE SONS OF SUCH A GODLY MAN AS SAMUEL TURN OUT BAD?

> *When Samuel became old, he made his sons judges over Israel. The name of his first-born son was Jo'el, and the name of his second, Abi'jah; they were judges in Beer-sheba. Yet his sons did not walk in his ways, but turned aside after gain; they took bribes and perverted justice. Then all the elders of Israel gathered together and came to Samuel at Ramah, and said to him, "Behold, you are old and your sons do not walk in your ways; now appoint for us a king to govern us like all the nations."*
>
> 1 Samuel 8:1–5 RSV

We all bear responsibility for our own actions, but sometimes when children turn out bad, it's partially the parents' fault. For example, Eli the high priest knew all about the terrible things his sons were doing, yet he didn't discipline them. He didn't take away their jobs as priests, even though their jobs gave them many opportunities to offend and hurt people (1 Samuel 2:12–17, 27–30; 3:13).

Sometimes, however, even when parents discipline their children and teach them the right way to live and set an example of honoring God, the children still choose to be disobedient. This is what happened with Samuel's sons. Unlike their father, they refused to walk with God (1 Samuel 8:1–5).

Every person is responsible for his or her own choices. Hezekiah was a godly king, yet his son Manasseh was an evil king. Then again, Manasseh's grandson Josiah truly loved God (2 Kings 18:1–7; 21:1–11; 22:1–2). No matter how good or how evil a king was, his sons made their own choices about whether to serve God.

"A wise son heeds his father's instruction," Proverbs 13:1 (NIV) says, "but a mocker does not listen to rebuke." And if a son (or daughter) ignores Dad's advice for too long, they might find themselves in this guy's situation!

KING SAUL WAS SUCH A GREAT LEADER IN THE BEGINNING. WHY DID HE END UP FAILING SO MISERABLY?

As a young man, Saul was tall and strong, yet he was very humble and shy. When he heard that he had been chosen as king, he hid himself (1 Samuel 9:2; 10:21–24). The Bible says that Saul was "small in his own eyes" (1 Samuel 15:17). Because he depended on God to help him, Saul was victorious in his battles with Israel's enemies (1 Samuel 11:6–11; 14:47–48).

But Saul had four weaknesses: He became impatient and fearful when God's prophet didn't show up on time; he began disobeying God's clear instructions; he valued the opinions of other people too much; and he became power hungry, insecure, and violent toward his competition (1 Samuel 13:1–13; 15:1–31; 18:1–12).

Instead of seeking and obeying God, Saul allowed these weaknesses to take over his life and develop into major problems, and that is why he fell.

"You acted foolishly," Samuel said. "You have not kept the command the LORD your God gave you; if you had, he would have established your kingdom over Israel for all time. But now your kingdom will not endure; the LORD has sought out a man after his own heart and appointed him leader of his people, because you have not kept the LORD's command."

1 SAMUEL 13:13–14 NIV

Like King Saul, Benedict Arnold was a military leader who fell into disgrace. A general in the Continental Army during the American Revolution, Arnold was angry that leaders in the colonies didn't seem to appreciate him—so he switched sides and joined the British. *Benedict Arnold* is now a name that means "traitor."

WHAT DID SAMUEL MEAN WHEN HE SAID, "OBEDIENCE IS BETTER THAN SACRIFICE"?

An evil tribe of raiders called Amalekites lived in the desert south of Israel. They were like a band of criminals. They hated God and had been terrorizing Israel for hundreds of years, killing and robbing and enslaving God's people. God finally had enough and had Samuel give King Saul very clear orders: Saul was to wipe out the Amalekites—every single one—and kill all their herds and flocks as well.

Saul disobeyed God. First, he allowed many Amalekites to escape, so that David had to fight them later (1 Samuel 30). Saul also decided to spare the king of the Amalekites and bring him back as a trophy; and he didn't destroy the Amalekites' herds and flocks. He brought the fattest calves and the lambs back to Israel to sacrifice to God.

The Lord was *not* pleased with Saul's sacrifice. He wanted Saul simply to do what He had told him to do.

But Samuel replied: "Does the Lord delight in burnt offerings and sacrifices as much as in obeying the voice of the Lord? To obey is better than sacrifice, and to heed is better than the fat of rams."

1 Samuel 15:22 NIV

Saul had other disobedience problems with Samuel—like the time Saul found a witch to call the dead Samuel's spirit. This painting, from the 1600s, shows Saul falling before a ghostly—and unhappy—Samuel. Read the whole story in 1 Samuel 28.

WHAT MADE KING DAVID ISRAEL'S GREATEST LEADER?

God said, "Up on your feet! Anoint him! This is the one."

1 Samuel 16:12 MSG

King Saul didn't love God wholeheartedly and disobeyed Him, so God rejected Saul as king. The prophet Samuel told Saul, "The Lord has sought out a man after his own heart" (1 Samuel 13:14 NIV). That man was David. This didn't mean that David was perfect or sinless. David made mistakes, too, but his heart was in the right place and he loved God intensely. When he sinned, he repented sincerely.

The apostle Paul shed more light on this when he quoted God, saying, "I have found David son of Jesse a man after my own heart; he will do everything I want him to do" (Acts 13:22 NIV). Saul constantly disobeyed and did very little of what God wanted him to do. David loved God and did everything God wanted him to do. Because of David's love and obedience, God made him Israel's greatest leader.

Four of the United States' greatest leaders—George Washington, Thomas Jefferson, Theodore Roosevelt, and Abraham Lincoln—are carved into the side of a rock hill in South Dakota. The presidents honored at Mount Rushmore were wise and strong leaders like the Bible's King David. But it was David's obedience to God that made him Israel's greatest leader.

WHAT DOES IT MEAN TO BE ANOINTED?....

Then Samuel took the horn of oil, and anointed him in the midst of his brethren.

1 SAMUEL 16:13 KJV

To "anoint" means to pour or spread oil on someone. There were three main reasons in the Bible for doing this:

1. People anointed themselves with perfume by spreading perfumed or scented oils on their bodies (Ruth 3:3; Esther 2:12). They also spread oil on their skin to make their faces shiny (Psalm 104:15).

2. Olive oil was poured on the heads of priests, prophets, and kings to dedicate them to God (Exodus 28:41; 1 Samuel 16:1, 13). The oil symbolized the presence of the Holy Spirit, who would then help the person.

3. In the New Testament, Christians anointed sick people with oil when praying for them to be healed (James 5:14).

WHY DID DAVID TAKE FIVE STONES WHEN HE WENT TO FIGHT GOLIATH, WHEN HE ONLY NEEDED ONE TO KILL HIM?.............

Then he took his staff in his hand, chose five smooth stones from the stream, put them in the pouch of his shepherd's bag and, with his sling in his hand, approached the Philistine.

1 SAMUEL 17:40 NIV

David was a good shot with the sling, but Goliath was covered with armor. He had a bronze helmet on his head and wore a coat of scale armor weighing 125 pounds. He even wore bronze shin guards. Another Philistine, carrying a shield, walked in front of Goliath (1 Samuel 17:4–7). David knew that he had to hit Goliath in the face, but there was no guarantee the stone would kill the giant; it might only wound him. Besides, there was the shield bearer to consider.

When David's first stone embedded in Goliath's forehead, the shield bearer apparently dropped the shield and ran. David ran up and found that the rock had killed the giant (1 Samuel 17:50–51). As it turned out, David didn't need the four extra stones, but he figured it would be wise to take them as a backup, just in case.

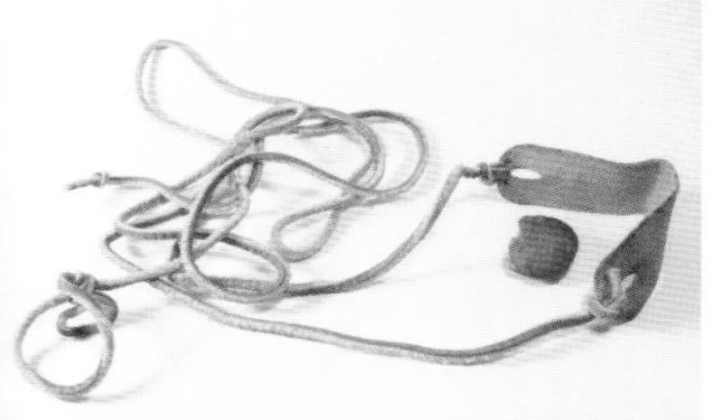

David's sling probably looked something like this. He would whirl it around and around until the stone inside the pouch had gained enough speed, then release one end of the string to let the rock fly. And David's first rock found its way right into Goliath's head!

WHY DID DAVID FIGHT SO MANY WARS?

David didn't *want* to fight all those wars. In almost every case, an enemy provoked him and David was forced to fight. After Saul died, David was God's choice as king, but one of Saul's generals declared Saul's son Ishbosheth to be king and fought against David. David finally united the kingdom of Israel peacefully (2 Samuel 2:1–9; 5:1–3).

Then the Philistines invaded Israel, but David defeated them (2 Samuel 5:17–25). Then the Ammonites disgraced David's ambassadors, and when they realized that they had started a war, they hired the Arameans to help crush David's armies—but David defeated them all (2 Samuel 8, 10). In later years, David's son Absalom led an army against him, and an Israelite named Sheba started a civil war, but David fought back and defeated them both (2 Samuel 15–20).

King David is known as a mighty warrior—and he was—but he was usually forced into that role. When you read the Psalms, you will see again and again that David prayed for God to protect him from his enemies who were plotting against him.

Now after this it came about that David defeated the Philistines and subdued them. . . .
2 Samuel 8:1 NASB

The weapons have changed over the years, but humans have been fighting wars almost since the beginning of history.

HOW DID DAVID GET AWAY WITH STEALING ANOTHER MAN'S WIFE AND KILLING THE MAN?...

Uriah, kneeling, takes a letter from King David, in a painting from the 1400s. Uriah delivered the secret message—which called for his own death!

> *David had her brought to his house, and she became his wife and bore him a son. But the thing David had done displeased the LORD.*
>
> 2 SAMUEL 11:27 TNIV

David did *not* get away with those things. The Bible tells us that David committed adultery with Bathsheba while her husband, Uriah, was away at war. When Bathsheba became pregnant and David couldn't cover his sin, he had Uriah sent into the heaviest fighting; then the rest of the army was ordered to retreat, leaving Uriah alone to die.

When God sent a prophet to confront the king about the terrible things he had done, David realized that God would have been justified to kill him for his crimes. You can read David's prayer of repentance in Psalm 51. God forgave David and said that he wouldn't die.

Nevertheless, God punished David by allowing Bathsheba's child to become sick and die. God also allowed David's adult son Absalom to wage war against him and to sleep with David's wives (2 Samuel 12:11–19).

David's handsome son Absalom gets his beautiful long hair caught in a tree branch—and soon loses his life.

WHY DID ABSALOM REBEL AGAINST HIS FATHER, KING DAVID, AND TRY TO BECOME KING IN HIS PLACE?....

> *Absalom sent secret messengers throughout all the tribes of Israel, saying, "As soon as you hear the sound of the trumpet, then say, 'Absalom is king at Hebron!'"*
>
> 2 SAMUEL 15:10 RSV

Absalom had two reasons. First, he despised his father for not doing justice when David's son Amnon raped Absalom's sister. David *was* furious with Amnon, but Absalom thought David didn't punish him enough—so he took the law into his own hands and murdered Amnon (2 Samuel 13).

David eventually forgave Absalom, but soon Absalom was telling every Israelite that David hadn't done what was right. Absalom said that if *he* were king, he would do justice (2 Samuel 15:1–6). Becoming king would mean murdering his own father and raping his father's wives, but Absalom didn't see anything unjust about that.

Second, Absalom was so handsome that everyone in Israel praised him. In fact, Absalom was in love with himself and was convinced that he was so royally good-looking that he surely ought to be king. He was especially proud of his long, pretty hair (2 Samuel 14:25–26), which eventually became his downfall.

WHY WAS IT SUCH A SIN FOR DAVID TO COUNT HOW MANY SOLDIERS HE HAD IN HIS ARMY?

> *"Go about now through all the tribes of Israel, from Dan to Beersheba, and register the people, that I may know the number of the people."*
>
> 2 SAMUEL 24:2 NASB

God didn't have a problem with the rulers of Israel counting how many fighting men they had. After all, in the past, God Himself had *twice* ordered Moses to conduct a census (Numbers 1:1–2; 26:1–2).

However, the Bible makes it clear that Satan was the one who inspired David to do this particular census, and God allowed it because God was upset with Israel for their disobedience (2 Samuel 24:1; 1 Chronicles 21:1). Why did David listen to the devil? Satan probably appealed to David's pride. After all, David had just finished conquering a huge empire that stretched from Egypt in the south to the Euphrates River in the north.

It wasn't the size of David's army that had won all those battles. David defeated those enemies because God was with him, helping him. By counting his fighting men, David was showing that he trusted in his soldiers more than in God.

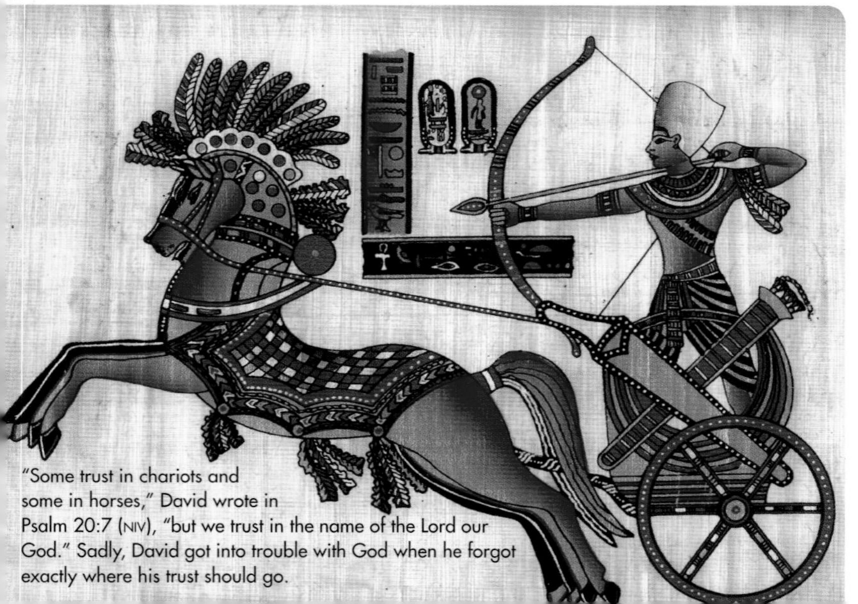

"Some trust in chariots and some in horses," David wrote in Psalm 20:7 (NIV), "but we trust in the name of the Lord our God." Sadly, David got into trouble with God when he forgot exactly where his trust should go.

"I will give you a wise and discerning heart, so that there will never have been anyone like you, nor will there ever be."
1 Kings 3:12 NIV

Can I Pray for Great Wisdom and Get It Like King Solomon Did?

You can certainly pray for wisdom. God has promised to give it to you. The Bible says, "If any of you lacks wisdom, you should ask God. . .and it will be given to you" (James 1:5 TNIV). But wisdom is not the same thing as intelligence or knowledge. God won't necessarily give you a bigger IQ than He already gave you, and He won't give you a supernatural download of math knowledge so you don't have to study for a test ever again. But He will give you more wisdom.

Solomon asked God for "a discerning heart. . .to distinguish between right and wrong" (1 Kings 3:9 TNIV), so that is exactly what God gave him. Solomon needed a lot of wisdom because he had so many people to govern. You probably don't need as much wisdom as Solomon did—but ask God for what you need.

Here's the classic example of Solomon's great wisdom: He threatens to cut a baby in half to learn which of the two women claiming the child is the real mom. When one woman shouts, "Give the baby to her!" Solomon knew she was the real mother. . . and gave the child to her. Read the whole story in 1 Kings 3:16–28.

WHY WAS THE TEMPLE COMPLETELY COVERED WITH GOLD INSIDE? SHOULDN'T THAT GOLD HAVE BEEN USED TO CARE FOR THE POOR?

So Solomon overlaid the house within with pure gold.

1 KINGS 6:21 KJV

God already had programs in place to care for widows, orphans, and the poor. In the villages and towns of Israel, the tithes of the Israelites were often distributed to feed the Levites and the poor. In Jerusalem the temple had a daily program to feed the poor. Besides, the law commanded Israelites to be generous and lend to the poor whatever they needed—and every seven years all debts were completely forgiven (Leviticus 25:35–37; Deuteronomy 14:28–29; 15:1–11).

The temple was where the Israelites met God and had their sins forgiven, so by giving valuable gold to the temple to make it beautiful, the Israelites showed that they placed great value on the place where they met God. King David was very rich, but he gave most of his gold to God, and the wealthy leaders of Israel gave generously also (1 Chronicles 29:1–9). These same rich people also gave to the poor.

Nobody knows exactly what Solomon's temple looked like, since it was destroyed almost 3,000 years ago! Other world religions still build fancy temples and cover them in gold or other shiny metals—like this Buddhist pagoda in Burma.

DID GOD ACTUALLY LIVE IN THE TEMPLE THAT SOLOMON BUILT?

"But will God really dwell on earth? The heavens, even the highest heaven, cannot contain you. How much less this temple I have built!"

1 KINGS 8:27 TNIV

God was present in the temple Solomon built, just as He was present in the tabernacle in the wilderness. God didn't permanently live in the tabernacle, but He met with the Israelites there. The tabernacle was made of cloth, and Solomon's temple was made of stone—but neither one was big enough for God to fit in.

Solomon admitted this when he said, "Not even all of heaven is large enough to hold you, so how can this Temple that I have built be large enough?" (1 Kings 8:27 GNT). It couldn't, of course. A Christian named Stephen pointed out that God doesn't dwell in man-made temples (Acts 7:48).

Nevertheless, for many centuries, God chose the temple in Jerusalem as the place where His people were to come worship Him and offer sacrifices for sin (1 Kings 8:29; 2 Chronicles 2:6).

That changed after Jesus died for our sins. Then believers no longer needed to sacrifice or worship in Jerusalem but could worship God wherever they were (John 4:19–24).

WHY DID GOD LET SOLOMON HAVE 700 WIVES?

Now King Solomon loved many foreign women. . . .
1 KINGS 11:1 RSV

God didn't want Solomon to have so many wives. In fact, He had warned Israel's kings *not* to do that (Deuteronomy 17:17). But Solomon disobeyed God. He even married women who worshipped evil gods. As a result, "his wives led him astray" and "his wives turned his heart after other gods" (1 Kings 11:3–4 NIV).

It was common in those days for kings to marry the daughters of important military allies and trade partners, and Solomon probably married for business reasons in a few cases—but seriously! There were nowhere near 700 kingdoms around Israel! Solomon simply married those women because he wanted to; and because he was king, no one could stop him. As Solomon confessed, "Anything I wanted, I got. I did not deny myself any pleasure" (Ecclesiastes 2:10 GNT).

"Not even all of heaven" could contain God, Solomon said (1 Kings 8:27). . . so God certainly wasn't limited to the Temple that Solomon built. But that was the place where God said He would meet with His special people, the Israelites.

HOW COME CHRISTIANS TODAY DON'T DO GREAT MIRACLES LIKE ELIJAH AND OTHER OLD TESTAMENT PROPHETS?

Wonder-workers like Elijah have always been unique. Back in Elijah's day, there was no one else doing amazing miracles either. A few other prophets, such as Moses and Elisha, did miracles, but *most* prophets just faithfully spoke God's Word and warned people to turn to God. Even the great prophet John the Baptist did no miracles, but he did tell people about Jesus (John 10:41).

However, just because you don't hear about big miracles like the Red Sea parting doesn't mean that God isn't doing miracles in modern times. He is! Around the world, every single day, Christians are praying in Jesus' name, and God is answering their prayers and doing hundreds of thousands of "small" miracles every single day.

The LORD heard Elijah's cry, and the boy's life returned to him, and he lived. Elijah picked up the child and carried him down from the room into the house. He gave him to his mother and said, "Look, your son is alive!"

1 KINGS 17:22–23 NIV

Ever hear of somebody who was so sick she wasn't expected to live—but then she got better? That's a kind of miracle, too!

Why did God send bears to kill some little children when all they did was tease Elisha?

The Bible says that as Elisha was passing the city of Bethel, "young lads came out from the city and mocked him." Then Elisha "cursed them in the name of the LORD. Then two female bears came out of the woods and tore up forty-two lads of their number" (2 Kings 2:23–24 NASB). Why would Elisha do such a thing?

The Hebrew word *yeled* translated as "young lads" actually means "youths." These were not elementary school kids playing in the school yard. This was a large gang of teenagers roaming around looking for trouble. Because there were more than 42 of them in the mob, Elisha probably felt threatened. He was alone and had no defense but God. The Lord sent two bears to punish and scare the boys. Fortunately, it seems that no one was killed. The youths most likely escaped with scratches and bites and hopefully learned a lesson.

From there Elisha went up to Bethel. As he was walking along the road, some youths came out of the town and jeered at him. "Go on up, you baldhead!" they said. "Go on up, you baldhead!" He turned around, looked at them and called down a curse on them in the name of the LORD. Then two bears came out of the woods and mauled forty-two of the youths.

2 KINGS 2:23–24 NIV

HOW DID GOD MAKE AN IRON AX HEAD FLOAT?

He cut off a branch and tossed it at the spot. The axhead floated up.

2 KINGS 6:6 MSG

God created the world and the entire universe, so we know that He has astonishing power and imagination. God not only created the physical things that we see, but also created the invisible rules of physics that we can't see. God made the natural laws that bind electrons, neutrons, and photons together. He created matter and antimatter. He designed energy to be able to change into matter and matter to change back into energy. God created gravity and gave the earth a magnetic field.

Really, when you think about it, how difficult would it have been for God to do a little anti-gravity miracle and make an iron ax head rise up from the bottom of a river?

Giant steel ships float. . .but only in very large bodies of water. It was really a miracle for a solid metal ax head to float in a small stream.

DOES GOD EVER TRICK PEOPLE INTO THINKING THAT SOMETHING IS TRUE WHEN IT REALLY ISN'T?

For the Lord had caused the army of the Arameans to hear a sound of chariots and a sound of horses. . . .

2 KINGS 7:6 NASB

Yes, He does. One time God tricked a huge enemy army in order to protect His people. The entire army of Aram had camped around the city of Samaria in Israel. They kept anyone from going in or out of the city and waited while the Israelites slowly ran out of food and began to starve.

But in the darkness of night, God "caused the Arameans to hear the sound of chariots and horses and a great army" (2 Kings 7:6 TNIV). There was so *much* noise that the Arameans were terrified, thinking that the two

Magicians specialize in tricking people—making them think a rabbit suddenly appeared in their hat or that they can saw pretty ladies in half without hurting them. Even God pulled a big trick on the Arameans one time!

greatest armies on earth—the Hittites and the Egyptians—had joined forces and were attacking them.

The Arameans fled, leaving everything behind, but there were no Hittites or Egyptian armies around. God had simply made a lot of noise.

WERE ALL THE VIOLENT THINGS KING JEHU DID GOOD OR BAD?....

When [Jehu] came to Samaria, he killed all who remained to Ahab in Samaria, until he had destroyed him, according to the word of the LORD which He spoke to Elijah.

2 KINGS 10:17 NASB

When a prophet anointed Jehu as king and told him to kill all the evil descendants of King Ahab and to uproot Baal worship from Israel, Jehu killed two evil kings and one truly wicked queen that same day. Then he ordered 70 of Ahab's male descendants beheaded. The next day, Jehu killed another 42 of Ahab's relatives. Then he called all the priests of Baal together for a "great festival" and killed them all.

God wanted to wipe out Baal worship in Israel, and Jehu did that (2 Kings 10:30). Jehu believed in God but still worshipped idols of the golden calf, so he was not a godly leader like King David.

But when God wanted to get rid of Baal worship, Jehu was the logical choice. He was an ambitious, get-results kind of man. Jehu had his own motivations for obeying God—namely, he wanted to be king—but God often has to use imperfect people to get the job done.

Violence is a big problem in today's world, and most of the violence that happens is *not* God's will, but the will of selfish, evil men.

Question & Answer

Saul took a sword, and fell upon it.
1 CHRONICLES 10:4 KJV

King Saul and his armor-bearer lie dead on Mount Gilboa while other soldiers look on. The painting, by Elie Marcuse, is from the mid-1800s.

WHY DOES THE BIBLE GIVE TWO DIFFERENT STORIES OF HOW KING SAUL DIED?

King Saul died in a battle against the Philistines. First Chronicles 10:1–6 says it happened this way: When Saul was mortally wounded by Philistine archers, he decided to end his own life. So he deliberately fell on his own sword and died. The Bible says that Saul's armor-bearer *saw* him die.

However, later on, an Amalekite who claimed to be part of the Israelite army brought Saul's crown to David and told him that he had seen Saul wounded but still standing. He claimed that Saul had ordered him to kill him—so the Amalekite claimed that is what he had done (2 Samuel 1:1–16).

The first version of the story is the true one. The Amalekite was lying. In the past, Saul had tried to kill David, so the Amalekite thought David would reward him for saying that he had killed Saul. He was wrong.

Uzzah falls backward dead—after touching the ark of the covenant.

WHY WAS UZZAH KILLED FOR MERELY TRYING TO KEEP THE ARK OF THE COVENANT FROM TIPPING OVER?........

God is holy, and when He comes to a physical location, that spot becomes holy also. When God appeared to Moses in the burning bush, He said, "Do not come any closer," and warned that Moses was standing on "holy ground" (Exodus 3:5 NIV). God wanted the Israelites to keep a respectful distance from the ark of the covenant as well, because His Spirit was often present there.

Uzzah *knew* that he shouldn't have touched the ark. He had *heard* the story: Several years earlier, the people of Beth Shemesh had become curious, lifted the lid, and peeked inside the ark—and 70 of them had died (1 Samuel 6:19–20).

David and the priests also should have known better: They shouldn't have carried the ark on an ox cart that was liable to tip. The Levites were supposed to carry the ark on poles (Exodus 25:12–15; 1 Chronicles 15:1–2), and even *they* were forbidden to touch it or they would die (Numbers 4:15). Everyone broke the rules that day, and Uzzah paid with his life.

> *David and all Israel went up to Baalah, that is, to Kiriath-jearim, which belongs to Judah, to bring up from there the ark of God, the LORD who is enthroned above the cherubim, where His name is called. They carried the ark of God on a new cart from the house of Abinadab, and Uzza and Ahio drove the cart. David and all Israel were celebrating before God with all their might, even with songs and with lyres, harps, tambourines, cymbals and with trumpets. When they came to the threshing floor of Chidon, Uzza put out his hand to hold the ark, because the oxen nearly upset it. The anger of the LORD burned against Uzza, so He struck him down because he put out his hand to the ark; and he died there before God. Then David became angry because of the LORD's outburst against Uzza; and he called that place Perez-uzza to this day. David was afraid of God that day, saying, "How can I bring the ark of God home to me?"*
>
> 1 CHRONICLES 13:6–12 NASB

ARE DROUGHTS AND FAMINES GOD'S JUDGMENT ON SIN?

Sometimes they are, but not always. For example, in King David's day, when a drought lasted for three years, God told David that it was punishment on Israel for Saul's slaughtering of the Gibeonites, Israel's allies. When David made things right, God sent rain (2 Samuel 21). Sometimes God withheld rain when His people neglected serving Him (Haggai 1).

Other times, droughts happened simply because of changing weather patterns and because all lands in the region were going through a dry spell. In those cases, both the righteous and the unrighteous were affected. The book of Genesis describes three great droughts and doesn't mention that any was a judgment for sin (Genesis 12:10; 26:1; 41:53 –54). However, God *did* use those droughts to work out His will.

When God sends rain, He sends it on both the just and the unjust (Matthew 5:45).

"When the heavens are shut up and there is no rain because your people have sinned against you, and when they pray toward this place and confess your name and turn from their sin because you have afflicted them, then hear from heaven and forgive the sin of your servants, your people Israel. Teach them the right way to live, and send rain on the land you gave your people for an inheritance."
2 Chronicles 6:26–27 NIV

Droughts dry out land, kill plants. . .and starve people.

HOW COULD KING JEHORAM BE SO CRUEL AS TO KILL ALL HIS BROTHERS?

> *When Jehoram had taken over his father's kingdom and had secured his position, he killed all his brothers along with some of the government officials.*
>
> 2 CHRONICLES 21:4 MSG

Jehoshaphat was a good king, but he made a terrible mistake when he allowed his son Jehoram to marry Princess Athaliah of Israel. Athaliah was a wicked Baal worshipper, and she completely corrupted Jehoram. Jehoram turned away from the Lord and embraced the demon-god Baal. After Jehoram became king of Judah, he murdered all his brothers to keep them from challenging him for the throne.

If you have a brother or sister, you've probably wished sometimes that you didn't. Just don't ever reach the point of sibling rivalry that Jehoram did!

Like many selfish, insecure rulers, he wanted no competition. Also, as the prophet Elijah pointed out, all of Jehoram's brothers were better than he was (2 Chronicles 21:13). Very likely, Jehoram worried that if he died, one of his brothers would become king and lead the people away from Baal worship and back to worshipping God.

God judged Jehoram for his evil deeds, and soon war broke out. Then the Arabs and the Philistines raided Judah and pillaged the palace. Finally, Jehoram died from a painful disease (2 Kings 8:16–22; 2 Chronicles 21).

HOW COULD GOOD KING JOASH TURN AGAINST GOD SO QUICKLY AND SO TOTALLY?

> *Now after the death of Jehoiada the princes of Judah came and did obeisance to the king; then the king hearkened to them. And they forsook the house of the LORD, the God of their fathers.*
>
> 2 CHRONICLES 24:17 RSV

Ever since Joash was young, he had been mentored by the high priest Jehoiada. As long as Jehoiada was alive, Joash worshipped God and did what was right. Jehoiada was a great influence for good, but many powerful officials of Judah worshipped idols. As long as Jehoiada was alive, they couldn't make their move; but as soon as he died, they influenced King Joash to worship idols—and he listened to them (2 Chronicles 24:17). Later, when Jehoiada's son spoke out against Joash's evil deeds, the palace officials plotted against him and got Joash to issue a death warrant against him.

Joash was weak and easily influenced. A later king of Judah, Zedekiah, also didn't have the backbone to resist ungodly advice (Jeremiah 38:4–6).

WHY IS THE NUMBER SEVEN SO SPECIAL?

> *And they brought seven bullocks, and seven rams, and seven lambs, and seven he goats, for a sin offering for the kingdom, and for the sanctuary, and for Judah. And he commanded the priests the sons of Aaron to offer them on the altar of the LORD.*
>
> 2 CHRONICLES 29:21 KJV

You will often hear people say, "Seven is God's number." Actually, *all* numbers belong to God. However, the number seven does have special significance in the Bible. The Israelites sacrificed seven bulls, seven rams, seven male lambs, and seven male goats to God (2 Chronicles 29:21). The apostle John describes seven stars, seven lampstands, seven spirits of God, seven seals, seven trumpets, and seven plagues (Revelation 1:12, 16; 4:5; 5:1; 8:6; 15:1). Even Jesus is described as a Lamb with seven horns and seven eyes (Revelation 5:6).

The number seven symbolizes completeness and perfection. It is based on the fact that seven days make one complete week, and that God rested on the seventh day "and made it holy" (Genesis 2:2–3).

IF WE KEEP ON SINNING, DOES THERE COME A POINT AT WHICH THERE IS NO MORE HOPE OF REPENTANCE AND MERCY?

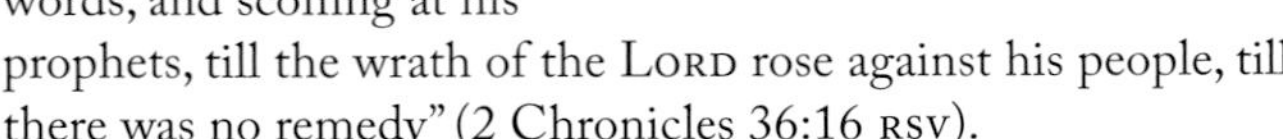

> *The wrath of the LORD was aroused against his people and there was no remedy.*
>
> 2 CHRONICLES 36:16 TNIV

In Jeremiah's day, the people of Judah were disobedient to the Lord. But because God had great compassion, He kept sending prophets to warn them. Still, they refused to change. "They kept mocking the messengers of God, despising his words, and scoffing at his prophets, till the wrath of the LORD rose against his people, till there was no remedy" (2 Chronicles 36:16 RSV).

God is love, and He gave His people many, many chances to change their ways. But when they stubbornly refused to listen, they had to suffer the consequences. Of course, *after* God punished His people and they finally woke up and repented, He once again had mercy on them and restored them.

Jeremiah was called the "weeping prophet" for the tears he cried over his people. Their stubbornness led to an invasion by a foreign country, and many of the Jewish people were carried off from their country.

WHY DID PERSIA'S KING CYRUS ALLOW THE JEWS TO RETURN TO THEIR HOMELAND?

The Babylonians uprooted people from their homelands if the people rebelled against them, and resettled them in distant lands to discourage them from rebelling again. The Persians were more tolerant, however. They believed that if they governed people fairly, the people wouldn't rebel. They even allowed captive peoples like the Jews to go back to their homelands.

This fulfilled a prophecy that God had given Isaiah. Hundreds of years before the Persian Empire existed, God prophesied that He would make a man named Cyrus set the Jews free to go rebuild Jerusalem (Isaiah 45:1–4, 13). When Cyrus came along, that is exactly what he did (Ezra 1:1–3).

In the first year of Cyrus king of Persia, in order to fulfill the word of the LORD spoken by Jeremiah, the LORD moved the heart of Cyrus king of Persia. . . .

EZRA 1:1 TNIV

EXILES RETURN TO JUDEA

The extent of the Persian Empire at the time of Ezra (c. 458 BC)

Judean exiles return under Zerubbabel's leadership

Judean exiles return under Ezra's leadership

Caspian Sea
ARARAT
Tushpa
Melidu
Tarsus
Carchemish
Haran
Gozan
Nineveh
MEDIA
Arpad
ASSYRIA
Asshur
Ecbatana
Habor River
Tigris River
Rezeph?
Euphrates River
Hamath
Paphos
Riblah
Tadmor
Mediterranean Sea
Tyre
Damascus
Cuthah
Babylon
Nippur
Susa
ELAM
BABYLONIA
Ezra leads the exiles along a shorter, more dangerous route without military escort
Samaria
Erech
Jerusalem
ARABIAN DESERT
Chebar River?
Ur
Zoan
Tahpanhes
JUDEA
EGYPT
Persian Gulf
Dumah
Memphis
Nile River
Elath
Tema
0 100 200 300 400 mi
0 100 200 300 400 500 600 km
N

WHY WAS IT SO IMPORTANT FOR THE JEWS TO REBUILD THE TEMPLE?

> *Let him go up to Jerusalem, which is in Judah, and build the house of the LORD God of Israel, (he is the God,) which is in Jerusalem.*
>
> EZRA 1:3 KJV

The Babylonians attacked Israel, tore down the temple of God, and took the Jews far away to Babylon. For 70 years, the Jews had no temple, so they began meeting together every Sabbath to pray, worship God, and read the Scriptures. That's how synagogues (meeting houses) began. When the Jews returned to Israel, they continued meeting in synagogues.

This was a good thing, but something was missing. The Messiah, Jesus, hadn't yet come to die for their sins—so the Jews still needed animal sacrifices to cover their sins and restore a relationship with God. The only place they were allowed to sacrifice was at the altar in the temple (Deuteronomy 12:5–14), so they had to rebuild the altar and the temple as soon as possible (Ezra 3:1–10).

WHY WAS EZRA SO ANGRY ABOUT JEWS MARRYING NON-JEWS?

> *"The people of Israel and the priests and the Levites have not separated themselves from the peoples of the lands. . . . For they have taken some of their daughters as wives for themselves and their sons."*
>
> EZRA 9:1–2 NKJV

More than 3,000 years ago, God made a rule for His people—the Jews—that they only marry other Jews. Here's what a Jewish wedding looked like a hundred years ago.

God had commanded the Israelites not to marry the people of Canaan (Deuteronomy 7:3–4). He explained why: "You shall not enter into marriage with them. . .for surely they will turn away your heart after their gods" (1 Kings 11:2 RSV). King Solomon, the wisest man on earth, thought that *he* could marry pagan wives and get away with it—but next thing you know, he was worshipping their wicked gods to please them (1 Kings 11:3–9; Nehemiah 13:26).

Later on, most Jews ended up worshipping pagan gods. This made God so angry that He allowed the Babylonians to attack Israel and take the people from their land for 70 years. Now that God had again shown mercy to the Jews and allowed them to return to their homeland, Ezra didn't want to see them fall back into idol worship.

WHY WAS IT SO IMPORTANT TO BUILD A WALL AROUND JERUSALEM?

The Jews were back in their own land and living in Jerusalem, but they were in great trouble because the walls of the city were broken down (Nehemiah 1:3). There were lots of Samaritans and Ammonites and Arabs and Philistines living around them who were harassing them. If their enemies attacked, the Jews needed to be able to flee inside a city with high stone walls around it to be safe. As long as Jerusalem's walls were broken down, they had no refuge.

Also, they needed to protect God's temple from enemies who despised God. That's why when Nehemiah became governor, he made it his first priority to rebuild the city's walls.

Daniel had prophesied that the wall would "be built again. . .in troublesome times" (Daniel 9:25 NKJV), and it was.

Then Eliashib the high priest rose up with his brethren the priests and they built the Sheep Gate. They consecrated it and set its doors; they consecrated it as far as the Tower of the Hundred, as far as the Tower of Hananel. And next to him the men of Jericho built. And next to them Zaccur the son of Imri built. And the sons of Hassenaah built the Fish Gate; they laid its beams and set its doors, its bolts, and its bars. And next to them Meremoth the son of Uriah, son of Hakkoz repaired. And next to them Meshullam the son of Berechiah, son of Meshezabel repaired. And next to them Zadok the son of Baana repaired. And next to them the Tekoites repaired. . . .

NEHEMIAH 3:1–5 RSV

If you visit the Holy Lands today, you'll see walls like this around the "old city" of Jerusalem.

WHY DID SOME PARENTS IN OLD TESTAMENT TIMES SELL THEIR CHILDREN AS SLAVES?......

Some parents sold their children as slaves because they were desperately poor and had no other way to get money for food or to pay their debts (2 Kings 4:1). Slavery is a terrible thing, but at least Jewish masters weren't allowed to make Jewish servants work too hard or do humiliating work. Also, the law said that Jewish servants had to be set free after seven years (Exodus 21:2; Leviticus 25:39–43).

Some parents complained to Nehemiah that they had been forced to sell their sons and daughters as slaves because rich Jews had taken over their farms—making them even poorer. And instead of giving them interest-free loans, the rich Jews had been charging them interest, forcing them even deeper into debt.

Nehemiah was furious and told the people that they hadn't paid to free Jewish slaves from the heathen just to see their children sold as slaves to fellow Jews. He demanded that the rich give the poor back their lands and stop charging interest (Nehemiah 5:1–12).

Now the men and their wives raised a great outcry against their Jewish brothers. Some were saying, "We and our sons and daughters are numerous; in order for us to eat and stay alive, we must get grain." Others were saying, "We are mortgaging our fields, our vineyards and our homes to get grain during the famine." Still others were saying, "We have had to borrow money to pay the king's tax on our fields and vineyards. Although we are of the same flesh and blood as our countrymen and though our sons are as good as theirs, yet we have to subject our sons and daughters to slavery. Some of our daughters have already been enslaved, but we are powerless, because our fields and our vineyards belong to others."

NEHEMIAH 5:1–5 NIV

Two girls protest the "slavery" of American children in 1909. . .the conditions that forced some families to send young kids into the workplace. Eventually, laws were made to prohibit "child labor." Jewish families of Old Testament times would have approved!

Why is God never mentioned in the book of Esther?

The word *God* or *Lord* appears in every book of the Bible except for the book of Esther. Some people worry that this means the book of Esther wasn't inspired by God. Or they think that Esther isn't a very spiritual book. Yet when you read it, you see that it is a very inspired book. When Esther and all the Jews were facing a life-and-death situation, they fasted for three days (Esther 4:15–16). They weren't fasting to lose weight; they were fasting and praying desperately for God to help them. In Jewish culture, fasting always meant "a fast before the LORD" (Jeremiah 36:9 NKJV). The good news is that God answered their prayers and saved the Jews from their enemies.

Mordecai talks with Esther, in a 1685 painting by Aert de Gelder.

Job, diseased and depressed, gets some advice from his wife: "Curse God and die!" (Job 2:9 NIV). It was bad advice, to be sure—but don't forget that she was driven insane with grief. Not only was her husband terribly sick; she'd also lost her 10 kids and all the family wealth.

WHY DID GOD ALLOW JOB TO SUFFER SO MUCH?

Job was a righteous man who tried his best to please God. The Lord in turn blessed Job with wealth and health, and put a protective barrier around him and everything he owned. The devil wanted to bring Job trouble and sickness but couldn't get through, so he argued that Job only feared God because God had blessed him. The devil insisted that if God took away Job's wealth and health, Job would curse Him (Job 1:1–12; 2:1–7).

God hated to see Job suffer, but to prove Satan wrong, He allowed Job to be tested. Job passed the tests and came out even stronger and more blessed than ever (Job 42:12–16).

God also allowed Satan to test the apostle Peter. Even though Peter failed the test and denied Jesus, in the end he, too, came out stronger and more pure-hearted and became the leader of the disciples (Luke 22:31–34; Acts 2:14).

"Naked I came from my mother's womb, and naked I will depart. The LORD gave and the LORD has taken away; may the name of the LORD be praised. In all this, Job did not sin by charging God with wrongdoing.

JOB 1:21–22 NIV

WERE JOB'S THREE FRIENDS RIGHT WHEN THEY SAID GOD WAS JUDGING JOB FOR HIS SINS?

No. They were wrong. Job was a righteous man who loved God. The Lord allowed Job to suffer because He knew that it would make Job a more deeply spiritual man. However, God *does* punish people for their sins. When people ignore God, He allows trouble to come into their lives. When they obey God, He blesses them. When they disobey, He judges them (Deuteronomy 28).

Job's friends knew these basic spiritual laws, so they assumed that God must be punishing Job. Even though they couldn't think of anything Job had done wrong, they insisted that there must be *some* sin! They then began falsely accusing Job of all kinds of terrible things.

Finally, a fourth friend became angry with the other three because they had condemned Job even though they couldn't prove he'd done anything wrong (Job 32:3).

The boastful may not stand before thy eyes; thou hatest all evildoers. Thou destroyest those who speak lies; the LORD abhors bloodthirsty and deceitful men.
PSALM 5:5–6 RSV

IF GOD IS LOVE, WHY DO THE PSALMS SAY THAT GOD HATES EVILDOERS?

The Bible tells us that "God is love" (1 John 4:8) and that God loved us so much that He sent Jesus to die for us (John 3:16). All people are sinners, yet God loves people even while they're sinning (Romans 3:23; 5:8). Yet the Bible also clearly states, "Thou hatest all evildoers. . . . The LORD abhors bloodthirsty and deceitful men" (Psalm 5:5–6 RSV).

How can God love sinners but hate evildoers? There's a difference. Some people sin from time to time, some people sin often, but *some* people are thoroughly wicked: They hate God, delight to do evil, and work hard at it all day long. They are sadistic, bloodthirsty people who enjoy murdering and causing pain. These are the evildoers God hates.

And yet, if they repent and turn from their evil ways, God can save even the wickedest people—like the apostle Paul (Acts 26:9–11; 1 Timothy 1:15).

A lightning bolt is a common image used for God's anger. . . just like King David wrote in 2 Samuel 22:15 (NIV)— "He shot arrows and scattered the enemies, bolts of lightning and routed them."

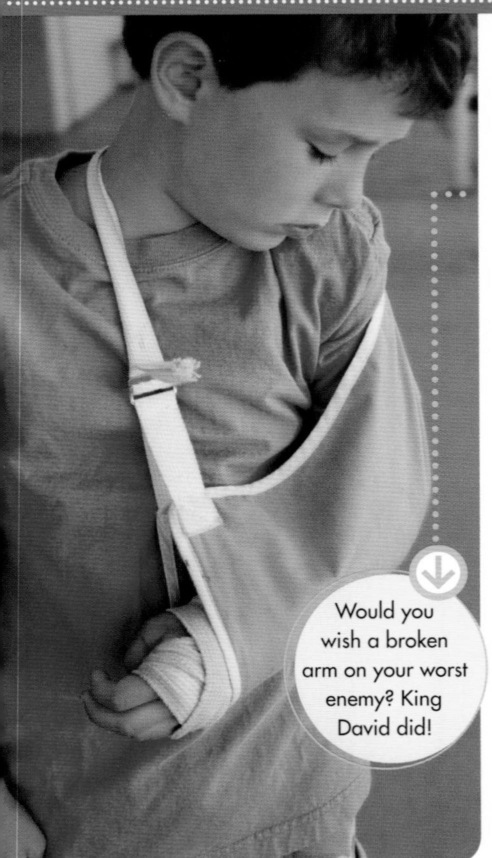

Would you wish a broken arm on your worst enemy? King David did!

WHY DID DAVID PRAY MEAN PRAYERS, SUCH AS, "GOD, BREAK THE ARMS OF THE WICKED"?

Break thou the arm of the wicked and evildoer; seek out his wickedness till thou find none.

Psalm 10:15 RSV

David prayed such a strong prayer for a very good reason. He wasn't praying against people who had simply knocked his books over or had said something mean to offend him. He was praying against hardened criminals. If you read the verses before this one, you will see that these men hunted down the weak, praised the greedy, cursed the Lord, proudly thought they were invincible, constantly told lies, threatened others, set ambushes to murder the innocent, and dragged off their helpless victims and crushed them. And while their victims were crying out to God, the wicked laughed, "God will never notice!" (Psalm 10:1–13 TNIV).

Of course David prayed, "Break the arms of the wicked and the evildoers!" If their arms were broken, they wouldn't be able to keep doing so much evil.

IF YOU TRULY LOVE GOD, WILL HE KEEP ALL TROUBLE OUT OF YOUR LIFE?

The righteous cry out, and the Lord hears them; he delivers them from all their troubles.

Psalm 34:17 NIV

David said, "The righteous call to the Lord, and he listens; he rescues them from all their troubles" (Psalm 34:17 GNT). Some Christians think—or they wish!—that this means that if they love God and live righteously, He will keep all trouble out of their lives. They then feel as if God has let them down when they go through periods of trouble. But this verse isn't saying our lives will always be easy. In fact, only two verses later, the Bible says, "Good people suffer *many* troubles, but the Lord saves them from them all" (Psalm 34:19 GNT, emphasis added). As a Christian, you can expect to face many troubles (Acts 14:22). It may

take time, and you may have to endure some troubles for a while, but God will "save" you from all of them—when He takes you to heaven, where there is no trouble at all!

The apostle Paul loved God—but he never escaped the problems of life: "Five times I received from the Jews the forty lashes minus one. Three times I was beaten with rods, once I was stoned, three times I was shipwrecked, I spent a night and a day in the open sea, I have been constantly on the move. I have been in danger from rivers, in danger from bandits, in danger from my own countrymen, in danger from Gentiles; in danger in the city, in danger in the country, in danger at sea; and in danger from false brothers" (2 CORINTHIANS 11:24–26 NIV).

WILL GOD ALWAYS SUPPLY EVERYTHING YOU WANT?....

David said, "Take delight in the LORD, and he will give you the desires of your heart" (Psalm 37:4 RSV). He also said, "Those who seek the LORD lack no good thing" (Psalm 34:10 RSV).

Delight yourself in the LORD and he will give you the desires of your heart.
PSALM 37:4 NIV

These verses seem to promise that if you love God and seek Him, He will give you whatever "good thing" you pray for—so if you desire a new PSP or iPod, God will see to it that you get it, right? Not necessarily. When you truly delight in God and His ways, your desires *change* from wanting fun things just for

No, God is not Santa Claus!

your own personal pleasure to wanting what God knows is best for you.

Besides, as Paul said, "My God will supply every need of yours" (Philippians 4:19 RSV). God will supply what you *need*, but He wants you to be content with what He gives you, whether it's exactly what you wanted or not, whether it's little or much (Philippians 4:11–12; 1 Timothy 6:6–9).

WOULD GOD REALLY "CAST AWAY" SOMEONE WHO BELIEVES IN HIM?

Because of your great wrath, for you have taken me up and thrown me aside.

PSALM 102:10 TNIV

Ever feel all alone? Lots of people in the Bible felt that way, too—but God has promised He'll always be with us.

In Psalm 102, a believer cries out to God, "You have lifted me up and cast me away" (verse 10 NKJV). Does this mean that God casts people away forever, not letting them enter heaven? No. The title of the psalm reads, "A prayer of the afflicted." When you read the entire psalm, it's clear that "afflicted" refers to people who are sick or being oppressed by their enemies; people who *feel* as if God is judging them, picking them up, and throwing them away.

Job felt the same way when he was sick. He said that God had picked him up and tossed him into the mud (Job 30:19). Had God actually done such a thing? No, but when God allowed Job to suffer, Job *felt* as if God had discarded him. In actuality, God has promised never to leave us nor forsake us (Hebrews 13:5).

Praise ye the LORD. Blessed is the man that feareth the LORD, that delighteth greatly in his commandments.

PSALM 112:1 KJV

WHY SHOULD WE FEAR GOD? ISN'T HE OUR LOVING FATHER?

David says, "Blessed is the man who fears the LORD" (Psalm 112:1 NIV). Many people wonder why it's a *good* thing to fear God. After all, God is compassionate and loves us; He's our heavenly Father and only wants good for us, so why should we fear Him? Isn't fear a negative thing?

No, not always. In this case "fear" means having a very healthy respect for God.

God is a loving God, but He is all-powerful and He hates sin, so we are very wise if we fear to disobey Him. You wouldn't throw stones at a tiger and then crawl into its cage, right? Having a healthy respect for the tiger is a wise thing. Well, God is far more powerful, and He tells us, "The fear of the LORD is the *beginning* of wisdom" (Proverbs 9:10 NIV, emphasis added). Yes, God loves you and sent Jesus to die for your sins, but it's not wise to deliberately anger Him.

WHY DO THE PSALMS TELL US OVER AND OVER TO PRAISE GOD? DOES GOD ENJOY HEARING US CONSTANTLY TELL HIM HOW GREAT HE IS?

God is so immensely powerful that He created the entire universe—every star, every planet, and every living thing. When we understand how mind-bogglingly awesome God is, and that He's the one who created us, it dawns on us that we should worship Him. And it's natural to *say* what we're thinking and praise Him.

Praising God is not like praising other people to make them feel good about themselves. God doesn't have an ego problem. We praise God because all the wonderful things we're saying about Him are *true*!

The most important commandment is this: "Love the Lord your God with all your heart and with all your soul and with all your mind" (Matthew 22:37 TNIV). If you love God *that* much, you're already worshipping Him. And if you love God with everything in you and appreciate all that He's done for you, how can you *help* but praise Him (2 Corinthians 4:13)?

Praise ye the LORD. Praise God in his sanctuary: praise him in the firmament of his power. Praise him for his mighty acts: praise him according to his excellent greatness. Praise him with the sound of the trumpet: praise him with the psaltery and harp. Praise him with the timbrel and dance: praise him with stringed instruments and organs. Praise him upon the loud cymbals: praise him upon the high sounding cymbals. Let every thing that hath breath praise the LORD. Praise ye the LORD.

PSALM 150 KJV

WHAT IS WISDOM?

> *The beginning of wisdom is this: Get wisdom. Though it cost all you have, get understanding.*
> PROVERBS 4:7 TNIV

Solomon writes, "Getting wisdom is the most important thing you can do" (Proverbs 4:7 GNT). Why is getting wisdom so important? And what exactly is wisdom? Well, wisdom is more than just getting knowledge or memorizing facts. If that were all it was, then studying history or science would be the most important thing you could do. Those things are important, but getting wisdom is the most important.

When Solomon prayed for wisdom, he asked God for "a discerning heart. . .to distinguish between right and wrong" (1 Kings 3:9 TNIV). To "discern" means to see into the heart of a matter. Real wisdom means to speak not only with knowledge but also with love. Anyone can memorize facts and figures, but a wise person understands how to use knowledge to solve problems and help others.

SHOULD MODERN WOMEN AND GIRLS BEHAVE LIKE WOMEN OF ANCIENT TIMES?

> *Charm is deceitful and beauty is passing, but a woman who fears the LORD, she shall be praised.*
> PROVERBS 31:30 NKJV

Some Christians believe that the Bible teaches that a husband should have the final say in any discussion—that wives should always submit to their husbands (Colossians 3:18). They believe that, even today, women are not supposed to teach men, nor even to speak out loud in church (1 Timothy 2:12; 1 Corinthians 14:34). Some even insist that women must cover their heads when they pray (1 Corinthians 11:5–6).

Other Christians agree that that's the way it (mostly) was in olden days, but that even in the Old Testament, women had freedom and led God's people (Proverbs 31; Judges 4:1–8). They especially believe that ever since Jesus died, there is no difference in the roles of males and females (Galatians 3:28), that husbands and wives are partners, "heirs together" of eternal life (1 Peter 3:7).

Different churches have different views, so it would be good to ask what your parents and pastors believe. They have probably thought about it a great deal.

These Amish girls in Lancaster, Pennsylvania, live an "old-fashioned" lifestyle compared to most modern women.

"Meaningless! Meaningless!" says the Teacher.
"Utterly meaningless! Everything is meaningless."
ECCLESIASTES 1:2 NIV

WHY IS ECCLESIASTES SUCH A SAD, DISCOURAGING BOOK?

Solomon writes, "Everything is meaningless. . . . I have seen all the things that are done under the sun; all of them are meaningless, a chasing after the wind" (Ecclesiastes 1:2, 14 TNIV). He asks what people gain from a lifetime of work, because one day they'll die and leave it behind. It's like chasing the wind: If you try to grab the air, in the end you have nothing. If this world is all there is, what's the point in living?

This life is *not* all there is. Solomon says at the end of Ecclesiastes that we should love and obey God, because one day God will judge us for every deed—good and evil (12:13–14).

So do good and be satisfied with what you have, "for we brought nothing into this world, and it is certain we can carry nothing out" (1 Timothy 6:7 NKJV). That's why Jesus said to store up spiritual riches in heaven rather than hoarding material things on earth (Matthew 6:19–21).

For Christians, the cemetery isn't the end—it's just the beginning of real life!

IF KNOWLEDGE BRINGS GRIEF AND SORROW, WHY GO TO SCHOOL?......

For with much wisdom comes much sorrow; the more knowledge, the more grief.

ECCLESIASTES 1:18 NIV

Solomon writes, "With much wisdom comes much sorrow; the more knowledge, the more grief" (Ecclesiastes 1:18 NIV). Some people ask, "If that's the case, why go to school? Why learn anything if knowledge just makes you sad?" But does that mean it's best to be ignorant?

No, that's not what Solomon meant. Knowledge is good. You need to get a good education, and Solomon himself says that wisdom is the most important thing you can have (Proverbs 4:7).

But as you grow up, you learn, as Solomon did, that there is a lot of injustice in the world. Life is often not fair (Ecclesiastes 3:16–17; 4:1–3). Good people suffer poverty and are oppressed by corrupt governments. Innocent people die in earthquakes. Murders and robberies happen every day. Knowing that 12 x 10 = 120 won't make you sad; but watch enough news on TV, and it's bound to make you "wiser but sadder."

WHY DOES SOLOMON SAY THAT THERE ARE TIMES TO KILL, TO TEAR DOWN, AND TO HATE?........

For everything there is a season. . . .

ECCLESIASTES 3:1 RSV

Solomon said there is a time for everything, a time for every different kind of activity and emotional reaction. There is "a time to be born and a time to die. . .a time to weep and a time to laugh. . .a time to keep silence and a time to speak" (Ecclesiastes 3:2, 4, 7 NIV). These things are true, right? You shouldn't stay silent when it's time to speak up, but you shouldn't butt in and speak when something is none of your business.

Every year is filled with seasons—and so is every life. Ecclesiastes teaches that every human emotion and activity has its own "season."

Just so, there is also a time to build and a time to tear down old, rotten buildings that are no longer safe to live in. There is a time for our nation to be at peace with other nations, and there are times when our armed forces must go to war and fight. There is a time to love someone's good deeds and a time to hate evil deeds and injustice. We need the wisdom to know how to react in different circumstances.

Ew, gross! Why do grown-ups have to be so mushy? You'll figure it out in a few years. . . .

WHY DID SOLOMON WRITE A BOOK ALL ABOUT ROMANCE?

Solomon wrote the words to a very long song called the Song of Songs. Today we have just the words without the music. Solomon wrote this beautiful, imaginative love song for his wife, and—no surprise—men and women who are in love and married often get a lot out of reading it. They're glad to learn that God is okay with them feeling romantic and sighing and kissing. They're happy to read that physical love between a husband and wife is pure in God's eyes. Just as there is a time for everything, when you are older, there will be a time for the Song of Songs.

The Song—best of all songs—Solomon's song! The Woman: Kiss me—full on the mouth! Yes! For your love is better than wine, headier than your aromatic oils. The syllables of your name murmur like a meadow brook. No wonder everyone loves to say your name!
Song of Songs 1:1–3 MSG

This building, called the Hagia Maria Sion Abbey, stands atop Mount Zion today.

WHAT IS THE MOUNTAIN OF THE LORD'S HOUSE?

Mount Zion is a very small mountain—really just a hill—inside the city of Jerusalem, on which Solomon's temple was built. Because the temple was also called "the Lord's house," "the mountain of the Lord's house" referred to Mount Zion, where the temple stood.

Isaiah prophesied, "The mountain where the Temple stands will be the highest one of all, towering above all the hills" (Isaiah 2:2 GNT). Isaiah didn't mean that the temple mountain would erupt like a volcano and grow bigger. He was using symbolic language to describe God reigning over all the earth. Physically, Mount Zion is not big, but spiritually, it is the highest mountain on earth, because God will reign there.

Many peoples will come and say, "Come, let us go up to the mountain of the LORD, to the house of the God of Jacob. He will teach us his ways, so that we may walk in his paths." The law will go out from Zion, the word of the LORD from Jerusalem.

ISAIAH 2:3 NIV

Want to know your future? Don't go to a fortune-teller!

WHAT DOES THE BIBLE SAY ABOUT GOING TO MEDIUMS?

And when they say to you, "Seek those who are mediums and wizards, who whisper and mutter," should not a people seek their God? Should they seek the dead on behalf of the living?

ISAIAH 8:19 NKJV

Today many people think that going to a medium is harmless and even helpful, but God condemns this. He says, "Do not turn to mediums or seek out spiritists, for you will be defiled by them" (Leviticus 19:31 NIV). *Defiled* means to become filthy. God warns that He will turn against those who consult mediums (Leviticus 20:6).

The ancient Egyptians constantly sought advice from spirits. To prove that He was God, the Lord said He would foil the Egyptians' plans and punish them (Isaiah 19:3–4). King Saul lost the kingdom, and his life, for consulting a medium at Endor (1 Samuel 28:5–19).

God said, "When someone tells you to consult mediums and spiritists, who whisper and mutter, should not a people inquire of their God?" (Isaiah 8:19 TNIV). The answer, of course, is a definite "Yes!" Pray to God. Stay far away from mediums.

"By his wounds we are healed" (ISAIAH 53:5 NIV).

WHY DO PEOPLE SAY THAT ISAIAH 53 IS A PROPHECY ABOUT JESUS?

Isaiah was a prophet, and he spoke accurately about things that would happen in the future. Some things he prophesied came to pass during his lifetime; other prophecies were fulfilled after he died.

Isaiah's most amazing prophecy is recorded in Isaiah 53. It was written some 700 years before Jesus lived, yet it describes Jesus' trial, death, and burial in astonishing detail. It even describes why He died—to take away our sins.

In the New Testament, the Gospels describe

how Jesus fulfilled Isaiah's prophecy. Compare Isaiah 53:1 with John 12:38, and Isaiah 53:7 with Matthew 27:12–14. An early Christian named Philip declared that Isaiah 53:7–8 refers to Jesus (Acts 8:32–33)—and it does! If you've never read Isaiah 53, read it today.

Surely he hath borne our griefs, and carried our sorrows: yet we did esteem him stricken, smitten of God, and afflicted. But he was wounded for our transgressions, he was bruised for our iniquities: the chastisement of our peace was upon him; and with his stripes we are healed.

Isaiah 53:4–5 KJV

IF PEOPLE WON'T STOP SINNING, DOES GOD REFUSE TO HEAR THEIR PRAYERS?

Look! Listen! God's arm is not amputated—he can still save. God's ears are not stopped up—he can still hear. There's nothing wrong with God; the wrong is in you. Your wrongheaded lives caused the split between you and God. Your sins got between you so that he doesn't hear.

Isaiah 59:1–2 MSG

Yes, if by "hear" you mean hear *and answer*. God sees everything people do and hears everything they say. But when people rebel against God and stubbornly refuse to obey Him, if they keep on sinning, at some point God stops answering their prayers. The Bible says, "Your iniquities have separated you from your God; and your sins have hidden His face from you, so that He will not hear" (Isaiah 59:2 NKJV). Once they repent, however, God forgives them and answers their prayers again.

Don't be quick to judge people, though. Just because God isn't answering someone's prayer (yet) doesn't mean that person is sinning. Remember, that's what Job's friends falsely accused him of. Sometimes it simply takes *time* for prayer to be answered. Perhaps God is testing that person's faith. Or perhaps what they're asking for isn't God's will for them, but He still loves them very much.

However, if people know that they're displeasing God, then, yes, they need to stop displeasing Him.

WHY DID GOD LET THE PAGAN BABYLONIANS CONQUER HIS OWN PEOPLE, THE JEWS?

> *I am calling all the tribes of the kingdoms of the north, says the LORD; and they shall come and every one shall set his throne at the entrance of the gates of Jerusalem.*
>
> JEREMIAH 1:15 RSV

God had promised in Moses' day—before the Israelites even entered the Promised Land—that as long as His people loved Him and obeyed Him, He would bless them and protect them. At the same time, however, God warned the Israelites that if they disobeyed Him and began to worship other gods, He would judge them. He would allow enemies to invade and conquer them and even take them from their land (Deuteronomy 28).

The Jews knew God's warning but willfully chose to disobey Him and worship other gods. So the Lord brought the Babylonians to conquer them (Jeremiah 1:14–16). This punishment taught the Jews a very good lesson. After they returned to their land 70 years later, they were determined to worship only God.

WHY DIDN'T THE JEWS LISTEN TO THE PROPHET JEREMIAH?

> *I am ridiculed all day long; everyone mocks me.*
>
> JEREMIAH 20:7 NIV

Many Jews worshipped Baal and other gods, so they didn't want to listen to a prophet of God telling them that they should destroy their "evil idols" and worship only the Lord. Many who worshipped Ishtar—the Queen of Heaven—believed that this goddess was blessing them and argued that if they stopped worshipping her, they'd lose their blessings (Jeremiah 44:15–18). They'd actually lost out by not worshipping God!

Also, many people in Judah were still going through the motions of worshipping God, so they thought that everything was okay. But God said, "Judah has not turned to Me with her whole heart, but in pretense" (Jeremiah 3:10 NKJV). Jeremiah added, "They always speak well of you, yet they do not really care about you" (Jeremiah 12:2 GNT).

Worse yet, some false prophets proclaimed that God would still bless them and convinced the disobedient Jews that they didn't need to listen to Jeremiah or repent (Jeremiah 28).

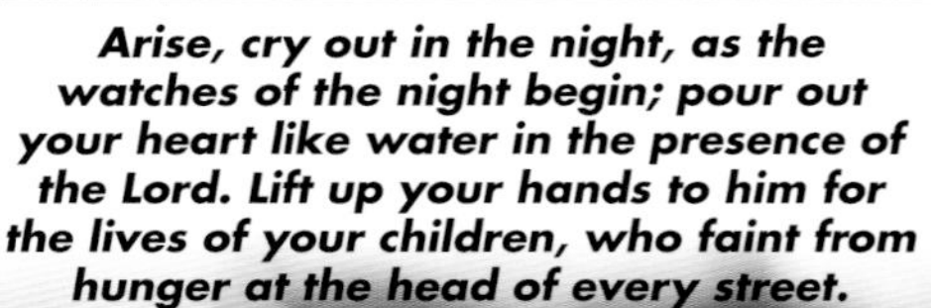

Arise, cry out in the night, as the watches of the night begin; pour out your heart like water in the presence of the Lord. Lift up your hands to him for the lives of your children, who faint from hunger at the head of every street.
LAMENTATIONS 2:19 NIV

IF GOD IS ALL-POWERFUL, WHY DOES HE ALLOW CHILDREN TO SUFFER?

Around the world, people are suffering and going hungry. In some nations, evil rulers fight wars that bring death and starvation to their people. Others foolishly waste money and cause poverty. If God is all-powerful, why doesn't He stop this? Why does He allow innocent people to suffer—even children? Well, God *will* set things right, when Jesus returns and rules righteously.

But what about disasters like droughts and earthquakes and the AIDS epidemic? Why does God allow such things? They happen because we live in an imperfect world. Rather than blame God for them, we need to pray. Jeremiah writes, "Pour out your heart like water before the presence of the Lord. . .for the lives of your children, who faint for hunger" (Lamentations 2:19 RSV).

God wants us to pray for those who suffer—*and* He wants us to help them. That's why Christians should work to overcome poverty, help discover cures for diseases, and find peaceful ways to settle conflicts. And that's why we should donate money, if we can, to help victims of earthquakes, famines, and other disasters (see James 2:15–16; 1 John 3:17–18). God will reward us for helping others (Matthew 25:31–40).

Many children around the world go to bed hungry, sick, and alone. Have you thanked God for all He's given you?

I am the man who has seen affliction by the rod of His wrath. He has led me and made me walk in darkness and not in light. Surely He has turned His hand against me time and time again throughout the day. He has aged my flesh and my skin, and broken my bones. He has besieged me and surrounded me with bitterness and woe.

LAMENTATIONS 3:1–5 NKJV

IS IT OKAY TO COMPLAIN TO GOD WHEN WE PRAY?

The apostle Paul said, "Do everything without complaining," and "Ask God for what you need, always asking him with a thankful heart" (Philippians 2:14; 4:6 GNT). The Lord doesn't enjoy hearing selfish prayers, such as, "God, if you don't give me a new game system, I won't love you anymore."

However, God understands that when some people go through very difficult experiences, they think that He doesn't love them anymore. He understands that when they're in pain, they cry out, asking why He allows them to suffer. Men in the Bible, such as Job and Ethan the Ezrahite, prayed gloomy prayers when they were suffering (Job 3; 9; Psalm 89:38–51), yet they still praised God (Job 1:21; Psalm 89:52).

Jeremiah complained that God had shut out his prayer and attacked him—yet he concluded that God was good and compassionate (Lamentations 3:1–36).

God doesn't like to hear complaints, but He also knows if you're only pretending to be trusting and cheerful. He'd rather you prayed an *honest* prayer, even when you're feeling miserable.

There were figures resembling four living beings. . . .
EZEKIEL 1:5 NASB

WHAT ARE CHERUBIM?

When Ezekiel had a vision of God on His throne, he saw four cherubim around Him. Each of the cherubim had a body like a man, but with four heads: one head like a man, another like a lion, another like an ox, and another like an eagle. The cherubim had four wings, and their entire bodies were covered with eyes. They had feet like oxen and hands like men, looked like burning coals of fire, and moved like flashes of lightning (Ezekiel 1:4–14).

When John saw them, the cherubim stood around God's throne like royal, ceremonial guards—sort of like the lions some kings kept chained near their thrones. The cherubim also never stop praising God (Revelation 4:6–9).

Many people think that cherubim are a kind of angel, but the Bible actually refers to them as "beasts" or "creatures" or "living beings." It would be best to think of the cherubim as awesome spiritual beings. (See also Ezekiel 10:1–17.)

Many people think of a "cherub" as a cute little angel with wings—but that's not how the Bible describes them!

In a way, Ezekiel was an actor—playing a role God had given him for the benefit of all who would watch him. Sadly, very few cared about his message.

WHY DID THE PROPHET EZEKIEL DO SO MANY STRANGE THINGS?

When you read the book of Ezekiel, you see how many unusual things God told Ezekiel to do. First, Ezekiel made a tiny, detailed model of the Babylonian army camped around Jerusalem. Then he lay on his left side for 390 days (that's more than a year!) staring at it. Next, he made a fire from cow dung and cooked his food over it. He also cut off his beard and shaved his head bald. Then Ezekiel dug a hole through the wall of his house and carried all his stuff out through the hole. Finally, when Ezekiel's beloved wife died, God told him not to publicly mourn her—so Ezekiel didn't (Ezekiel 4; 5; 12; 24:15–27).

God had Ezekiel do these startling "skits" to get the Jews' attention. The prophet Jeremiah had warned them for many years what would happen to them if they continued to disobey God, but the Jews hadn't listened. So God gave Ezekiel not only messages to speak but messages to act out. Ezekiel told the disobedient Jews that what he was doing was a symbol of what God would do to them (Ezekiel 12:11).

Dig thou through the wall in their sight, and carry out thereby. In their sight shalt thou bear it upon thy shoulders, and carry it forth in the twilight: thou shalt cover thy face, that thou see not the ground: for I have set thee for a sign unto the house of Israel. And I did so as I was commanded: I brought forth my stuff by day, as stuff for captivity, and in the even I digged through the wall with mine hand; I brought it forth in the twilight, and I bare it upon my shoulder in their sight. And in the morning came the word of the LORD unto me, saying, Son of man, hath not the house of Israel, the rebellious house, said unto thee, What doest thou? Say thou unto them, Thus saith the Lord GOD; This burden concerneth the prince in Jerusalem, and all the house of Israel that are among them. Say, I am your sign: like as I have done, so shall it be done unto them: they shall remove and go into captivity. And the prince that is among them shall bear upon his shoulder in the twilight, and shall go forth: they shall dig through the wall to carry out thereby: he shall cover his face, that he see not the ground with his eyes.

EZEKIEL 12:5–12 KJV

WHAT DOES EZEKIEL'S WEIRD VISION ABOUT DRY BONES MEAN? . . . .

This was one of the weirdest visions Ezekiel ever had, yet it is filled with beautiful meaning. Through the Holy Spirit, God took Ezekiel to a valley full of scattered, dry bones. Then, when Ezekiel spoke the word of the Lord to them, the bones came together into skeletons and were covered with flesh. Then life came into the bodies and they stood up, alive again!

Here's what it means: The Israelites had been carried far away from their land and were living in exile in Babylon. They were saying, "Our bones are dried up and our hope is gone" (Ezekiel 37:11 NIV). It was true. They hadn't been listening to the word of the Lord and were spiritually dried up and dead. But God showed them that even though it looked like all hope was gone, He still loved them and was going to do a miracle: They would one day hear and obey God, and He would bring them back to their own land—and He did!

And as I was prophesying, there was a noise, a rattling sound, and the bones came together, bone to bone. I looked, and tendons and flesh appeared on them and skin covered them, but there was no breath in them. Then he said to me, "Prophesy to the breath; prophesy, son of man, and say to it, 'This is what the Sovereign LORD says: Come, breath, from the four winds and breathe into these slain, that they may live.'" So I prophesied as he commanded me, and breath entered them; they came to life and stood up on their feet—a vast army.

EZEKIEL 37:7–10 TNIV

This engraving of Ezekiel's vision of dry bones was made by Gustave Dore around 1870.

WHY DID DANIEL AND HIS FRIENDS REFUSE TO EAT FOOD FROM THE KING'S TABLE?....

The Babylonian official taking care of the four Jewish youths couldn't understand why they wouldn't eat the delicious food prepared by the king's own cooks or drink the best wine in Babylon. Why did they say that the king's food was defiled and choose to eat only vegetables and drink water? There were two good reasons.

First, the Babylonians ate many unclean animals that God had forbidden the Jews to eat. And even clean animals like sheep and cattle had not been slaughtered and bled properly (Leviticus 11; 17:10–14).

Second, the king's food was defiled because the Babylonians worshipped demonic gods, and a portion of the meat and wine was given to the idols, dedicating the entire meal to their idols. Since Daniel and his friends were dedicated to the true God, they didn't want to eat such food.

But Daniel resolved that he would not defile himself with the king's rich food, or with the wine which he drank; therefore he asked the chief of the eunuchs to allow him not to defile himself. . . . Then Daniel said to the steward whom the chief of the eunuchs had appointed over Daniel, Hananiah, Mishael, and Azariah; "Test your servants for ten days; let us be given vegetables to eat and water to drink."

DANIEL 1:8, 11–12 RSV

Daniel turning down King Nebuchadnezzar's food would be like kids today saying "No thanks" to a pizza buffet. But Daniel knew he was making the right decision.

WHAT DO DANIEL'S VISIONS AND PROPHECIES MEAN?

"The dream is certain, and its interpretation is sure."

DANIEL 2:45 NKJV

Many believe that some of Daniel's prophecies described Alexander the Great, the Greek conqueror who lived about 300 years after Daniel.

God gave Daniel several dreams, visions, and prophecies, and though each was different, they all described the great empires that would arise in the future. The Babylonian Empire ruled the Middle East during most of Daniel's life. Then came the Persians. The Grecian Empire arose next, and finally the Roman Empire took over.

This is all ancient history now, but in Daniel's day, most of these empires were still in the future. When the prophecies came true, people were amazed that God had accurately described these empires *before* they conquered the world.

Most Christians believe that the book of Daniel also gives a detailed description of the worldwide empire of the Antichrist, which will conquer the entire world during the end times.

HOW DID DANIEL SURVIVE IN A DEN FULL OF LIONS?

Then the king commanded, and they brought Daniel, and cast him into the den of lions.

DANIEL 6:16 KJV

It wasn't because Daniel was the "lion whisperer." He wasn't. Besides, their keepers made sure that those lions were kept ferociously hungry. As soon as Daniel was pulled up out of the pit, the king commanded that Daniel's *enemies* be thrown in—and before they even reached the floor of the pit, the lions attacked and killed them.

Daniel explained to the king how he had survived the night in the lions' den: "My God sent his angel and shut the lions' mouths" (Daniel 6:22 RSV).

Of course, many Christians in the early church *were* killed by lions in the Roman arena. God could have shut those lions' mouths as well, but He didn't. God knew that the way that the Christian martyrs died, gladly giving up their lives for Jesus' sake, would be a great witness to the Romans who were watching. (See Revelation 12:11.)

DOES GOD STILL SPEAK TO PEOPLE IN DREAMS AND VISIONS?

In the Bible, God often gave people messages or warnings through dreams and visions—and He can still do that today if He chooses. However, it's important to remember that just because you had an unusual dream doesn't mean that God is speaking to you. After all, even dogs dream.

Most of our dreams are jumbled-together bits and pieces of things that we have been thinking about during the day. Often we dream about things we really want (Ecclesiastes 5:3, 7; Isaiah 29:8). It would be a mistake to think that such dreams are a message from God.

Some Christians think that now that the Bible is written, God doesn't speak to believers through dreams and visions anymore. Other Christians believe that God is still perfectly able to give a message that way if He chooses. However, if a message in a dream doesn't line up with what the Bible says, don't pay attention to it.

In the first year of Belshazzar king of Babylon, Daniel had a dream, and visions passed through his mind as he was lying on his bed. He wrote down the substance of his dream.

DANIEL 7:1 NIV

Artist Michael Willmann (1630–1706) painted this picture of Jacob's dream of angels climbing up and down a ladder to heaven. God definitely spoke to people by dreams in Bible times. He can today, too—though we have the Bible now to tell us what He wants us to know.

DID JONAH REALLY SPEND THREE DAYS AND THREE NIGHTS IN THE BELLY OF A GREAT FISH?

> *Now the LORD provided a huge fish to swallow Jonah, and Jonah was in the belly of the fish three days and three nights.*
>
> JONAH 1:17 TNIV

Yes, he did, though it's not certain what kind of fish this was. The Hebrew word in Jonah 1:17 and the Greek word in Matthew 12:40 both mean "great aquatic animal"—so it could have been a sperm whale or a giant white shark—or a whale shark, which can grow up to 50 feet long. All of these giant sea animals have swallowed animals as big as humans.

Another thing, the expression "three days and three nights" can also refer to one whole day and *parts* of two other days. So Jonah didn't necessarily spend a full 72 hours in the sea creature's belly. He could have spent 40 hours—which probably still seemed like forever—and had enough oxygen to survive until the sea creature vomited him up.

Don't forget also that "the LORD had prepared a great fish to swallow up Jonah" (Jonah 1:17 KJV). So even though God used a natural creature, He performed a miracle to make sure Jonah survived the voyage.

Could this be the last thing Jonah saw before he was swalled by the "great fish"?

DOES GOD ACTUALLY CHANGE HIS MIND ABOUT THINGS?

God doesn't change His mind like people do. Some people say one thing, but when they find out the full facts, they change their mind. Or they promise they'll do something, and then change their mind and don't keep their word. God always knows the full facts before He speaks. He always keeps His word.

God says clearly that He will bless people for obeying and punish them for disobeying. However, He *also* says that if a wicked man repents and changes his ways, he will live (Ezekiel 18:1–23). This is because God is a compassionate God and loves to show mercy instead of judgment (Psalm 103:8–10).

God showed mercy to the city of Nineveh when the people there repented. God sent Jonah to Nineveh and told him to warn them that within 40 days Nineveh would be destroyed. Yet when the people turned from their evil ways, God relented—had compassion—and didn't bring the disaster He'd threatened to bring upon them (Jonah 3; see also Exodus 32:1–14).

> *[God] relented and did not bring on them the destruction he had threatened.*
>
> JONAH 3:10 TNIV

WHY DOES GOD SOMETIMES TAKE SO LONG TO ANSWER OUR PRAYERS?.....

> *How long, O LORD, must I call for help, but you do not listen? Or cry out to you, "Violence!" but you do not save? Why do you make me look at injustice? Why do you tolerate wrong? Destruction and violence are before me; there is strife, and conflict abounds.*
>
> HABAKKUK 1:2–3 NIV

Habakkuk once complained, "Oh Lord, how long must I call for help before you listen?" (Habakkuk 1:2 GNT). In the book of Revelation, even the Christian martyrs felt that God was taking a very long time to answer prayer (6:10–11). God told them to wait a little longer and He would answer.

When we experience a huge problem or an injustice or we feel we just can't stand a situation much longer, we want God to answer our prayers right away. But when He doesn't answer quickly, our patience is tested. And that's one reason why God sometimes makes us wait: to teach us more faith and patience.

God also wants to teach us to be persistent and never give up. That's why Jesus said, "Men always ought to pray and not lose heart" (Luke 18:1 NKJV). In 1 Kings 18:41–45, when God didn't immediately answer Elijah's prayers, the prophet kept praying and praying and praying until God finally did answer.

WILL GOD REFUSE TO BLESS US IF WE DON'T GIVE MONEY TO THE CHURCH?

> *Thus says the* Lord *of hosts, "Consider your ways! Go up to the mountains, bring wood and rebuild the temple, that I may be pleased with it and be glorified," says the* Lord.
>
> Haggai 1:7–8 NASB

In Ezra's day, after the Jews started to rebuild God's temple, their enemies forced them to stop (Ezra 3:8–10; 4:23–24). Some 16 years later, the Jews had basically accepted that they would never have a place to worship God. They built their own houses and planted fields and vineyards but no longer tried to rebuild God's house. So God sent a drought to get their attention. The prophet Haggai told the people they had to rebuild the temple if they expected God to bless them.

In the New Testament, Christians met in homes and had no church buildings, so no one was asked to give to a building fund. The offerings they gave were used to feed and care for the poor (Romans 15:26; 16:3–5).

However, if your family meets in a church building, it is only fair that you contribute something to help build it and keep a roof overhead. God won't necessarily refuse to bless you if you don't, but the Bible does say that He will bless you for giving as much as you're able (2 Corinthians 8:12; 9:6–8).

Many churches hand out envelopes to remind their members to give regularly. And though giving is good, remember that you'll never be able to buy God's love with money—He showed His great love for you by sending Jesus to die on the cross for your sins!

HOW COULD A VIRGIN BECOME PREGNANT?

The Bible clearly states that Mary's fiancé, Joseph, hadn't slept with her yet, so we know that Joseph wasn't Jesus' actual father. We also know that Mary was a virgin and that she hadn't slept with any *other* man, so God did a miracle to get Mary pregnant (Matthew 1:18–20).

We don't really know how He did it. In fact, Mary herself didn't see how it was possible. When the angel told her that she would conceive and give birth to the Son of God, she asked, "How will this be, since I am a virgin?" The angel simply explained, "The Holy Spirit will come on you, and the power of the Most High will overshadow you" (Luke 1:34–35 TNIV).

Since the Holy Spirit is the Spirit of God, and God created all human beings to begin with, He certainly had the power to cause Mary to become pregnant and give birth to baby Jesus.

Then Joseph woke up. He did exactly what God's angel commanded in the dream: He married Mary. But he did not consummate the marriage until she had the baby. He named the baby Jesus.

MATTHEW 1:24–25 MSG

Some think Mary might have been as young as an early teenager when God called her to become the mother of Jesus.

WHAT DOES IT MEAN TO REPENT?

> *In those days came John the Baptist, preaching in the wilderness of Judaea, and saying, Repent ye: for the kingdom of heaven is at hand.*
>
> MATTHEW 3:1–2 KJV

The Bible talks a lot about our need to repent. John the Baptist preached, "Repent, for the kingdom of heaven is at hand!" and Jesus preached, "Repent, and believe in the gospel" (Matthew 3:2; Mark 1:15 NKJV). Later, the apostle Peter also told people to repent (Acts 2:38).

Think of repentance as a U-turn—you're going in one direction (the wrong one) and you completely turn around to the right way!

What exactly does the word *repent* mean? Well, the Greek word *metanoeō*, from which we get our English word, means "to have another mind." In other words, to repent means to totally change your way of thinking, to stop thinking that sin and selfishness are cool, and to start obeying God.

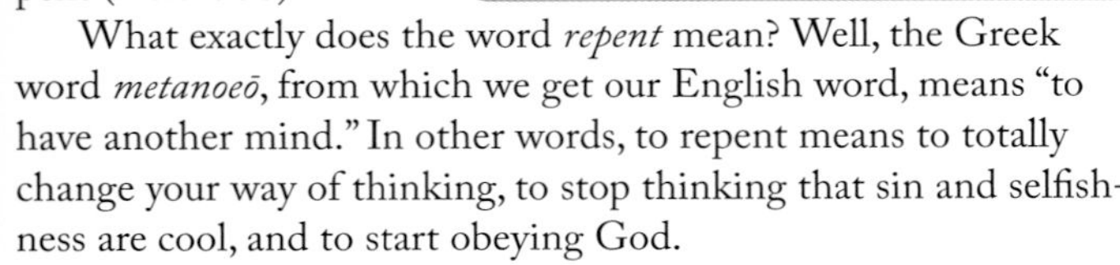

The first thing to do when you repent is to believe in the gospel, and when you do that, Jesus' Spirit comes into your life and gives you the power to change your way of thinking. And when you change your old selfish ways and start living a new life, your actions will be the "good fruit" that *shows* that you've had a change of heart (Luke 3:8–14).

WHY DID JESUS SAY, "IF YOUR RIGHT EYE CAUSES YOU TO SIN, PLUCK IT OUT AND THROW IT AWAY"?

> *"If your right eye causes you to sin, pluck it out and throw it away; it is better that you lose one of your members than that your whole body be thrown into hell."*
>
> MATTHEW 5:29 RSV

Seems like pirates are always missing an eye for some reason—but probably not because they were following Jesus' advice in Matthew 5:29!

If you don't have the willpower to control what you look at, you're going to end up in trouble, because "the lust of the eyes" (1 John 2:16 KJV) is one of the world's biggest problems. For example, guys can't help but notice a beautiful girl pass by. That's not a problem. But if they allow themselves to *desire* her, their minds will fill with lustful thoughts, which might lead to sinful actions.

This applies to other things as well. For example, if a girl desires someone else's iPod, she may begin coveting (lusting for) what belongs to someone else and end up stealing it. That's why the Bible says, "You shall not covet. . .*anything* that belongs to your neighbor" (Exodus 20:17 NIV, emphasis added).

So how do you stop "the lust of the eyes"? Literally gouge them out? No. Jesus was speaking in a parable. David said he had a bridle on his mouth so he wouldn't blurt out the wrong thing (Psalm 39:1). You don't think the king of Israel sat on this throne with a horse's bridle in his mouth, right? In the same way, Jesus' point was that you should do what you have to do to control your eyes. (See also Job 31:1.)

WHAT DID JESUS MEAN WHEN HE SAID, "RESIST NOT EVIL"? ARE WE SUPPOSED TO LET PEOPLE WALK ALL OVER US?

"But I say to you, Do not resist one who is evil. But if any one strikes you on the right cheek, turn to him the other also."

MATTHEW 5:39 RSV

Jesus said, "You have heard that it was said, 'An eye for an eye, and a tooth for a tooth.' But I tell you not to resist an evil person" (Matthew 5:38–39 NKJV). The Law of Moses called for very strict justice: If you were in a fight and someone knocked out your top left tooth, the judges would order his top left tooth knocked out. If he burned you, the officers of the law burned him in the exact same place (Exodus 21:22–25).

Jesus didn't mean that you shouldn't even defend yourself if someone starts slapping or punching you. You *should* defend yourself. But you shouldn't go looking for a fight. If someone slaps you, don't do the exact same thing back to that person just to get even. "Do not say, 'I'll do to him as he has done to me; I'll pay that man back for what he did" (Proverbs 24:29 NIV).

Defend yourself, yes, but don't seek revenge. Let God take care of paying someone back. (See Romans 12:17–21.)

Jesus followed His own advice the night He was arrested, allowing the "bad guys" to take Him to an unfair trial and, ultimately, the Crucifixion. But Jesus knew that there was a much bigger purpose to His pain—and He suffered for all of us.

DOES JESUS REALLY EXPECT US TO BE PERFECT?

> *"You, therefore, must be perfect, as your heavenly Father is perfect."*
>
> MATTHEW 5:48 RSV

Jesus said, "Be perfect, therefore, as your heavenly Father is perfect" (Matthew 5:48 TNIV). The word *perfect* doesn't mean to be totally without sin. It literally means "complete"—in other words, we are to act completely the way God acts.

Jesus had just finished saying, "Love your enemies" (verse 44). He then went on to explain that even though *we* may have difficulty loving those who mock or hurt us, *God* still loves them. He sends them rain and sunshine as much as He sends these blessings to good people (verse 45).

So if we say that we are God's children, we should act the way that God acts toward our enemies. We should love them and do good things to them.

WHY DID JESUS SAY NOT TO USE "VAIN REPETITIONS" WHEN WE PRAY, YET HE PRAYED THE EXACT SAME WORDS THREE DIFFERENT TIMES?

> *"And when you pray, do not keep on babbling like pagans, for they think they will be heard because of their many words."*
>
> MATTHEW 6:7 TNIV

Jesus said, "When you pray, do not use vain repetitions as the heathen do. For they think they shall be heard for their many words" (Matthew 6:7 NKJV). Notice that Jesus *didn't* say, "Do not repeat yourself at all." He said, "Do not use *vain* repetitions." Vain means "worthless" or "insincere." His point was that you aren't to keep on repeating words you don't really mean, babbling on and on, just to make your prayer last longer. God isn't impressed by what kind of prayer show you put on.

But if you're really desperate and you're praying with all your heart and not just for show, it's fine if you repeat yourself. Sometimes those are just about the only words you can think of. When

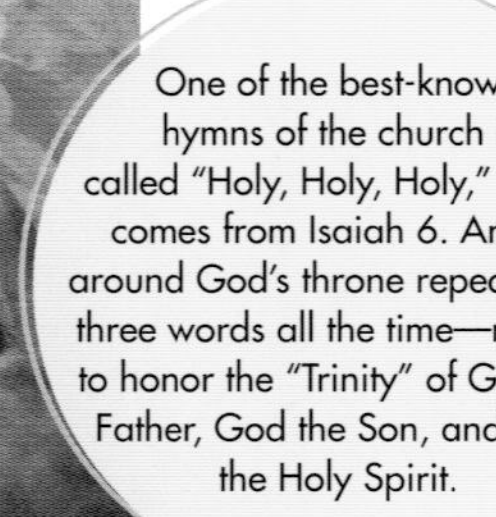

Jesus was in the Garden of Gethsemane, just before He was crucified, He was in such deep agony that He was sweating blood, and He repeated the same prayer three times (Mark 14:32–41; Luke 22:44).

DOES JESUS REALLY WANT US TO BE LIKE THE BIRDS AND NOT WORK AT ALL OR SAVE ANY MONEY, BUT JUST TRUST HIM TO SUPPLY OUR NEEDS?

"Therefore I tell you, do not worry about your life, what you will eat or drink; or about your body, what you will wear. Is not life more important than food, and the body more important than clothes? Look at the birds of the air; they do not sow or reap or store away in barns, and yet your heavenly Father feeds them. Are you not much more valuable than they?"

MATTHEW 6:25–26 TNIV

Who says birds don't work? Sure, if they live in captivity and get their food from a bird feeder, they don't have to search for food. But most birds in the world work hard much of the day. An average bird has to eat its body's weight worth of insects every day, and that means a lot of flying and hunting. And parents feeding growing chicks are on the go from morning to night to find enough food.

God takes care of this cardinal by having a caring human fill a bird feeder. Other birds, in the wild, rely on God in other ways. However they eat, God provides!

Jesus' point was that God provides food for the birds, and because people are worth much more than birds, He will also provide for us. Jesus didn't say, "Do not work." He said, "Do not worry" (Matthew 6:25). We will still have to work for what we get—and like the birds, maybe work hard—but we should trust God and not worry. If we do our part and pray, God will provide our needs.

DO WE ALL HAVE GUARDIAN ANGELS WHO CONSTANTLY WATCH OVER US?

"Watch that you don't treat a single one of these childlike believers arrogantly. You realize, don't you, that their personal angels are constantly in touch with my Father in heaven?"

MATTHEW 18:10 MSG

The Bible tells us that God has put His angels in charge of caring for us and protecting us "in *all* [our] ways" (Psalm 91:11 NKJV). It certainly does sound like His angels are with us all the time, constantly watching over us. But are they the same angels all the time, or is it always a new angel?

Some parents think their kids give guardian angels are real workout! This 1656 painting, by Pietro da Cortona, shows a guardian angel walking a child through danger.

Jesus was talking about children when He said, "Do not despise one of these little ones; for I tell you that in heaven their angels always behold the face of my Father who is in heaven" (Matthew 18:10 RSV). Because Jesus said "*their* angels," it sounds like each angel "belongs" to the person he is guarding. That's definitely what the early Christians believed (Acts 12:15).

Many Christians believe that there are one or two angels assigned to each person. This could well be, but we don't know for certain.

DID JESUS REALLY MEAN IT WHEN HE SAID THAT IF WE BELIEVE WHEN WE PRAY, WE'LL RECEIVE WHATEVER WE PRAY FOR?

Jesus said, "If you believe, you will receive whatever you ask for in prayer." He also said, "Everything is possible for the person who has faith" (Matthew 21:22; Mark 9:23 GNT). Far too many people pray wishfully, without really expecting that God will answer. They just pray because, well, praying is something that Christians do. When you pray like that, you won't receive anything (James 1:6–7). You need to believe when you pray.

And you need to believe *in God* if you want Him to do something for you. But no matter how much you pray, God won't give you something if it's not His will for you to have it (1 John 5:14–15).

Also, it may not be God's time—yet (Revelation 6:10–11). Sometimes, God's answer is on the way, but the devil is fighting your receiving it (Daniel 10:12–13). So pray and believe. *Keep* praying and believing.

Crossing your fingers and wishing real hard. . .no, that's not what prayer is all about!

But Jesus was matter-of-fact: "Yes—and if you embrace this kingdom life and don't doubt God, you'll not only do minor feats like I did to the fig tree, but also triumph over huge obstacles. This mountain, for instance, you'll tell, 'Go jump in the lake,' and it will jump. Absolutely everything, ranging from small to large, as you make it a part of your believing prayer, gets included as you lay hold of God."

MATTHEW 21:21–22 MSG

ARE WE LIVING IN THE END TIMES?.....

> *Watch therefore: for ye know not what hour your Lord doth come.*
>
> MATTHEW 24:42 KJV

Christians have different opinions about the end times. Some Christians, called *idealists*, don't believe there will be end times at all; they think the events in Matthew 24 and Revelation symbolize the eternal struggle between good and evil. Others, called *preterists*, believe that Matthew 24 was fulfilled when the Romans destroyed Jerusalem in AD 70. *Historicists* believe that the events in Matthew 24 and Revelation describe the fall of the Roman Empire and other major events in history.

Christians who believe that the end times are yet to come are called *futurists*—and they have many different ideas about the last days. Some believe that we're already living in the end times. Others believe that the end can begin any day now. Others believe that it's still a ways off.

Some futurists believe that the church has to conquer the world before Jesus can return. Others believe that the world must first conquer the church. As you can see, Christians have many different opinions about the end times.

HOW DID JESUS RISE FROM THE DEAD?.....

> *He has risen, just as He said.*
>
> MATTHEW 28:6 NASB

Roman soldiers pass out in terror as Jesus comes back to life, in this painting from the 1500s.

Jesus was definitely dead. He suffered terribly from being beaten and lost so much blood that, when He was nailed to a cross Friday at noon, He died after only a few hours. His disciples buried Him just before sundown, and Jesus' body lay in a cold tomb Friday evening, all that night, all day Saturday, all Saturday night, and Sunday morning until the sun rose.

Then the Spirit of God did an outstanding miracle and brought Jesus' dead body back to life (Romans 8:11). This was no ordinary miracle. What's more, Jesus wasn't just raised back to life in a normal body as Lazarus had been (John 11:38–44). Jesus was resurrected in an eternal, powerful body—never to die again.

This was such a great miracle that Paul said it was proof that Jesus is the Son of God (Romans 1:3–4).

"I baptize you with water, but he will baptize you with the Holy Spirit."
MARK 1:8 NIV

The Holy Spirit (represented by the dove) fills Jesus' followers at Pentecost (Acts 2:1–4). The flames above each person show the Spirit's baptizing work.

WHAT DOES IT MEAN TO BE BAPTIZED WITH THE HOLY SPIRIT?

John the Baptist said, "I baptize you with water, but he [Jesus] will baptize you with the Holy Spirit" (Mark 1:8 GNT). Christians have two main opinions about what the baptism of the Holy Spirit is.

First, many Christians believe this is talking about salvation—because the moment we accept Jesus as Lord, God sends the Spirit to live in our hearts (Galatians 4:6). Since all Christians must have the Spirit of Christ to be saved (Romans 8:9), they say that being baptized with the Spirit means becoming a Christian.

Other Christians agree that the Holy Spirit "seals" believers (sets God's mark of ownership on them) when they are saved (Ephesians 1:13–14). But they insist that being "baptized with the Holy Spirit" is often a separate event. This is when a believer is filled with the Spirit and speaks in tongues. They point out that, in the Bible, people sometimes received the Holy Spirit after they became Christians (Acts 8:14–17; 19:1–6).

Jesus whips the money changers in the temple, in this 1626 painting by the classic artist Rembrandt.

HOW COULD JESUS HAVE NEVER SINNED WHEN THE BIBLE SAYS THAT HE SOMETIMES GOT ANGRY?

He looked around at them in anger. . . .
MARK 3:5 NIV

Many Christians think that it's a sin to become angry, no matter what the reason. So when they read in the Bible that Jesus looked around at the Pharisees with anger, grieved at how hard-hearted they were, they mistakenly imagine that Jesus must have sinned. This is not the case. The Bible says, "If you become angry, do not let your anger lead you into sin" (Ephesians 4:26 GNT). There are sometimes *good* reasons to get angry—like when you see a bully tormenting a smaller kid. But even though you get angry, don't lose control and do something foolish.

WHY DID JESUS IGNORE THE PHOENICIAN WOMAN WHEN SHE BEGGED HIM TO HELP HER?

Now the woman was a Greek, a Syrophoenician by birth. And she begged him to cast the demon out of her daughter. And he said to her, "Let the children first be fed, for it is not right to take the children's bread and throw it to the dogs."
MARK 7:26–27 RSV

One day, when Jesus traveled to the region of Tyre, a Phoenician woman, a non-Jew, heard that He was there and repeatedly begged Him to drive a demon out of her daughter (Mark 7:24–30). At first, Jesus ignored the woman. When she persisted, He finally told her that He was "sent only to the lost sheep of Israel." When she continued to beg Him to help her, He said that He couldn't take the children's bread and give it to the dogs (Matthew 15:21–28). Why did He do that?

Jesus loves Gentiles (non-Jews) as much as Jews, but God had specifically promised the Jews that He would send the Savior to them first, and that afterward the Savior would be a blessing to the whole world. God's Son had to care for the children of God (the Jews) before the non-Jews.

Jesus cared for the woman. He was simply taking the gospel *first* "to the lost sheep of Israel" (Matthew 10:5–6 NIV; see also Romans 1:16). But because the woman had such great faith, Jesus eventually responded to her request and healed her daughter.

IS THE DEVIL RESPONSIBLE FOR CAUSING ALL SICKNESS AND DISEASE?

> *"Deaf and dumb spirit, I command you, come out of him and enter him no more!"*
>
> MARK 9:25 NKJV

Many Christians think that the devil and his demons are responsible for causing all sicknesses, from the AIDS virus to the common cold. Every time a person is born deaf or blind, they think the devil caused it to happen. This is because the Bible often tells us that Jesus cast out an evil spirit at the same time He healed people's diseases or handicaps (Mark 9:25–26).

Though it is true that evil spirits directly cause *some* illnesses, it's important to remember that there are countless germs and viruses running loose around the world that are perfectly capable of causing sickness all on their own.

Also, many times, Jesus simply healed sickness—from fevers to leprosy—without needing to cast out demons. He healed people because He has power over disease as well as power over demons (Mark 1:29–31, 40–42; 3:1–5; 5:25–29).

Some of the Bible's descriptions of hell sound a bit like the hot lava oozing from a volcano.

IF GOD IS LOVE, WHY WOULD HE SEND SOMEONE TO A PLACE AS HORRIBLE AS HELL?

When Jesus described hell, He used the word *gehenna* and said it was a place "where their worm does not die, and the fire is not quenched" (Mark 9:48 RSV). Therefore, many Christians think that hell is a literal "lake of fire" (Revelation 20:15) where sinners are tormented for all eternity.

However, the name Gehenna comes from the word *ge-hinnom* (the Valley of Hinnom), which was Jerusalem's garbage dump. So hell may be more like a stinky dump.

Many people have difficulty believing that God would let people burn in fire forever. Billy Graham said that he thought that the fire mentioned in the Bible is a burning thirst for God that can never be quenched. He added, "I think that hell. . .is separation from God forever." In other words, people end up separated from God, because that's what they choose—then later they regret their decision forever.

Whether you believe that hell is a lake of fire, a smoking garbage dump, or a lonely separation from God, know this: People *don't have to go there*! Jesus offers us eternal life with God in heaven instead.

> *"If your hand or your foot gets in God's way, chop it off and throw it away. You're better off maimed or lame and alive than the proud owner of two hands and two feet, godless in a furnace of eternal fire. And if your eye distracts you from God, pull it out and throw it away. You're better off one-eyed and alive than exercising your twenty-twenty vision from inside the fire of hell."*
>
> MARK 9:43–44 MSG

WHY DOES MARK SAY THAT THE WOMEN SAW ONE ANGEL INSIDE JESUS' TOMB, BUT LUKE SAYS THE WOMEN SAW TWO ANGELS THERE? IS THAT A CONTRADICTION?

Early Sunday morning, Mary Magdalene and a group of women went to Jesus' tomb, and to their shock they found that the huge stone blocking the opening of the tomb had been rolled away. The Roman guards were sprawled on the ground unconscious (Matthew 28:1–4). The tomb was like a cave, so the women walked inside to see Jesus' body—but it was missing! Just then they saw an angel who told them that Jesus had risen from the dead (Mark 16:1–7).

Fra Angelico, an artist in the 1400s, went with Mark's description of one angel in Jesus' empty tomb.

Luke tells the same facts, except he says there were *two* angels in the tomb (Luke 24:1–7). Why the difference? Obviously, one of the angels was doing most of the speaking, so he's the only angel Mark mentioned. Luke, who was a stickler for details, mentioned that a second angel was there as well. Often, one Gospel writer includes facts that another writer doesn't mention.

> *As they entered the tomb, they saw a young man dressed in a white robe sitting on the right side, and they were alarmed.*
>
> MARK 16:5 NIV

Why Didn't Jesus' Disciples Believe at First That He Had Risen from the Dead?. . . .

Jesus' disciples believed that God could do miracles, but they also knew that Jesus had been killed. John had even watched Jesus die (John 19:33–35). Jesus was dead and buried, so when the women came running, all talking at once, telling the disciples that they'd seen Jesus and that angels had told them Jesus was alive, "they did not believe the women, because their words seemed to them like nonsense" (Luke 24:11 GNT). They thought the women were seeing things.

When the disciples saw Jesus with their own eyes, that's when they finally believed that He was alive. Thomas was the hardest to convince. He thought the other disciples were either hallucinating or seeing Jesus' ghost. But when Jesus showed up again and told Thomas to touch Him and see that He wasn't a ghost, Thomas was convinced too (John 20:24–28).

Now when Jesus was risen early the first day of the week, he appeared first to Mary Magdalene, out of whom he had cast seven devils. And she went and told them that had been with him, as they mourned and wept. And they, when they had heard that he was alive, and had been seen of her, believed not. After that he appeared in another form unto two of them, as they walked, and went into the country. And they went and told it unto the residue: neither believed they them. Afterward he appeared unto the eleven as they sat at meat, and upbraided them with their unbelief and hardness of heart, because they believed not them which had seen him after he was risen.

Mark 16:9–14 KJV

Have you heard of a "Doubting Thomas"? The nickname comes from one of Jesus' disciples—Thomas—who wouldn't believe Jesus had come back to life unless he could actually touch the nail holes in Jesus' hands and His spear wound!

Nobody knows what they really looked like, but painter Jacob Jordaens imagined Matthew, Mark, Luke, and John like this in the 1600s.

Many have undertaken to draw up an account of the things that have been fulfilled among us, just as they were handed down to us by those who from the first were eyewitnesses and servants of the word. With this in mind, since I myself have carefully investigated everything from the beginning, I too decided to write an orderly account for you, most excellent Theophilus, so that you may know the certainty of the things you have been taught.

LUKE 1:1–4 TNIV

WHY ARE THERE FOUR GOSPELS?

We don't know why God decided that there should be *four* different accounts of Jesus' life, death, and resurrection in the Bible. We can only be glad that there are. Mark tells the entire gospel story quickly in very descriptive, action-packed words, but he skips many interesting parables and stories.

That's where the Gospel of Matthew really shines. It is filled with all kinds of parables, stories, and conversations that Mark left out.

Then Luke researched and wrote his Gospel some years later. He admitted that others had already written about Jesus but still felt that God wanted him to write his version. We're sure glad he did! Luke told many details that both Matthew and Mark left out.

Finally, 60 years after Jesus' resurrection, the apostle John wrote the fourth and final Gospel, and it added a ton of new information about Jesus that we otherwise never would have known.

WHO IS THE HOLY SPIRIT?

> *The angel answered and said to her, "The Holy Spirit will come upon you, and the power of the Most High will overshadow you; and for that reason the holy Child shall be called the Son of God."*
>
> LUKE 1:35 NASB

God is made up of three Persons—God the Father, God the Son (Jesus Christ), and God the Holy Spirit. The Holy Spirit is also called the Spirit of God and the Spirit of Christ (Romans 8:9).

The Bible describes the Holy Spirit as being "like a dove" (Mark 1:10)—but it doesn't say the Holy Spirit *is* a dove.

Some people have the idea that the Holy Spirit is just some kind of power or force, some kind of "it," but the Bible makes it clear that the Spirit is a person—and, in fact, is equal in power and wisdom and holiness to God the Father.

The Spirit knows everything that God knows (1 Corinthians 2:10–11). That's why He is also called "the Spirit of truth" (John 16:13).

IF JOHN THE BAPTIST TOLD THE ROMAN SOLDIERS TO "DO VIOLENCE TO NO MAN," HOW CAN CHRISTIANS BE POLICE OFFICERS OR SOLDIERS?

> *Then some soldiers asked him, "And what should we do?" He replied, "Don't extort money and don't accuse people falsely—be content with your pay."*
>
> LUKE 3:14 TNIV

The King James Version of the Bible is a good translation, but it is 400 years old, so some of its expressions are a bit unclear today. When John the Baptist told the Roman soldiers, "Do violence to no man" (Luke 3:14 KJV), it was tied to his next two pieces of advice, "Neither accuse any falsely; and be content with your wages."

The words "Do violence to no man" literally mean "*Do not shake any man.*" In John's day, many Roman soldiers were unhappy with their wages and would "shake down" people and falsely accuse them of crimes to scare them into paying protection money. This is called extortion. In fact, some modern translations, such as Today's New International Version, say: "Don't extort money."

This has nothing to do with soldiers and police officers using necessary force to keep law and order or to defend their country from enemies.

WHY WERE THE PHARISEES SO FOCUSED ON OBEYING TINY LITTLE LAWS?

"But woe to you Pharisees! for you tithe mint and rue and every herb, and neglect justice and the love of God; these you ought to have done, without neglecting the others."

LUKE 11:42 RSV

The Pharisees started out with the right idea. In the past, the Jews had ignored God and disobeyed His law, so the Pharisees decided that they would *always* do their best to obey *every* single rule and commandment. For example, they were so careful to tithe 10 percent of their income that they snipped off one-tenth of tiny garden herbs like mint and rue to give to God.

They got so focused on the tiny details, however, that they lost sight of the big, important commandments, such as loving God and being compassionate toward others (Luke 11:42). They acted holy by praying long prayers in public, but meanwhile they were overcharging poor widows rent (Matthew 6:5; 23:14).

They made sure everyone knew all about it whenever they turned around and gave money to the poor—but because they didn't truly love God and their fellow man, it was all an empty, religious show (Matthew 6:1–2).

Jesus' story of the Good Samaritan (Luke 10:25-37) made it clear that God wants people to love each other—not worry about lots of man-made rules.

WHY WERE THE RELIGIOUS LEADERS OF ISRAEL SO OFFENDED BY WHAT JESUS TAUGHT AND DID?

The chief priests, the scribes, and the leaders of the people sought to destroy Him.

LUKE 19:47 NKJV

The religious leaders enjoyed their positions of power and authority. They really liked it when people called them "Rabbi" or "Master" and moved aside to give them the most important seats at feasts (Matthew 23:6–7). Their attitude was completely opposite of what Jesus taught—namely, that a good leader should serve the people who were under him (Luke 22:24–26).

Because of their wrong attitude, the religious rulers lost touch with the common people and thus became very jealous when Jesus became popular with the crowds. They became afraid that people would follow Jesus instead of them and they'd lose their positions. They finally became so envious of Jesus that they decided to kill Him (Matthew 27:18).

Another reason they were offended by Jesus was because He constantly broke the little religious laws that were so important to them. They argued, therefore, that He must be a bad person.

Judas betrays Jesus with a kiss—it was a signal to Jesus' enemies indicating who they should arrest.

WHY DID JESUS PICK A DISCIPLE (JUDAS) WHO WOULD BETRAY HIM?

> *That's when Satan entered Judas, the one called Iscariot. He was one of the Twelve.*
>
> LUKE 22:3 MSG

Jesus knew that Judas would eventually betray Him and turn Him over to His enemies. So why did He pick Judas as a disciple in the first place? Jesus certainly did not look forward to being beaten, crucified, and killed. He wanted to avoid such a painful death if possible (Matthew 26:38–39).

However, Jesus knew that it was *not* possible. He had to die to pay the price for our sins. He also knew that the Psalms prophesied that a close friend would be the one to betray Him (Psalm 41:9; John 13:18). Judas was that betrayer.

That didn't mean Judas did a good thing, however. Jesus said, "The Son of Man will die as the Scriptures say he will, but how terrible for that man who will betray the Son of Man!" (Matthew 26:24 GNT).

WHAT KIND OF BODY DID JESUS HAVE AFTER HIS RESURRECTION?

> *Behold my hands and my feet, that it is I myself: handle me, and see; for a spirit hath not flesh and bones, as ye see me have. And when he had thus spoken, he shewed them his hands and his feet.*
>
> LUKE 24:39–40 KJV

God raised Jesus up in the same physical body He'd had before. It was the same body, yes—He even had the nail wounds from His crucifixion. But His body was also very different. If Jesus had been brought back to life in His normal body, He eventually would have grown old and died again. God's Spirit not only resurrected Jesus' natural body, but totally transformed it into a supernatural body (1 Corinthians 15:42–44). Jesus' new, resurrected body was still flesh and bones, but it was now also powerful and eternal.

Sometimes Jesus looked just like the ordinary man His disciples had always known (John 20:24–27), but other times He shone in His full glory. (See Revelation 1:14–16.)

In the beginning was the Word, and the Word was with God, and the Word was God.
JOHN 1:1 KJV

IS JESUS GOD'S SON, OR IS HE GOD HIMSELF?

Jesus is both. He said many times in the Gospels that He was the Son of God and that God was His Father. This is very clear. In fact, God the Father declared, "This is My beloved Son, in whom I am well pleased" (Matthew 3:17 NKJV). But being God's Son doesn't mean that Jesus is *less* than God. Jesus is equal with His Father.

John called Jesus the Word of God and stated, "The Word became a human being" (John 1:14 GNT). But Jesus has always existed, for all eternity, even before He was born on earth. Before the beginning of time, Jesus was already in existence. "In the beginning the Word already existed; the Word was *with* God, and the Word *was* God" (John 1:1 GNT, emphasis added). How could Jesus be God if His Father is God? Well, He's one with His Father (John 10:30).

Isaiah said that the Savior—that's Jesus—would be born as a child but would be called "Mighty God, Everlasting Father, Prince of Peace" (Isaiah 9:6 RSV).

You are not your father. . .and your father is not you. But with God the Father and His Son, Jesus—well, it's different!

WHAT DID JESUS MEAN WHEN HE SAID, "YOU MUST BE BORN AGAIN"?

> *Do not be amazed that I said to you, "You must be born again."*
>
> JOHN 3:7 NASB

We have all been born physically. That's why our physical bodies are alive in this world. That's the *first* birth. But the spirit that lives inside your body needs to come alive as well. Before God's Holy Spirit enters your life, you're not spiritually alive. That's why Jesus said, "You must be born again" (John 3:7 NASB). He said "again" because spiritual birth is the *second* birth.

Jesus explained, "That which is born of the flesh is flesh, and that which is born of the Spirit is spirit" (John 3:6 NASB). Being "born again" means being "born of the Spirit." This happens when you receive Jesus Christ as your Lord and Savior, and God sends the Spirit into your heart and gives you eternal life. "It is the Spirit who gives life" (John 6:63 NKJV).

WHY ARE THERE SO MANY HYPOCRITES IN THE CHURCH?

> *"Stop judging by mere appearances, but instead judge correctly."*
>
> JOHN 7:24 TNIV

There *are* hypocrites in church today, of course, just as there were hypocrites in Jesus' day (Matthew 23). Because a hypocrite is someone who's play-acting, pretending to be something they're not, even we—if we're honest—must admit that we are hypocrites at times.

Often, however, when we think someone else is a hypocrite, we're just being quick to judge. For example, if we see a woman dressed in a very nice outfit and wearing expensive rings, we might be tempted to think, *If she were really a Christian, she'd give lots of money to feed the poor!* Yet maybe she *is* giving a great deal to do just that—only we don't *know* about it.

That's why Jesus said, "Do not judge according to appearance, but judge with righteous judgment" (John 7:24 NKJV).

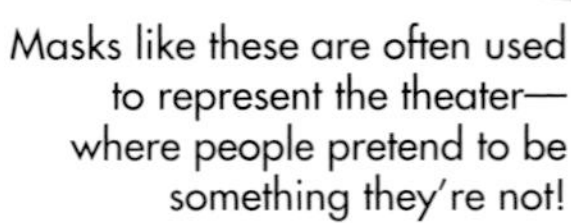

Masks like these are often used to represent the theater—where people pretend to be something they're not!

IS JESUS THE ONLY WAY TO GOD?

Jesus saith unto him, I am the way, the truth, and the life: no man cometh unto the Father, but by me.

JOHN 14:6 KJV

Yes, He is. Jesus said, "I am the way, and the truth, and the life; no one comes to the Father, but by me" (John 14:6 RSV).

Most religions teach some good morals and some truth about God—so you should respect them for that—but that doesn't make them a "way to God." They only have part of the truth and thus can only take people *part way* to God. They can't take anyone all the way, because they can't get across the vast canyon called sin that separates humanity from God.

Jesus is the truth, because everything He taught is true. Jesus is the way, because when He died for your sins, He created a way where there was no way—a bridge across the gap of sin—all the way to God. That's why Jesus is the only one who can save us and give us eternal life. There is no other way to get to heaven.

The early Christians said, "There is salvation in no one else, for there is no other name. . .by which we must be saved" (Acts 4:12 RSV).

WHAT DOES THE HOLY SPIRIT DO?

But the Comforter, which is the Holy Ghost, whom the Father will send in my name, he shall teach you all things, and bring all things to your remembrance, whatsoever I have said unto you.

JOHN 14:26 KJV

The Holy Spirit does many things. When we believe in Jesus, God sends the Spirit of His Son to dwell in our hearts (Galatians 4:6). We are "born of the Spirit" when this happens (John 3:6). The Holy Spirit then assures us that we belong to God (Romans 8:16).

Like the early apostles, modern-day preachers speak in the power of the Holy Spirit. But you don't have to be a preacher to tell others about Jesus—the Holy Spirit will help you, too!

He helps us to know how to live for God and gives us the power to live as Christians and tell others about Jesus (Acts 1:8). The Spirit also gives us wisdom (Luke 12:11–12) and fills our hearts with love, joy, peace, and hope (Galatians 5:22–23; Romans 15:13). When we feel discouraged, the Holy Spirit, who is also called the Comforter, encourages us (John 16:7).

The Holy Spirit gives us many more wonderful gifts, so ask God to send more of His Holy Spirit into your heart today.

WHY DO CHRISTIANS SUFFER PERSECUTION?..

Jesus said, "If the world hates you, just remember that it has hated me first" (John 15:18 GNT). We know from the Gospels that although many people loved Jesus and obeyed His teachings, He also had enemies who resented what He said and hated what He stood for. Soon they were speaking evil things about Jesus and trying to harm Him physically. That's called persecution.

"If the world hates you, you know that it hated Me before it hated you. If you were of the world, the world would love its own. Yet because you are not of the world, but I chose you out of the world, therefore the world hates you. Remember the word that I said to you, 'A servant is not greater than his master.' If they persecuted Me, they will also persecute you. If they kept My word, they will keep yours also. But all these things they will do to you for My name's sake, because they do not know Him who sent Me."

JOHN 15:18–21 NKJV

Jesus warned those who believe in Him, "If people persecuted me, they will persecute you too" (John 15:20 GNT). Being a Christian means living as Jesus lived as much as possible. It means taking a stand for what is right instead of compromising and going along with the crowd. When you do that, people may insult you and avoid you or try to shove you around (Luke 6:22–23).

Many Christians in other countries suffer much more serious persecution than we do. When you are persecuted, remember that Jesus promised to reward us greatly in heaven if we suffer for His sake (Matthew 5:11–12).

A man named Stephen was the first Christian killed for following Jesus. You can read the whole story in Acts 6–7.

IF JESUS WAS GOD, WHY DID HE PRAY TO GOD? WASN'T HE JUST TALKING TO HIMSELF?.....

Holy Father, keep them in thy name, which thou hast given me, that they may be one, even as we are one.

JOHN 17:11 RSV

There is one God, but He consists of three different persons—God the Father, God the Son (Jesus), and God the Holy Spirit. The three-in-one God is called the Trinity.

When Jesus was in heaven before He came to earth, He communicated with His Father all the time, instantly and perfectly. After Jesus became a man, He still spoke with His Father, but now that He had a limited human body, His communication was limited as well. So He prayed using human words. Prayer simply means talking to God.

We talk to God, too, but we definitely can't talk to God the Father on the same level that Jesus could. If you read John 17:1–5, you will see that Jesus talked to the Father as an equal.

The idea of the Trinity has confused people for centuries—but here's one way to explain it: You know how water can be a liquid, a solid (ice), or a gas (steam), like you see in this picture taken near Greenland? God is kind of like that—one God, but in three different "persons."

Peter replied, "Repent and be baptized, every one of you, in the name of Jesus Christ for the forgiveness of your sins. And you will receive the gift of the Holy Spirit."
ACTS 2:38 NIV

WHY IS IT SO IMPORTANT TO BE BAPTIZED?

The apostle Peter said, "Repent and be baptized, every one of you, in the name of Jesus Christ for the forgiveness of your sins" (Acts 2:38 NIV). Down through the ages, when people put their faith in Jesus, repented of their sins, and declared that they would follow Jesus, they were baptized in water.

Now, the water doesn't wash away your sins. When Jesus enters your life, His blood cleanses you from sin (1 Peter 3:21; 1 John 1:7). Just the same, it's very important to be baptized. It's an outward declaration that you have had an inward change.

Jesus didn't need to repent of any sins, yet even He allowed John the Baptist to baptize Him, because He wanted to show that it was an important thing to do (Matthew 3:13–15).

Men line up to be baptized in the Jordan River—the same water in which Jesus was baptized by John the Baptist.

ARE CHRISTIANS SUPPOSED TO GIVE UP ALL THEIR MONEY AND WORLDLY POSSESSIONS?

> *All the believers were together and had everything in common. Selling their possessions and goods, they gave to anyone as he had need.*
>
> Acts 2:44–45 NIV

Jesus *does* call some people to give up all their worldly possessions. He told the rich young ruler, "Go, sell everything you have and give to the poor. . . . Then come, follow me" (Mark 10:21 NIV). Many missionaries today give up jobs and possessions in order to preach the gospel.

Usually, however, God wants you to start working, in order to earn an honest living for yourself and to be able to help the poor (Ephesians 4:28)—and that includes having money to help support missionaries.

Jesus commanded His disciples to give generously, so when many poor people and widows in Jerusalem became Christians and were in desperate need, wealthy Christians sold their extra lands and houses to raise money for the emergency (Acts 2:44–45). They probably didn't sell the houses they were living in, but they did give generously. Whether we give up everything we own or just a portion of it, we should give generously to God and others.

WHAT DOES IT MEAN TO BELIEVE IN JESUS CHRIST?

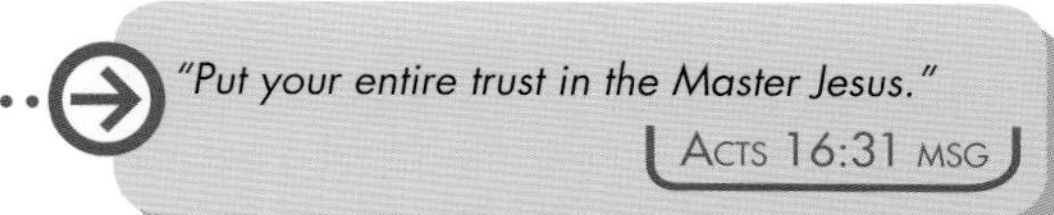

> *"Put your entire trust in the Master Jesus."*
>
> Acts 16:31 MSG

When the jailer in Philippi asked, "What must I do to be saved?" Paul answered, "Believe in the Lord Jesus, and you will be saved" (Acts 16:30–31 RSV). Now, surveys show that 88 percent of American adults believe that Jesus Christ was a real person who actually walked the earth. But only 82 percent believe that Jesus is the Son of God and that He died for our sins. So are 88 percent of Americans saved—or is it 82 percent? How many *are* saved? And what exactly does it mean to believe?

The Greek word for believe (*pisteuō*) means "to trust, to rely on, to stick to." It's not enough simply to agree that Jesus exists. It's not even enough to know that He is the Son of God and that He died for our sins. To be saved, you must believe that *you* have sinned and that Jesus died for *your* sins. You must accept Jesus as your Savior and trust Him to save you.

The Bible's book of James says even the demons "believe" in God (2:19)—but they're *not* saved.

IS EVERYBODY IN THE WORLD A SINNER—EVEN GOOD, MORAL PEOPLE?

For all have sinned, and come short of the glory of God.
ROMANS 3:23 KJV

Many people think that only criminals, drug addicts, or sexually immoral people are sinners because they think that "sin" means only the worst kind of behavior and lawbreaking.

But the Greek word for sin (*hamartanō*) means "to err, to miss the mark." So when Romans 3:23 says, "All have sinned and fall short of the glory of God," it's saying that all of us miss the mark and fall short. None of us is perfect. All of us—in big or small ways—have disobeyed God. All of us have done selfish things or hurt others.

So, yes, everybody in the world is a sinner, even moral people who are good *most* of the time. Jesus was the only one who never sinned. That's why only He can save us.

HOW IS SALVATION A FREE GIFT?

For the wages of sin is death; but the gift of God is eternal life through Jesus Christ our Lord.
ROMANS 6:23 KJV

Many people have the idea that they have to *earn* their salvation. They figure that if they try to keep the Ten Commandments and do more good deeds than bad deeds, God will reward them for living a (mostly) good life and allow them into heaven.

But salvation is not like a wage or a reward. You can't earn it. We're all sinners, and "the wages of sin is death" (Romans 3:23; 6:23 KJV). Instead of earning eternal life, we earn death as our "wages."

Fortunately, there is *more* to this verse. The second half reads, "But the gift of God is eternal life through Jesus Christ our Lord." What we could never possibly earn, God will give us for *free* if we simply trust Jesus to save us. Salvation is a gift from a generous, loving God. We can't earn a gift. We can only accept it.

ARE WE SUPPOSED TO SUBMIT TO GOVERNMENTS AND AUTHORITIES EVEN WHEN THEY'RE WRONG?

Let every soul be subject unto the higher powers. For there is no power but of God: the powers that be are ordained of God.

ROMANS 13:1 KJV

When Jesus returns and sets up His kingdom on earth, it will be a perfect government. But until that day, nations will be ruled by imperfect rulers. Some of them govern well, but even the best leaders make decisions that cause hardships or suffering. And, sad to say, some governments are run by corrupt, selfish rulers. Most authorities are somewhere in the middle.

Some Christians in 1940s Germany felt they had to oppose their government. . . and many of them were killed for standing up to Adolf Hitler and the Nazis.

Just the same, the Bible tells us, "Be a good citizen. All governments are under God. Insofar as there is peace and order, it's God's order. . . . God also has an interest in keeping order, and he uses them to do it" (Romans 13:1, 4 MSG). According to Paul, there are two main reasons to avoid breaking the law: to avoid being punished by the authorities, and because it's the right way to live.

The only times we should not obey a government is if it commands us to do something wrong, deny our faith, or forbids us to tell others about Jesus (Daniel 3:1–18; 6:1–13; Acts 4:18–20).

WERE THERE OUTSTANDING WOMEN IN THE NEW TESTAMENT?

I commend to you our sister Phoebe. . . .

ROMANS 16:1 NASB

Yes, there were. The Virgin Mary gave birth to the Savior (Luke 1:26–33).

Mary Magdalene helped support Jesus, and she was the first person to see Him after He rose from the dead (Mark 16:9; Luke 8:1–3).

Mary the mother of Mark owned a large house in Jerusalem where many Christians met to pray (Acts 12:11–12).

Priscilla and her husband, Aquila, were Paul's close coworkers. Often when the couple is mentioned, Priscilla's name is mentioned first (Acts 18:1–3, 18; Romans 16:3).

Phoebe, the woman who delivered Paul's letter to the church in Rome, was a deacon of the church of Cenchrea. Paul instructed the Romans, "Assist her in whatever business she has need of you" (Romans 16:1–2 NKJV).

Euodia and Syntyche were Christians in Philippi, and Paul urged the church to "help these women who labored with me in the gospel" (Philippians 4:2–3 NKJV).

My brothers and sisters, some from Chloe's household have informed me that there are quarrels among you. What I mean is this: One of you says, "I follow Paul"; another, "I follow Apollos"; another, "I follow Cephas"; still another, "I follow Christ." Is Christ divided? Was Paul crucified for you? Were you baptized into the name of Paul?
1 CORINTHIANS 1:11–13 TNIV

Christians come from many different backgrounds and worship in different ways—but if Jesus is their focus, they're all on the same team!

CHRISTIANS HAVE MANY DIFFERENT DOCTRINES AND CHURCHES. IS THAT WRONG?

Paul warned Christians against divisions, scolding them because some of them were insisting, "I follow Paul." Others were arguing, "I follow Peter," and others were boasting, "I follow Apollos." Paul asked, "Was Paul crucified for you?" (1 Corinthians 1:12–13 NIV). Of course not. *Jesus* was crucified for us, so we should all follow Jesus.

You should also respect every person who truly follows Jesus, no matter which pastor they prefer to listen to or which church they attend. You might think that your pastor is the best, but it's wrong to think that only the people in your church are true Christians.

You should accept other Christians who have different opinions (Romans 14:1–6). After all, if we agree on the important things about Jesus and the Christian faith, we can be in unity with each other and love each other (Ephesians 4:3–6).

When We Get to Heaven, Will We Be Rewarded for Our Good Deeds and Punished for Our Bad Deeds?

For no other foundation can any one lay than that which is laid, which is Jesus Christ. Now if any one builds on the foundation with gold, silver, precious stones, wood, hay, straw—each man's work will become manifest; for the Day will disclose it, because it will be revealed with fire, and the fire will test what sort of work each one has done. If the work which any man has built on the foundation survives, he will receive a reward. If any man's work is burned up, he will suffer loss, though he himself will be saved, but only as through fire.

1 Corinthians 3:11–15 RSV

Doing good deeds won't get us into heaven. However, even though we are saved, we will be judged for what we have done. "We must all appear before the judgment seat of Christ, that everyone may receive what is due them. . .whether good or bad" (2 Corinthians 5:10 TNIV). Jesus will reward us for the good we've done, but what about the bad things?

Paul compares our lives to building a house and says that if we build with materials such as gold, silver, and precious stones, when the fire of judgment comes, they won't be affected, and we'll receive a reward.

But if we build with cheap things like wood, hay, and straw, when the fire comes, they'll be burned up. The Bible promises, "If anyone's work is burned, he will suffer loss; but he himself will be saved" (1 Corinthians 3:15 NKJV).

Joseph runs away from his boss's wife, in this 1631 painting by Guido Reni.

Why Does the Bible Tell Us to Flee Sexual Immorality?

Flee from sexual immorality. All other sins a man commits are outside his body, but he who sins sexually sins against his own body.

1 Corinthians 6:18 NIV

Some people play around the edges of sexual temptation, enjoying lustful thoughts or looking at pornographic photos, while telling themselves that they'll never actually cross the line and sin sexually. They tell themselves that they're strong enough to resist the actual temptation. But many a young man or woman has been surprised—and ashamed afterward—by how they have given in to temptation in the end.

So don't even get started down that path. Turn away from it. The Bible says: "Do not set foot on the path of the wicked. . . . Avoid it, do not travel on it; turn from it and go on your way" (Proverbs 4:14–15 NIV).

If you find temptation coming out to meet you, flee from it and head the other way (1 Corinthians 6:18). Joseph actually physically ran away when Potiphar's wife tried to tempt him (Genesis 39:11–12).

WHAT IS THE PURPOSE OF COMMUNION?

Jesus celebrated the Lord's Supper (Communion) with His disciples just before He was arrested and crucified, so that's why it's also called the Last Supper. Jesus gave the disciples some bread to eat, telling them that it represented His body that was broken for them. He also gave them wine to drink, which represented His blood poured out for the forgiveness of their sins (Matthew 26:26–28).

For I have received of the Lord that which also I delivered unto you, that the Lord Jesus the same night in which he was betrayed took bread: And when he had given thanks, he brake it, and said, Take, eat: this is my body, which is broken for you: this do in remembrance of me. After the same manner also he took the cup, when he had supped, saying, this cup is the new testament in my blood: this do ye, as oft as ye drink it, in remembrance of me. For as often as ye eat this bread, and drink this cup, ye do shew the Lord's death till he come.

1 CORINTHIANS 11:23–26 KJV

Jesus said, "Do this in memory of me" (Luke 22:19 GNT). He wanted His disciples to continue celebrating the Lord's Supper. He said, "This cup is God's new covenant, sealed with my blood. Whenever you drink it, do so in memory of me" (1 Corinthians 11:25 GNT).

Paul explained that every time we take Communion, we're reminding ourselves that Jesus died for us. We are to keep doing this right up until the day that Jesus returns.

WHAT DOES "NEW TESTAMENT" MEAN?

In Jesus' day, the Jews called the Law of Moses and the other Scriptures "the Law and the Prophets" (Matthew 7:12 NKJV). These Scriptures talked about the covenant (agreement) that God had made with Israel. The Israelites were His holy, chosen people, and as long as they loved and obeyed Him, God would bless and protect them.

However, the prophet Jeremiah prophesied that one day God would make a "new covenant" with His people (Jeremiah 31:31–33). When Jesus came, He made this covenant by dying on the cross for our sins. At the Last Supper, He offered His disciples a cup of wine, which symbolized His blood, and said, "This cup is the new covenant in My blood" (1 Corinthians 11:25 NKJV).

In the King James Version of the Bible, the words for new covenant are "new testament," so that's why we call the Christian writings the New Testament and the Law and the Prophets the Old Testament.

> *After the same manner also he took the cup, when he had supped, saying, this cup is the new testament in my blood: this do ye, as oft as ye drink it, in remembrance of me.*
>
> 1 CORINTHIANS 11:25 KJV

WHO CAN HAVE AS MUCH LOVE AS THE BIBLE SAYS WE'RE SUPPOSED TO HAVE? ISN'T THAT UNREALISTIC?

The kind of love Paul describes in 1 Corinthians 13 is so great that you might think that ordinary people will never be able to set aside all their anger, jealousy, and prejudices and have that kind of love.

Well, you might not have that much love at the beginning, but as you grow in your Christian faith, you become more loving. You get love by yielding your heart to God. It helps to read 1 Corinthians 13 often.

Showing love to other people is one of the proofs that you have

> Here's the ultimate example of love: "But God demonstrates his own love for us in this: While we were still sinners, Christ died for us" (ROMANS 5:8 NIV).

God's Spirit in your life (Galatians 5:22). "God's love has been poured into our hearts through the Holy Spirit which has been given to us" (Romans 5:5 RSV). So pray for God to give you more love.

Love is patient, love is kind and is not jealous; love does not brag and is not arrogant, does not act unbecomingly; it does not seek its own, is not provoked, does not take into account a wrong suffered, does not rejoice in unrighteousness, but rejoices with the truth; bears all things, believes all things, hopes all things, endures all things. Love never fails.

1 CORINTHIANS 13:4–8 NASB

WHAT DOES THE BIBLE MEAN WHEN IT SAYS THAT WE WILL BE RESURRECTED?

Some people think that Jesus saves just their *spirit*, so when their body dies, they leave it behind forever and just their spirit lives eternally in heaven. They guess that it sort of floats around on clouds forever because it is just a spirit, after all.

Christians' spirits *do* go to heaven at first, but God has a long-range plan: He wants to save your physical body, too, and reunite it with your spirit. To do this He will resurrect your body. To resurrect means to bring back to life. For your body to live forever, God must *change* it to make it powerful and indestructible and eternal—just like Jesus' resurrection body (Philippians 3:20–21; 1 John 3:2).

The resurrection will happen at the very end of time when Jesus returns (1 Thessalonians 4:14–17). To learn more, read 1 Corinthians chapter 15.

But now is Christ risen from the dead, and become the firstfruits of them that slept. For since by man came death, by man came also the resurrection of the dead. For as in Adam all die, even so in Christ shall all be made alive. But every man in his own order: Christ the firstfruits; afterward they that are Christ's at his coming.

1 CORINTHIANS 15:20–23 KJV

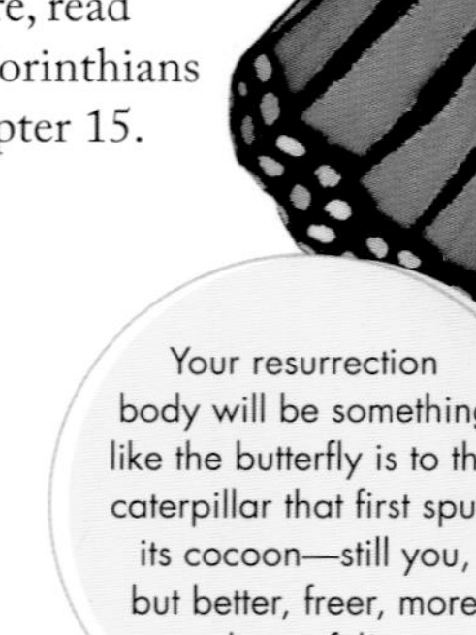

Your resurrection body will be something like the butterfly is to the caterpillar that first spun its cocoon—still you, but better, freer, more beautiful!

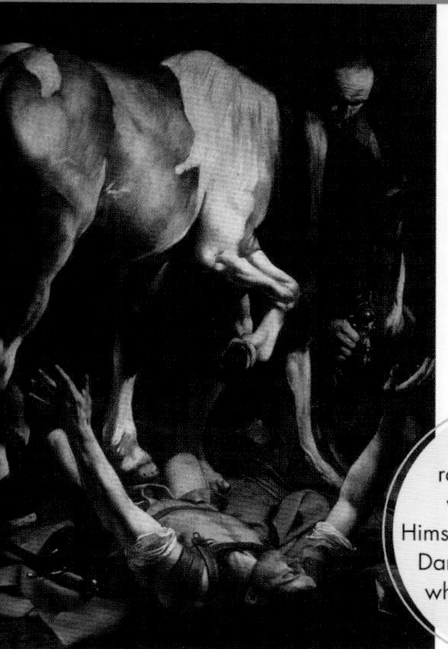

Why was the Apostle Paul beaten up so much?

> *What they did to Jesus, they do to us—trial and torture, mockery and murder. . . .*
>
> 2 Corinthians 4:10 msg

Paul said, "Anyone who wants to live all out for Christ is in for a lot of trouble; there's no getting around it" (2 Timothy 3:12 msg). Paul definitely lived all out for Christ. He preached the gospel boldly and very publicly in many cities, so he had many opportunities to lead people to faith in Jesus Christ.

Paul's first rough encounter was with Jesus Himself—on the road to Damascus. Read the whole story in Acts 9:1–19.

This also meant, however, that he had a greater-than-average amount of run-ins with religious people who hated his message. These enemies didn't want to lose control over the people, so they tried to stop Paul from preaching the gospel. Sometimes they beat Paul themselves; sometimes they talked gangs of thugs into doing it; other times they got the city rulers to do it (Acts 14:19; 16:16–24; 17:5).

What does it mean not to be unequally yoked with unbelievers?

> *Do not be yoked together with unbelievers.*
>
> 2 Corinthians 6:14 niv

In the Old Testament, God commanded the Jews, "Do not plow with an ox and donkey yoked together" (Deuteronomy 22:10 niv). They're unequal. The ox is larger and stronger and takes bigger steps, and the donkey can't keep up. The ox pulls the plow one direction while the donkey pulls it another, and they can barely plow a straight line. It doesn't make sense to expect them to work well together.

In the same way, Paul said that it just doesn't work when a Christian and an unbeliever are together in a close relationship. Unbelievers think and live differently from the way a Christian thinks and lives, and they'll end up pulling you off track.

Of course, you can be friends with someone who isn't a Christian, but your closest friends should be people who share your faith and values.

HOW CAN WE BE SONS AND DAUGHTERS OF GOD? ISN'T JESUS GOD'S ONE AND ONLY SON?.....

Adoption brings a non-related person into a family—and gives her an official, permanent place!

> *"I will be a Father to you, and you will be my sons and daughters, says the Lord Almighty."*
>
> 2 CORINTHIANS 6:18 NIV

The Bible tells us that Jesus is God's "one and only Son" (John 3:16 NIV). However, God also says to believers, "I will be a father to you, and you shall be sons and daughters to Me" (2 Corinthians 6:18 NASB). How can this be?

Well, Jesus is God's only *natural* Son—made of the same substance as God the Father, and equal with God—but God loved us so much that once Jesus Christ died for our sins, God forgave us and *adopted* us. We weren't His natural children, but He adopted us as His sons and daughters and sent His Spirit to live in our hearts. That's why we can call God our Father (Romans 8:15; Galatians 4:4–6).

WHAT WAS PAUL'S "THORN IN THE FLESH"?......

> *In order to keep me from becoming conceited, I was given a thorn in my flesh, a messenger of Satan, to torment me.*
>
> 2 CORINTHIANS 12:7 TNIV

Paul said that God gave him a "thorn in the flesh" (2 Corinthians 12:7 KJV) that he couldn't get rid of. Most Bible scholars believe that this was a long-lasting illness or disability that God used to keep Paul humble. It wasn't an actual thorn that had worked its way into Paul's flesh.

Most likely it was some kind of eye disease, because Paul complained that his sight was so bad that he had to write in very large letters. He also said that the Christians in Galatia loved him so much that they gladly would have plucked out their own eyes and given them to him if it would have helped (Galatians 4:15; 6:11). Whatever this illness was, Paul had it his whole life.

This close-up of a rose stem shows a lot of sharp thorns. Real thorns probably weren't Paul's problem, but you can imagine how much his problem hurt.

WHY DID PAUL WRITE SO MUCH ABOUT TRUSTING IN JESUS INSTEAD OF RELIGIOUSLY TRYING TO OBEY THE LAW OF MOSES?....

O foolish Galatians! Who has bewitched you, before whose eyes Jesus Christ was publicly portrayed as crucified? Let me ask you only this: Did you receive the Spirit by works of the law, or by hearing with faith?

GALATIANS 3:1–2 RSV

Until Jesus came, the Law of Moses was all the Jews had to teach them how to live as God's people. They tried very hard to keep all its commandments because they thought that's how they could earn eternal life (John 5:39).

When they sinned, they had to sacrifice an animal, and the blood covered their sins. The problem was that such sacrifices couldn't permanently forgive their sins. When Jesus died on the cross and poured out His blood, all people had to do was to believe in Him and all their sins would be forgiven and they'd have eternal life (Hebrews 10:11–14).

However, some Jewish teachers insisted that people still had to keep the Law of Moses to be saved (Acts 15:1). These teachers went to the churches in Galatia and confused the new Christians, so Paul made it very clear that just believing in Jesus was enough for salvation.

Hebrews 3 describes Jesus as being greater than Moses—who came back from heaven to see Jesus' transfiguration. Read the whole story in Matthew 17:1–8.

We say a good figure skater is "graceful"—smooth in movement and pleasing to watch. That's one definition of the word, but not the one the Bible uses.

WHAT IS GRACE?

For it is by grace you have been saved, through faith—and this is not from yourselves, it is the gift of God.

EPHESIANS 2:8 TNIV

Grace means several things in the New Testament. When we say that someone is "gracious" or "full of grace," we mean that they are good, kind, and merciful. This is what John meant when he said that Jesus was "full of grace and truth" (John 1:14 KJV).

In New Testament times, *grace* also meant the kindness and mercy of a master toward a servant. The Bible says, "By grace you have been saved through faith, and that not of yourselves; it is the gift of God" (Ephesians 2:8 NKJV). We have been saved from hell by God's kindness and mercy. He doesn't expect us to work for eternal life or to do enough good deeds to earn such a reward. We couldn't earn eternal life no matter how hard we worked, so God graciously gave us salvation free, as a gift.

HOW SHOULD CHILDREN TREAT THEIR PARENTS?

Children, obey your parents in the Lord, for this is right. Honor your father and mother (which is the first commandment with a promise), so that it may be well with you, and that you may live long on the earth. Fathers, do not provoke your children to anger, but bring them up in the discipline and instruction of the Lord.

EPHESIANS 6:1–4 NASB

The fifth commandment reads: "Honor your father and your mother" (Exodus 20:12 NIV). In the New Testament, Paul writes, "Children, obey your parents in the Lord, for this is right" (Ephesians 6:1 NIV).

Parents not only care for their kids physically; they also teach them about the Lord. If children don't honor their father and mother, they definitely won't honor the invisible God their parents are teaching them about. John writes, "If any one says, 'I love God,' and hates his brother [or his parents], he is a liar; for he who does not love his brother [or his parents] whom he has seen, cannot love God whom he has not seen" (1 John 4:20 RSV).

Loving and honoring and obeying go hand in hand. If you love your parents, you will honor and obey them; children who honor their parents are taking the first step toward loving and obeying God.

WHAT IS THE ARMOR OF GOD?

The early Christians were familiar with the armor that Roman soldiers wore. It was quite impressive-looking and very effective in protecting the soldiers from their enemies. Paul explained that Christians have a spiritual enemy who hates us—the devil—and we need to cover our bodies with *spiritual* armor.

Just as a Roman soldier had a breastplate—iron armor covering his chest and stomach—we need Christ's righteousness to cover our hearts. We need the helmet of salvation protecting our heads and the shield of faith to stop the flaming arrows of the devil from hitting and wounding us.

We also need the belt of truth, the sword of the Spirit (the Word of God) with which to attack the enemy, and sturdy shoes so we are ready to preach the gospel. We can't skip one piece of armor. Paul said twice to "put on the *full* armor of God."

Put on the whole armour of God, that ye may be able to stand against the wiles of the devil. For we wrestle not against flesh and blood, but against principalities, against powers, against the rulers of the darkness of this world, against spiritual wickedness in high places. Wherefore take unto you the whole armour of God, that ye may be able to withstand in the evil day, and having done all, to stand. Stand therefore, having your loins girt about with truth, and having on the breastplate of righteousness; and your feet shod with the preparation of the gospel of peace; above all, taking the shield of faith, wherewith ye shall be able to quench all the fiery darts of the wicked. And take the helmet of salvation, and the sword of the Spirit, which is the word of God.

EPHESIANS 6:11–17 KJV

WHY WAS PAUL IN PRISON?

> *My imprisonment here has had the opposite of its intended effect.*
> PHILIPPIANS 1:12 MSG

When Paul visited Jerusalem to take money to the poor Christians there, he was attacked by religious enemies and arrested by the Romans. The Roman governor, Felix, would have released Paul if he had paid a bribe, but Paul refused to do that. Paul knew that God wanted him to go to Rome to preach the gospel to the emperor and his court. (See Acts 21:27–34; 23:11; 24:26.)

At first other Christians thought it was a huge defeat that Paul was in prison, but Paul said, "I want you to know, my friends, that the things that have happened to me have really helped the progress of the gospel" (Philippians 1:12 GNT).

After Paul preached in Rome, it appears he was released from prison and was free to travel to Spain to preach the gospel there as well (Romans 15:24, 28).

DID JESUS GIVE UP HIS POWER AS GOD WHEN HE CAME TO EARTH?

> *Who, being in very nature God, did not consider equality with God something to be grasped, but made himself nothing. . . .*
> PHILIPPIANS 2:6–7 NIV

"Though he was in the form of God. . .[Jesus] emptied himself, taking the form of a servant, being born in the likeness of men" (Philippians 2:6–7 RSV). When Jesus was born as a baby in a limited, mortal human body, that body simply couldn't contain all the power and glory of God.

Jesus didn't stop being God. He didn't stop being the Son of God. But He had to set aside most of His divine power. He had to "empty himself" of much of the glory that He'd had when He was with His Father in heaven (John 17:5).

Once Jesus was raised from the dead in a powerful, eternal body, however, He was once again able to contain all the power of God. After Jesus' resurrection, "his eyes were like blazing fire. His feet were like bronze glowing in a furnace, and his voice was like the sound of rushing waters" (Revelation 1:13–15 NIV).

It's hard to be more powerless than a newborn baby—which is exactly how Jesus came to earth!

HOW IS JESUS CHRIST DIFFERENT FROM EVERY OTHER FAMOUS MAN WHO STARTED A RELIGION?

Every religious leader who has ever lived has claimed to have some new revelation from God, or has preached a new set of commandments that, if you will obey them, will supposedly make you good enough to go to heaven. Some, like Confucius, simply taught morals to make people better citizens. And one after another, all of these religious leaders died. They were mere men who could not give eternal life, even to themselves.

Jesus was not just a man, "for by him all things were created" (Colossians 1:16 NIV). That means that He was God who created the heavens and the earth in the beginning (Genesis 1:1). When Jesus was on earth, He was God in the body of a human being (John 1:1, 14).

Though Jesus' enemies killed His physical body, He only allowed that so He could pay the price for our sins. When His work was finished, Jesus was raised back to life by the Spirit of God, never to die again. No other religious teacher has come even close to doing any of these things.

He is the image of the invisible God, the first-born of all creation; for in him all things were created, in heaven and on earth, visible and invisible, whether thrones or dominions or principalities or authorities—all things were created through him and for him.

COLOSSIANS 1:15–16 RSV

This statue of Confucius stands near a lake in Yueyang, China.

HOW COME SATAN IS ALLOWED TO HINDER GOD'S PLANS?

For we wanted to come to you—certainly I, Paul, did, again and again—but Satan stopped us.

1 THESSALONIANS 2:18 NIV

The devil is powerful, but not more powerful than God. And one day, it will be God's angels who defeat Satan and his demons (see Revelation 12:7–8).

Paul told the Christians in Thessalonica, "We wanted to come to you—even I, Paul, time and again—but Satan hindered us" (1 Thessalonians 2:18 NKJV). The Greek word translated "hinder" means "to cut in, to interrupt." Satan fought God's plans very hard. He cut in and tried to block Paul, like a bully cutting in front of him on a racetrack to bump him off course or slow him down.

Satan didn't fight only Paul, however. He has been fighting all of God's people for centuries, including us today.

Why does God allow Satan to cause so much trouble in the world? There are many reasons. First, God allows Satan to test us so that we will come out stronger. God is able also to bring good out of the evil Satan tries to do (Genesis 50:20; Romans 8:28).

However, God doesn't give us a full explanation to this question. He *does*, however, warn us to be alert to the fact that the devil is out to fight and destroy us (1 Peter 5:8). That's why we need to pray and stay close to Jesus.

WHAT IS THE RAPTURE?

Then we which are alive and remain shall be caught up together with them in the clouds.

1 THESSALONIANS 4:17 KJV

One day Jesus will return and will send His angels around the world to gather all believers together to meet Him in the clouds of heaven (Matthew 24:30–31). In the blink of an eye, our bodies will be transformed into supernatural, eternal bodies.

Being "caught up together. . .in the clouds" (1 Thessalonians 4:17 NIV) is called the Rapture. *Rapture* comes from the Latin word *rapere*, which means "to seize." It describes the angels seizing and snatching us up from the earth.

Some people spend a lot of time trying to figure out when the Rapture will happen, but they can only guess. Jesus said that nobody except for God knows the day or the hour that He will return. Even the angels who will be doing the actual snatching don't know when the Rapture will happen (Matthew 24:36).

IS IT WRONG TO BE RICH?

> *Lust for money brings trouble and nothing but trouble.*
>
> 1 Timothy 6:9 MSG

It is wrong to be rich if you *become* rich by cheating people and taking advantage of the laborers working for you (James 5:1–6). Unfortunately, this is how many selfish people become wealthy. David once confessed that he was envious of the rich oppressors—until God showed him how they would come to a terrible end (Psalm 73:3–20). Paul warns Christians not to love money and says that those who desire to be rich end up straying from the faith (1 Timothy 6:9).

Yet money itself is not evil. Many good Christians have become wealthy through honest business practices; they pay fair wages to their employees; they give generously to help spread the gospel, and they donate to charities that help the poor. Paul advised rich Christians to be "rich in good works, ready to give, willing to share" (1 Timothy 6:17–18 NKJV). As long as they're doing that, there's nothing wrong with their wealth.

WHAT DOES IT MEAN THAT THE BIBLE IS INSPIRED BY GOD?

> *All Scripture is God-breathed and is useful for teaching, rebuking, correcting and training in righteousness.*
>
> 2 Timothy 3:16 TNIV

Older Bible translations say, "All scripture is given by inspiration of God" (2 Timothy 3:16 KJV). That already tells us a lot—that the entire Bible was thought up by God.

But the meaning of the verse goes even deeper. The verse literally means "All scripture is God-breathed." The Bible was not just an idea that God had something to do with. Rather, the Word of God came from God's own mouth. God spoke it and breathed it out.

An angel whispers God's words into the ear of the Gospel writer Matthew, in a painting by the famous artist Rembrandt.

Most of the time, God's Spirit filled godly men and women and used their mouths to speak His words. "For prophecy never came by the will of man, but holy men of God spoke as they were moved by the Holy Spirit" (2 Peter 1:21 NKJV). In New Testament times, God's Spirit filled the minds of the apostles and told them what to write.

A man that is an heretick after the first and second admonition reject.
TITUS 3:10 KJV

WHAT IS HERESY?

These days, we normally understand *heresy* to mean "false teaching," and that's what it does mean. Originally, however, a heresy meant a "choice" or a "sect."

A heresy wasn't just a Christian's harmless opinion of what a verse meant. It was a choice to believe something false, something that was different from the plain, clear teaching of the Bible. A heretic was an opinionated person who chose to follow his own divisive ideas even if he had to twist Scripture to make it line up with his opinions.

Paul described heretics as "savage wolves" tearing apart the flock. He warned the church, "From among yourselves men will rise up, speaking perverse things, to draw away the disciples after themselves" (Acts 20:29–30 NKJV).

This is how the apostle Paul described heretics—scary, huh?

IN THE BIBLE, A CHRISTIAN NAMED PHILEMON OWNED A SLAVE. DOES THAT MEAN GOD APPROVES OF SLAVERY?

Perhaps the reason he was separated from you for a little while was that you might have him back for good—no longer as a slave, but better than a slave, as a dear brother. He is very dear to me but even dearer to you, both as a man and as a brother in the Lord.
PHILEMON 15–16 NIV

There were slaves in Old Testament times, and God put up with man-made customs for quite a while, because people were too hard-hearted to change (Matthew 19:3–8). Nevertheless, foreign slaves who ran away from their masters and made it to Israel automatically became free people (Deuteronomy 23:15–16).

There were millions of slaves in the Roman Empire, and if Paul had insisted that all slaves be freed, he would have had to stop preaching the gospel to start leading an armed slave revolt—and the church would have been crushed. So Paul advised slaves to seek their freedom if they could, but to be content if they couldn't (1 Corinthians 7:21). He told masters to treat their slaves well, knowing that they, too, had a Master in heaven (Colossians 4:1).

Nevertheless, when writing to a friend who owned a slave, Paul told the master to receive the slave "no longer as a slave but more than a slave—a beloved brother" (Philemon 16 NKJV). Centuries later, Christians acted on this very principle and pushed to free all slaves.

Christians were a strong force in ending slavery in England and the United States.

WHAT DO ANGELS DO?

One of the angels' main jobs is to guard human beings. This is why people call them "guardian angels" (see Psalm 91:11). They sometimes rescue people in trouble (Genesis 19:4–16; Acts 5:17–25) and bring God's judgment on the disobedient (2 Samuel 24:13–16).

However, angels do much more than that. They also carry important messages to people (Matthew 1:20–21; Acts 27:23–24), and they spend a great deal of time praising God and His Son, Jesus (Revelation 5:11–12).

God also sends angels to minister to Christians (Hebrews 1:14). To "minister to" means to serve or care for. For example, after the devil had tempted Jesus, angels came and ministered to Him; and when Jesus was praying desperately in the Garden of Gethsemane, an angel strengthened Him (Matthew 4:11; Luke 22:42–44).

And did he ever say anything like this to an angel? Sit alongside me here on my throne until I make your enemies a stool for your feet. Isn't it obvious that all angels are sent to help out with those lined up to receive salvation?
HEBREWS 1:13–14 MSG

An angel comforts Jesus the night

WHAT DOES IT MEAN TO HARDEN YOUR HEART?

While it is said, To day if ye will hear his voice, harden not your hearts, as in the provocation.

HEBREWS 3:15 KJV

God wants His people to hear what He says and to receive His Word in their hearts (Deuteronomy 6:6). That's why Jesus described God's Word as a seed of grain and people's hearts as soil. He said some soil was rocky, some was trampled down hard, some was choked with thorns, but some was soft "good earth"—the kind of heart where God's Word will grow and bring forth a good crop (Matthew 13:3–8, 18–23).

David says in the Psalms, "Today, if you would hear His voice, do not harden your hearts" (Psalm 95:7–8 NASB; see also Hebrews 3:15). Don't make your heart as hard as solid, dry earth so that the Word of God can't even enter in and grow. Keep your heart soft and ready to receive.

WHY DOES GOD ALLOW US TO GO THROUGH HARD TIMES?

And have you forgotten the exhortation which addresses you as sons?—"My son, do not regard lightly the discipline of the Lord, nor lose courage when you are punished by him. For the Lord disciplines him whom he loves, and chastises every son whom he receives."

HEBREWS 12:5–6 RSV

Christians have wondered this for the past 2,000 years: "If God loves me so much that He sent His own Son to die for my sins, why does He let me go through hard times? Why does He take so long to answer my prayers when I need His help?"

Well, God sends hardship precisely because He *does* love you! God allows you to endure difficulties, because that is His way of disciplining and training you. Think of an athlete with a no-nonsense trainer who puts him on a strict diet and has him go through long, repetitive workouts to build up muscles and speed.

For Christians, God's discipline produces righteousness, peace, and holiness (Hebrews 12:10–11). It also teaches us patience.

So cheer up! Tough times are *proof* that God loves you! "No discipline seems pleasant at the time, but painful" (Hebrews 12:11 NIV), but "do not lose heart when he rebukes you, because the Lord disciplines those he loves" (Hebrews 12:5–6 NIV).

Hard things can make us stronger!

WHY DOES JAMES SAY THAT SIMPLY BELIEVING IN GOD IS NOT ENOUGH? DOESN'T THIS CONTRADICT WHAT PAUL TAUGHT?

Paul said, "Believe in the Lord Jesus, and you will be saved" (Acts 16:31 RSV). Paul also said that God's grace alone saves us, without our doing any good works or good deeds (Romans 10:9–10). Yet James said, "What does it profit, my brethren, if someone says he has faith but does not have works. Can faith save him?. . . Faith by itself, if it does not have works, is dead" (James 2:14, 17 NKJV).

There's no contradiction here, despite how it might seem. When you truly believe in Jesus, you naturally want to obey Him (1 John 5:1–3). You make Him the center of your life. When Jesus is the center of your life, you will naturally do good works and good deeds. "Our love should not just be words and talk; it must be true love, which shows itself in action" (1 John 3:18 GNT). So, although good deeds can't save you, if you have true faith, your faith will cause you to do good works. That's the proof that you have genuine faith.

Martin Luther, a great Christian leader from the 1500s, wondered if the book of James should even be part of the Bible—because he thought it contradicted salvation by faith. But James was really just saying that true faith leads to good works.

What use is it, my brethren, if someone says he has faith but he has no works? Can that faith save him?

JAMES 2:14 NASB

Do You Need to Be Baptized in Order to Be Saved?

This water symbolizes baptism that now saves you. . . .

1 Peter 3:21 NIV

Peter said, "Repent and be baptized. . .in the name of Jesus Christ for the forgiveness of your sins" (Acts 2:38 TNIV). Some Christians therefore believe that unless you are baptized, you are not saved.

However, Peter later compared baptism and salvation to Noah and his family being safe on the ark and talked about them being "brought safely through the water." Then he added, "Corresponding to that, baptism now saves you—not the removal of dirt from the flesh, but an appeal to God for a good conscience" (1 Peter 3:20–21 NASB).

The water doesn't wash away your sins. Jesus' blood is what cleanses your sins and washes your guilty conscience (1 John 1:7). Just the same, it's very important to be baptized as a symbol of your salvation.

Jesus told a thief, dying on a cross beside Him, "Today, you will be with me in paradise" (Luke 23:43)—but there's nothing in the Bible about that thief being baptized!

How Can We Be Sure That the Stories About Jesus Are True?

We have not followed cunningly devised fables. . . .

2 Peter 1:16 KJV

About 30 years after Jesus' crucifixion and resurrection, the apostle Peter said, "We have not followed cunningly devised fables, when we made known unto you the power and coming of our Lord Jesus Christ, but were eyewitnesses of his majesty" (2 Peter 1:16 KJV).

The Greek Christians had grown up hearing fables about the so-called Greek gods—Zeus, Hercules, Hades, and others. They knew that those stories were definitely made up. Peter said that Jesus was different. He was a real person who had actually lived, and Peter and the other disciples had seen Him.

About 60 years after Jesus' crucifixion, the apostle John, who was also an eyewitness to those events, wrote a Gospel (John 19:33–35; 21:24). John declared that he and the other disciples had heard Jesus, seen Him with their own eyes, and even touched Him—so they knew good and well that Jesus was real and that He actually did and said the things that the Gospels say He did and said (1 John 1:1).

GOD LOVES THE WORLD, AND WE ARE TOLD TO IMITATE GOD. WHY THEN ARE WE WARNED NOT TO LOVE THE WORLD?

Do not love the world or the things in the world. If anyone loves the world, the love of the Father is not in him. For all that is in the world—the lust of the flesh, the lust of the eyes, and the pride of life—is not of the Father but is of the world. And the world is passing away, and the lust of it; but he who does the will of God abides forever.

1 JOHN 2:15–17 NKJV

God loved the world *so much* that He sent His only Son to die on the cross, so that whoever believes in Jesus can have eternal life (John 3:16). We are told to love just like God loves. Yet in a later letter, John says, "If anyone loves the world, the love of the Father is not in him" (1 John 2:15 NKJV). Which of these statements is true?

They both are. When John said that "God so loved the world," he was talking about the *people* in the world. We are to love people—our fellow human beings. However, Jesus *didn't* love the power and riches and glory of the world's kingdoms. When Satan offered these things to Him, Jesus refused (Matthew 4:8–10).

We are to love people as much as we love our own selves, but we are not to love the riches and power and human glory that the world offers.

Here's another way to "love the world"—taking care of its natural resources. What God doesn't want you to love is the sinful ways the world works.

WHAT DOES THE WORD ANTICHRIST MEAN?

Here's how you test for the genuine Spirit of God. Everyone who confesses openly his faith in Jesus Christ—the Son of God, who came as an actual flesh-and-blood person—comes from God and belongs to God. And everyone who refuses to confess faith in Jesus has nothing in common with God. This is the spirit of antichrist that you heard was coming. Well, here it is, sooner than we thought!

1 JOHN 4:2–3 MSG

The devil whispers into the Antichrist's ear, in a painting from the early 1500s.

Antichrist means "against Christ." A person who is *antichrist* knows what Jesus stands for yet hates Him and fights against Him. Sometimes people who *say* they love Jesus are actually against Him, because they teach lies about Him or deny some of the basic truths of the gospel.

When John talks in this verse about people being antichrist, he means people who deny that Jesus lived on earth in a human body (1 John 4:2–3).

Christians also believe that there will be one final world dictator called the Antichrist in the end times, because John wrote, "It is the last hour; and as you have heard that the Antichrist is coming, even now many antichrists have come" (1 John 2:18 NKJV). This Antichrist is also called "the man of sin" and "the beast" (2 Thessalonians 2:3–4; Revelation 13).

WHO WERE THE GNOSTICS?

Little children, it is the last time: and as ye have heard that antichrist shall come, even now are there many antichrists; whereby we know that it is the last time.

1 JOHN 2:18 KJV

In John's day, a false teaching arose in the church. Many Greeks believed that all physical things were evil—rocks, trees, air, water, and human bodies. Only spiritual things were good. They thought that man's "good spirit" was trapped in his "evil body," so dying was a good thing.

These Greeks liked Jesus' message of love and brotherhood, but they couldn't believe that such a good Savior would come to earth in an "evil body." They therefore said that Jesus *appeared* to have a body, but He'd really only been a spirit. These teachers were called Gnostics.

John argued that he had not only seen and heard Jesus, but even *touched* Him (1 John 1:1). John had a blunt warning to the Gnostics: He said that anyone who admitted that Jesus Christ came in the flesh as a human being was of God, but that anyone who denied this was not saved (1 John 4:2–3).

HOW CAN WE KNOW WHEN SOMEONE IS A FALSE TEACHER?

> *For certain men have crept in unnoticed, who long ago were marked out for this condemnation, ungodly men, who turn the grace of our God into lewdness and deny the only Lord God and our Lord Jesus Christ.*
>
> JUDE 4 NKJV

Jesus said to "beware of false prophets." Even if they speak pretty and wise-sounding words, what their words lead people to believe and do is what matters (Matthew 7:15–20). Some corrupt teachers teach that you can live as you please and sin all you want, that it's no big deal to God and He'll quickly forgive you (2 Peter 2:18–19). Those kinds of false teachers are obvious, but some are less easy to spot.

Others might teach that you have to do some kind of good deeds to be saved (Acts 15:1–5). That *sounds* like common sense, but remember that God clearly explained that we are saved only by His mercy, not by our good deeds (Ephesians 2:8–9).

Don't be too quick to judge someone as a false teacher just because he teaches doctrines that your church doesn't teach. As long as he believes in the important truths of the Christian faith, minor differences are just a matter of opinion (Romans 14:1–10).

Some false teachers are like politicians who say just what people want to hear. Always be sure what a preacher says is what the Bible says!

HOW COULD THE STARS OF HEAVEN FALL TO THE EARTH?

After John saw his visions of the end of world events, he wrote down on a scroll what he had seen. Some of his visions were very unusual, but he described them as best he could. At one point, John wrote, "The stars of heaven fell to the earth, as a fig tree drops its late figs when it is shaken by a mighty wind" (Revelation 6:13 NKJV).

The Greek word *astēr* not only means "star," but also means "luminous meteor." (Our modern word *asteroid* comes from *astēr*.) John was probably describing a meteor shower, not giant stars falling.

It's also important to remember that many of John's visions weren't describing real objects but symbols of something else. For example, when John saw Jesus in a vision, Jesus was holding seven stars in His right hand, and Jesus told him, "The seven stars are the angels of the seven churches" (Revelation 1:16, 20 NKJV).

The stars in the sky fell to earth, as late figs drop from a fig tree when shaken by a strong wind.
REVELATION 6:13 NIV

WHAT IS THE GREAT TRIBULATION?.....

> *And I said unto him, Sir, thou knowest. And he said to me, These are they which came out of great tribulation, and have washed their robes, and made them white in the blood of the Lamb.*
>
> REVELATION 7:14 KJV

Jesus mentioned the Great Tribulation when He told His disciples about the end times and His second coming (Matthew 24:21). *Tribulation* means "trouble," so Jesus was warning that a time of great trouble was coming upon the earth. Even though the Great Tribulation will be a time of hardship and suffering for Christians, a great multitude will come out of it (Revelation 7:14).

Many different verses in the Bible tell us that the Tribulation will last 42 months, or 1,260 days (Revelation 11:2–3). This is about three and a half years.

Christians disagree about whether the Great Tribulation will happen soon and, if so, when it will begin. Some believe it has already happened. Others believe that it's a symbol of the suffering that Christians have had to endure down through the ages and are suffering even now in countries like China.

Christians have faced a lot of "tribulation" over the years—like when the Romans fed them to hungry animals as a form of entertainment. But many believe the "Great Tribulation" will be beyond the imagination.

DOES THE DEVIL REALLY LOOK LIKE A DRAGON?

Then another sign appeared in heaven: an enormous red dragon with seven heads and ten horns and seven crowns on its heads. . . . The great dragon was hurled down—that ancient serpent called the devil, or Satan, who leads the whole world astray. He was hurled to the earth, and his angels with him.

REVELATION 12:3, 9 TNIV

This dragon statue is part of a bridge in Ljubljana, Slovenia.

John describes the devil as a giant red dragon with seven heads and a long tail, and with seven crowns, one on each head (Revelation 12:3, 9). Is this how Satan actually looks, or is it a symbol? It's a symbol.

John also describes the church as a woman, nine months pregnant, "clothed with the sun" (Revelation 12:1–2), and we know that all the people in the church don't look like *that*.

Also, John saw Jesus, the Lamb of God, as a slain lamb with seven horns and seven eyes (Revelation 5:6), and we know for certain that Jesus doesn't actually look like that. Revelation is filled with many symbols, and these are some of them.

WHAT IS THE MARK OF THE BEAST, AND WHAT DOES THE NUMBER 666 MEAN?

And it was given to him to give breath to the image of the beast, so that the image of the beast would even speak and cause as many as do not worship the image of the beast to be killed. And he causes all, the small and the great, and the rich and the poor, and the free men and the slaves, to be given a mark on their right hand or on their forehead, and he provides that no one will be able to buy or to sell, except the one who has the mark, either the name of the beast or the number of his name. Here is wisdom. Let him who has understanding calculate the number of the beast, for the number is that of a man; and his number is six hundred and sixty-six.

REVELATION 13:15–18 NASB

Many Christians today take the book of Revelation literally and believe that a dictator called the Antichrist—also known as the Beast—will arise in the near future and take over the world. The Beast will demand that everyone worship him as if he were God, and will insist that everyone receive "a mark in his right hand or on his forehead. . .which is the name of the beast or the number of his name. . . . His number is 666" (Revelation 13:16–17 NIV). People will not be able to buy or sell unless they have the mark of the Beast.

The early Christians believed that this mark would be an actual brand. Many Christians today believe it will be a miniature computer chip inserted under a person's skin.

Others say that the mark of the Beast is spiritual, representing people who worship money and materialism; they point out that Christians receive a different mark, the name of God and Christ, on their foreheads (Revelation 7:3; 9:4; 22:3–4), and this mark is surely spiritual.

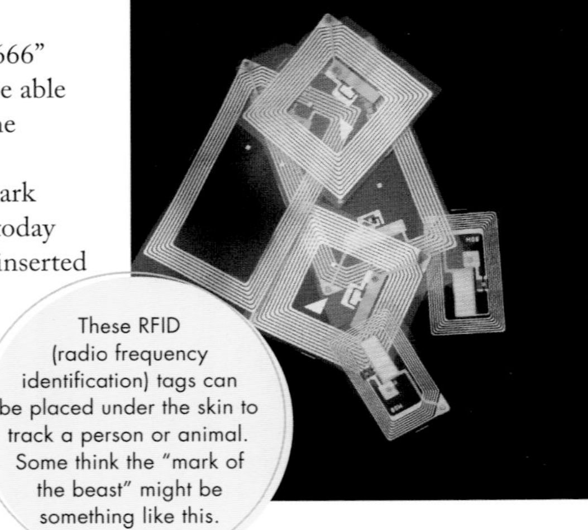

These RFID (radio frequency identification) tags can be placed under the skin to track a person or animal. Some think the "mark of the beast" might be something like this.

WHAT IS THE MILLENNIUM?

Millennium comes from the two Latin words *mille* and *ennium*, which together mean "a thousand years." The apostle John describes the Christians who went through the Great Tribulation and refused to receive the mark of the Beast, and says that "they lived and reigned with Christ a thousand years" (Revelation 20:4 KJV).

Many Christians believe that Jesus will return to this world, defeat the Antichrist and His armies in the battle of Armageddon, and set up His kingdom on earth. They also believe that this will be a tremendous time of peace when the nations will not "learn war anymore" (Isaiah 2:4 NKJV), and even animals will be at peace with each other (Isaiah 11:6–9).

Other Christians agree that Jesus will rule on earth one day but disagree when this will happen. They also say that "a thousand years" may not be literally one thousand years, but simply symbolic of a very long time.

And I saw thrones, and they sat upon them, and judgment was given unto them: and I saw the souls of them that were beheaded for the witness of Jesus, and for the word of God, and which had not worshipped the beast, neither his image, neither had received his mark upon their foreheads, or in their hands; and they lived and reigned with Christ a thousand years.

REVELATION 20:4 KJV

WHAT WILL HEAVEN BE LIKE?

John saw a vision of "the holy city, new Jerusalem" (Revelation 21:2 KJV) coming down out of the heavens, and a voice announced that God would now be living on earth among humans. Most Christians therefore believe that this heavenly city is the place where God Himself dwells, where His throne is, and that heaven itself will one day be on earth.

Revelation 21 and 22 give a beautiful, detailed description of this city, and you should read them if you want to be encouraged.

We don't know for certain if the streets will actually be made of gold that looks like transparent glass (Revelation 21:21), or whether this simply symbolizes the great beauty and riches of heaven. But we do know that we will live there forever with God and Jesus and that heaven will be wonderful and beautiful beyond our wildest dreams (1 Corinthians 2:9).

Now I saw a new heaven and a new earth, for the first heaven and the first earth had passed away. Also there was no more sea. Then I, John, saw the holy city, New Jerusalem, coming down out of heaven from God, prepared as a bride adorned for her husband. And I heard a loud voice from heaven saying, "Behold, the tabernacle of God is with men, and He will dwell with them, and they shall be His people. God Himself will be with them and be their God. And God will wipe away every tear from their eyes; there shall be no more death, nor sorrow, nor crying. There shall be no more pain, for the former things have passed away."

REVELATION 21:1–4 NKJV

GENESIS

EXODUS

LEVITICUS

NUMBERS

DEUTERONOMY

JOSHUA

JUDGES

RUTH

1 SAMUEL

2 SAMUEL

1 KINGS

2 KINGS

1 CHRONICLES

2 CHRONICLES

EZRA

NEHEMIAH

ESTHER

JOB

PSALMS

PROVERBS

ECCLESIASTES

SONG OF SONGS

ISAIAH

JEREMIAH

LAMENTATIONS

EZEKIEL

DANIEL

JONAH

HABAKKUK

HAGGAI

MALACHI

MATTHEW

MARK

LUKE

JOHN

ACTS

ROMANS

1 CORINTHIANS

2 CORINTHIANS

GALATIANS

EPHESIANS

PHILIPPIANS

COLOSSIANS

1 THESSALONIANS

2 THESSALONIANS

1 TIMOTHY

2 TIMOTHY

TITUS

PHILEMON

HEBREWS

JAMES

1 PETER

2 PETER

1 JOHN

JUDE

REVELATION

AP Photo/Damian Dovarganes: Page 170 (top)

Barbour Publishing: Page 168, 198, 229

iStockphoto.com: Page 164–165, 167, 171–172, 171–182, 183 (both), 184—185, 187–188, 189 (both), 190–193, 194 (both), 195–197, 200 (top), 204, 205 (both), 206–208, 211 (top), 213 (both), 214, 216–221, 222, (both), 223, 226–227, 231, 235–236, 237 (bottom), 238–239, 241–242, 244, 245 (both), 246–253, 256–259, 260 (both), 262 (top), 263, 264 (bottom), 266, 268, 270, 272 (top), 273–279, 281–282, 284, 286–288, 290 (both), 291–295, 298–299, 301–302, 304, 306–307, 309–311

Kelly McIntosh: Page 174

Model Maker R Walsh@www.noahs-ark.net: Page 170 (bottom)

Robert Walton: Page 272 (bottom)

Sunset Boulevard/Corbis: Page 210

WikiMedia: Page 169 (both), 175–176, 186 (bottom), 199, 202, 209, 211 (bottom), 212, 215 (both), 224–225, 228, 230, 232, 237 (top), 254, 264 (top), 265, 283, 285, 289, 297, 300, 303, 305, 308

WM/Bantosh: Page 280

WM/Gabriel L. Find: Page 186 (top)

WM/Jastrow: Page 283, 271

WM/Laurom: Page 262 (bottom)

WM/The CAD Expert: Page 240

WM/The Yorck Project: Page 166, 173, 233–234, 243, 255, 261, 267, 269, 299

WM/Truor: Page 200 (bottom)

(WM=WikiMedia)